Confessions of a
School Reformer

For Sam,

WITH AFFECTION,
RESPECT, AND
ADMIRATION.

Larry

Confessions of a School Reformer

LARRY CUBAN

Harvard Education Press
Cambridge, MA

Paperback ISBN 978-1-68253-695-7

Library of Congress Cataloging-in-Publication Data is on file.

Published by Harvard Education Press,
an imprint of the Harvard Education Publishing Group
Harvard Education Press
8 Story Street
Cambridge, MA 02138

Cover Design: Wilcox Design
Cover Image: stevegeer/E+ via Getty Images

The typefaces in this book are Minion Pro and Myriad Pro

For Treasured and Trusted Friend
Joel "Yus" Merenstein (1934–2019)

Contents

Introduction

Just see wherever we peer into the first tiny springs of the national life, how this true panacea for all of the ills of the body politic bubbles forth—education, education, education.

—ANDREW CARNEGIE, 1886[1]

School houses do not teach themselves—piles of brick and mortar and machinery do not send out men. It is the trained, living human soul, cultivated and strengthened by long study and thought, that breathes the real breath of life into boys and girls and makes them human, whether they be black or white, Greek, Russian or American.

—W. E. B. DU BOIS, 1903[2]

At the desk where I sit in Washington, I have learned one great truth: The answer for all our national problems comes down to one single word: education.

—PRESIDENT LYNDON B. JOHNSON, 1964[3]

[E]ducation is the silver bullet. Education is everything. We don't need little changes, we need gigantic, monumental changes. Schools should be palaces. The competition for the best teachers should be fierce. They should be making six-figure salaries. Schools should be incredibly expensive for government and absolutely free of charge to its citizens, just like national defense. That's my position. I just haven't figured out how to do it yet.

—SAM SEABORN, *THE WEST WING*, 2000, SEASON 1, EPISODE 18[4]

ACCORDING TO INDUSTRIALIST ANDREW CARNEGIE, scholar and activist W. E. B. Du Bois, President Lyndon B. Johnson, and a character in the award-winning television drama *The West Wing*, education ends poverty, leads to wealth, makes a person a full human being, and should be cherished.

They were not the only ones to urge fellow citizens to grab the brass ring of education that circled on the American carousel. Mexican immigrant Celia, who lives in a central Texas city, tells an interviewer what she does for Daniel, her ten-year-old son:

> Up to now, that Daniel is in fourth grade, I'll say all his teachers have been excellent teachers and I get along with them very well, I communicate. The first day of classes, and even before sometimes, I introduce myself, I ask them for their home phone number in case of an emergency, or in case the boy wants to lie and I have [to] doubt him, I ask them, I tell them, but it is not that I am bothering them. And teachers like to communicate, they ask for parents to go. For me, up to now, I don't know if I will have a problem later, but up to now not, they ask for parents to go. When I can I am there for an hour, and I am there to read in Spanish. Or if they have something to do I help them, but . . . I like to work with them, but if I see that they are not good I tell them.[5]

My mother, Fanny Janofsky, immigrated from Kiev, then part of Czarist Russia, to America in 1910. My father, Morris Cuban, also from Kiev, arrived in New York in 1912. They met through family connections and married in 1919. They had three sons, of whom I was the youngest.

Neither my father nor my mother completed school in Russia. My father worked in restaurants and delicatessens, and he and my mother had a small grocery store before he ended up as a jobber in Pittsburgh selling deli products from a paneled truck. He earned enough to house, feed, and clothe us for decades. Because my brothers were born in the 1920s, the Great Depression and World War II limited their schooling to getting high school diplomas. They eventually went into business after 1945.

I was born in 1934, and from the time I was a toddler, my mother drummed into me that since my brothers did not go beyond high school, I had to go to college to be a doctor or lawyer. I became neither. I did go to college, working at different part-time jobs to pay tuition and have spending money while living at home. I graduated and became a teacher. My mother's message about getting an education was clear and constant.

As important as getting an education is to presidents, corporate leaders, scholars, Celia, and my mother, the screenwriter who put the words "I just haven't figured out how to do it yet" into Sam Seaborn's mouth captured the complexity of sussing out what direction schools should move and getting schools to go on that path. Generation after generation of American reformers over the past century believed in the power of tax-supported schools to enrich individuals and remedy national problems. Some writers have characterized this faith in education as a secular religion that Americans worship. Because of this devotion to schooling as an all-purpose solvent for parents, communities, and the nation, reformers again and again have tried to figure out, in Seaborn's words, "how to do it."[6]

It would be a grave mistake, however, to think that American reformers looked only at schools as targets for change.

Reforming individual Americans to be better persons has been in the American bloodstream since the *Mayflower* arrived. Ditto for reforming community institutions to be better places within which to live and work. Perfecting individuals and community institutions while solving problems of urban slums, corrupt city governments, poverty, racial segregation, corporate overreach, and anemic economic growth has been steady work for reformers. Time and again these reform movements reached far beyond schools.[7]

As predictable as climbing up a ladder to clean leaves from roof gutters every season, reforms have regularly swept across the nation. Since the early 1900s, three overlapping social, political, and economic movements have churned across the US and left marks on government, business, and community institutions, including public schools: the Progressive movement (1900s–1950s), the civil rights struggle (1950s–1970s), and binding schools to the economy (1980s–present).[8]

REFORM MOVEMENTS

Each of these political and social movements sought multiple goals, one of which included school reform. Early twentieth-century Progressives sought to remedy municipal corruption, corporate exploitation of workers and consumers, and inefficient institutions including traditional, lockstep schooling.

Both Black and white civil rights advocates sought equal treatment for Blacks in every institution. They pressured federal and state governments to eliminate segregated hospitals, pools, motels, playing fields, and toilets. They demanded unencumbered voting rights. And they wanted urban and rural schooling equal to what white suburban parents received for their children.

And in the closing decades of the twentieth century, business leaders, alarmed by an economy falling behind Germany and Japan, restructured their industries, outsourced labor, and lobbied state and federal legislators to deregulate industries and lower taxes. Corporate leaders, seeking profits and returns to their investors, also pushed equal opportunity for minorities to achieve the American Dream. These business-minded reformers saw US public schools creating human capital necessary for the nation to compete economically in an increasingly interconnected global marketplace. Higher graduation requirements, common curriculum standards, and accountability for student test scores were reform-driven policies for producing that all-important human capital.

Binding together these seemingly different reform movements coursing through the American bloodstream over the past century were three common features:

- Reformers had a serene faith in better schools ridding society of individual and societal injustices, including crime, discrimination, and economic inequities. They believed schooling could create successful individuals and render American institutions havens of democracy, sources of economic growth and social justice.
- Reformers insisted that state and federal governments remedy political, social, and economic ills and be held accountable for the actions they take (or do not take).
- In pursuit of these multiple goals, reformer sought deep policy and practice changes in public schools, yet they left untouched the existing age-graded school structure and its "grammar of schooling." Thus, each generation of school reformers unknowingly ended up preserving, not altering, the basic structures of primary and secondary schooling.

Without skipping a beat, each generation of policy elites and activist leaders sought major reforms in government through federal and state legislation, including reconfiguring schools. And they succeeded to a degree. The rhetoric of school reform in each generation included a to-do list of past failures that had to be corrected (e.g., hidebound traditional curriculum and practices; inefficient, unproductive schools churning out unskilled graduates). Each generation's talk and political action did alter some official policies and increased access to public schools, but inflated rhetoric followed by downsized policies left intact fundamental structures (e.g., the age-graded school and the grammar of schooling). And as each movement wound down, another cohort of school reformers shouted rhetoric, redefined problems, and pushed policies that the previous one had chased while leaving largely unaffected existing school structures.

And so, the last century of reform in America has been the story of these three political and social movements featuring feverish policy talk, limited policy actions, and erratic implementation spilling over public schools decade after decade. Beyond these reformers achieving a few of their intended goals in each era, what often go unnoticed are some of the unintended—even perverse—effects of reform talk, adopted policies, and their uneven execution.

PERVERSE OUTCOMES OF SCHOOL REFORMS

Consider the massive effort by civil rights reformers to desegregate schools between the 1960s and 1980s following the US Supreme Court's *Brown v. Board of Education* decision (1954).

Where students went to school in the US depended on where their families lived. In most cities and suburbs, neighborhoods were segregated, producing schools that were nearly all-white, Black, or Latino. Activists used both direct action, such as boycotts and marches, and legal strategies to get urban and suburban districts to desegregate through busing, building schools that straddled city and county attendance boundaries, and taking school boards to federal court for maintaining segregated schools—strategies that civil rights reformers believed would bring minority and white children together to learn.[9]

Migration of white, Black, and Latino families moving into and out of urban residential areas where racial covenants and banking practices kept neighborhoods segregated led to resegregated schools where mostly minority children enrolled—often coming from families in poverty. Suburban schools often became white enclaves. The unintended effect of direct actions and court-driven desegregation decisions, then, was to speed up resegregation of poor and minority students by the 1990s. Few policy makers after the *Brown* decision anticipated the return of racial and ethnic separation of whites from African American and Latino schoolchildren.[10]

Consider that in the 1980s and 1990s, policies aimed at tying schools closer to the nation's economy—raising state high school graduation requirements, strengthening curriculum standards, using tests to determine how well students achieved those standards, and holding students, teachers, schools, and districts responsible for student academic outcomes—would have dire effects upon US schools and students. Recall that state and local reform-minded policy makers and political leaders cheered the passage of the federal No Child Left Behind Act (2001–2015), which contained many of these features, because reformers believed that such policies would help students and forge tighter links between schools and the economy.

The documented record, however, is mixed as to whether those reforms, including No Child Left Behind (NCLB), aimed at producing skilled graduates who could enter an information-driven workplace, achieved the intended goals. Since the early 2000s, high school graduation rates have risen. And, yes, the percentage of high school graduates attending college has increased. But test score gains sufficient to close the achievement gap between minorities and whites have not improved. Nor is there much evidence that graduates are better prepared to enter the workplace than an earlier generation. Furthermore, the promise that higher standards and accountability would alter historic inequalities between minorities and whites remains unfulfilled. Unemployment and wages for African Americans have remained largely unequal and stagnant during economic growth and recessions.[11]

Documenting the intended effects of school reforms is tough enough. But when researchers investigated the unintended or unexpected results of school reform, unusual outcomes became apparent.

Few reformers, for example, thought that NCLB, with its mandated state tests and its required reporting of Adequate Yearly Progress in test scores, would push state and local policy makers to manipulate student results. State officials fiddled with numbers setting the threshold for a passing score on its tests to avoid many schools being tagged as "failing." Additionally, many districts across the nation pressed teachers to taper their lessons to fit what was on these state tests. Schools set aside school time to prepare students for end-of-year exams. These unintended outcomes became obvious within a few years of NCLB's passage.[12]

Even worse, in the wake of NCLB many urban and suburban districts found that their schools had failed to meet the law's criteria for improvement. States published districts' test scores, and districts announced school-by-school scores identifying those schools that were in danger of closing if results didn't improve. Each year, shame and blame exponentially spread across the US as more schools flunked NCLB requirements. Local and state officials complained annually about the unfairness of such measures applied without acknowledging demographic differences in districts and schools. They lobbied their legislators to alter the federal law. The deluge of complaints and meager student outcomes led the US Congress to dump NCLB and pass the Every Student Succeeds Act (ESSA) delegating the power to determine school success and failure to each state. President Barack Obama signed ESSA into law in 2015. In effect, the 2001 reform was re-formed in 2015.[13]

None of this, of course, is new. Policy researchers and historians are well aware of how hard it is to show unvarnished success of reform-driven policies over time in districts and schools. They are equally aware of how commonly unexpected outcomes accompany these very same policies. Nor is it new that these unanticipated outcomes seldom loosened decision makers' embrace of reform-driven policies, simply because of the pervasive faith that Americans had in the power of schooling to uplift those who historically have done poorly in public schools—immigrants, rural migrants, and low-income children of color.

ROCK-HARD FAITH IN THE POWER OF SCHOOLING

Nonetheless, each generation of reformers believed in their hearts that they could solve thorny social, political, and economic problems. They knew what had to be done and had the answers. Public schools, they held, were the chief, if not the sole, determiner of individual and national success. Schooling was the great equalizer shaping the life journey that individual children and youth traveled. Mirroring the deeply embedded and traditional belief that American institutions can indeed make people better, the school, like the church and family, was an instrument for not only reforming individuals and institutions but also curing societal ills such as illiteracy, poverty, and economic slowdowns.[14]

Recall that industrial magnate Andrew Carnegie endowed the Foundation for the Advancement of Teaching in 1905 and funded the construction and maintenance of nearly 1,700 free libraries across the country between 1883 and 1929.[15] Recall also that President Lyndon B. Johnson had as the centerpiece of his War on Poverty the Elementary and Secondary Education Act (1965), which provided billions of dollars to poor and minority children then called "disadvantaged." And it is precisely on this point of faith about the curative powers of schooling that one pillar of that belief has wobbled and remains contested in 2021, even amid the COVID-19 pandemic. For many decades, there has been an enduring struggle among educators, parents, policy makers, and public officials over how much students' backgrounds shape school effects.

For true believers, schooling improves everyone regardless of family circumstances. Yet (and this is a very big "yet") much evidence has piled up over the past century that social class matters when it comes to who sails through age-graded schools and who stumbles along the way. Consider, for example, that the majority of urban districts in the US now house mostly minority and poor children. More than half of African American children and six out of ten Hispanic children and youth attended schools in 2017 that were at least 75 percent minority students. Most of these schools are located in urban districts and historically segregated southern rural districts. Note further than in 2013 researchers found that over half of US students are poor.[16]

Moreover, the research literature on children's academic performance has shown time and again that anywhere from over half to two-thirds of minority and white students' test scores—lower, middle, and upper class—can be attributed to their family's socioeconomic background.[17]

Yet many educators in public traditional and charter schools in poor neighborhoods either ignore or dispute those research findings. They continue to operate on the principle that engaged and committed staff unaccepting of "excuses" (e.g., low-income family, all-minority enrollment, neighborhood crime) could lift students out of poverty through helping them become academic achievers, enter college, and secure well-paid jobs. Both evidence of the crippling effects of poverty on academic achievement and findings that singular urban schools can produce high-achieving students are available and rich.[18]

The issue, then, of how much family background and ethnic and racial school demography affect student achievement has to consider a large body of evidence of schools graduating low-income minority students who enter higher education. Hovering over all of this point-counterpoint argument is another uncomfortable and inescapable fact: formal schooling occupies only a small portion of a child's day. Consider that children and youth attend public schools about 1,100 hours a year for thirteen years (or just under 15,000 hours). That time represents less than 20 percent of a child's and teenager's waking time for all of those years in school. Hence, most of a student's time is spent outside of school in the family, the neighborhood, religious settings, and the workplace.[19]

Important as time spent in school is, economically and socially, in accumulating content and skills and diplomas for jobs and careers, it is often given far more weight—recall the basic faith that Americans have in the power of schooling—than life lived outside of school in assessing not only how a child becomes an adult but also what kind of adult.

So two fundamental questions past generations of reformers in these three movements neglected, sometimes considered, but seldom wrestled with publicly are about the connection between individuals, schools, and society, questions that remain unanswered to contemporary crusaders:

- How much of a child's academic success or failure in school is due to family background?
- Can schools, reflecting the larger society's faith in perfecting individuals and institutions, not only alter the effects of family background but also reform society?

There are many ways to answer these questions in trying to determine the degrees of impact that these reform movements have had on children and youth, including poor and minority students. Individual memoirs (e.g., Roger Wilkins' *A Man's Life: An Autobiography*), case studies (e.g., Alex Kotlowitz's *There Are No Children Here*), surveys (e.g.,

Coleman Study, 1966), longitudinal research on groups of children (e.g., Perry Preschool Project), and many other designs have established general statements, more often than not challenged by other researchers and, especially, policy makers. No design is invulnerable, including what I offer in this book, a mix of research, analysis, and experiential data.[20]

Confessions of a School Reformer is one person's direct experiences in the three reform movements that have swept over the nation's public schools over the past century. Other accounts may arrive at different answers than what I present here. So be it. Using direct experiences informed by a broad and deep knowledge of the history of schooling, I delve into each of these reform movements to make sense of a complex community institution and its effects on my life.

The book is ambitious. I connect larger, swirling reform movements with my experiences as a student, teacher, superintendent, and researcher. I confess errors in beliefs and stumbles in practices. And I draw conclusions that often challenge mainstream wisdom about school reforms over the past century. The book, then, is both a policy history of school reforms over the past century and a memoir. It is a tricky combination, and readers will determine to what degree I succeed.

I have organized the book in alternating chapters of historical analysis and memoir to answer four sets of questions:

- How did the Progressive movement (1890s–1940s) shape public schooling in governance, organization, curriculum, and instruction, both nationally and in the Pittsburgh schools that I attended as a student (ch. 1)? As a student between 1939 and 1951, what do I recall and make of my experiences in three Pittsburgh schools in the fading years of Progressive school reform (ch. 2)?
- How did the civil rights movement (1950s–1970s) shape public schooling in governance, organization, curriculum, and instruction, both nationally and locally in the Cleveland and Washington, DC, school systems (ch. 3)? As a teacher in Cleveland and Washington, DC (1956–1972), what classroom and school reforms did I design and implement during the civil rights movement (ch. 4)?
- How did the standards, testing, and accountability movement (1970s–present) shape public schooling in governance, organization,

curriculum, and instruction nationally and in Arlington, Virginia (ch. 5)? As the Arlington County superintendent between 1974 and 1981, what district reforms did the Arlington School Board and I design, adopt, and implement during the standards, testing, and accountability movement (ch. 6)?

- As a former practitioner and historian of education, which reforms did I research and study and what were my conclusions? (ch. 7)

The four memoir chapters will contain one additional feature that calls to mind the title of this book. When I describe my direct experiences as a teacher, administrator, and researcher during surges of reform, I will elaborate my primary beliefs at the time and detail any mistaken ideas and slipups in practice that I pursued and committed. Thus, *Confessions of a School Reformer*.

For example, following the chapter analyzing the standards, testing, and accountability movement, I render a personal account of being Arlington's school chief during the early years of this national reform movement. I believed that the district, not the school or classroom, was the primary unit of school reform to improve schooling, especially for children of color. While that belief has substantial merit—and I specify those merits in the chapter—I have also learned that a district strategy of reform is too narrow. Surely, the district as a key piece to any strategy for improving governance, curriculum, and instruction is worthy, but such school reform fails to account for the larger social and political contexts (e.g., the impacts of poverty, racism, and the political vulnerability of tax-supported public schools in the community, state, and nation). That omission was an error in my thinking.

The following chapters document how perfecting imperfect individuals and a flawed society drove American reformers over the past century to mount three movements targeting public schools for improvement. Historically, faith in formal schooling as paving the road to personal success and national prominence has been an enduring motif. From Andrew Carnegie to Lyndon B. Johnson to a character in the popular drama *The West Wing*, education has been touted as essential not only to becoming a successful individual who is noticed, recognized, and approved but also to strengthening communities and, finally, maintaining a democratic nation committed to equal opportunity. American faith in schooling, while occasionally tarnished, remains steadfast even during and after the 2020–2021 pandemic.

Schooling was surely important to me as I traversed eight decades as a student, teacher, administrator, and researcher immersed in these larger reform movements. Just how important it has been in my life and the events that shaped who I am is a question I explore in the ensuing chapters.

CHAPTER 1

The Progressive Movement (1890s–1940s)

THERE IS A "SHORT" AND A "LONG" STORY to American reform movements. Consider the Progressive movement. Most historians find its beginnings in the closing decades of the nineteenth century, when reformers identified serious problems arising from an emergent industrial economy, burgeoning cities with corrupt municipal governments, and crowds of immigrants congregating in slums.[1]

Because traditional schools of the time were out of step with the changed economy and society, Progressive educators sought to remake schools into efficient places that looked at the whole child and prepared that child to enter an entirely different workplace and civic life than their parents and grandparents ever knew. Historians generally agree that this Progressive movement lasted through the Great Depression and the New Deal, winding down by World War II. This is the "short" story of a national reform movement that included efforts to transform traditional schools to meet new economic, political, and social demands.

But there is a "long" story to the educational side of the Progressive movement. That long story takes one back to the eighteenth century, when Jean-Jacques Rousseau wrote *Emile* and Swiss educator Johann Heinrich Pestalozzi penned *How Gertrude Teaches Her Children*, and to the nineteenth century, when German educator Friedrich Froebel introduced the concept of the *kindergarten*. All of these European writers sought a schooling that centered on the head, heart, and hands of children to explore their interests and to get them to think and engage with the world outside of the classroom. School was more than a preparation for life or work, they believed.[2]

Their ideas crossed the Atlantic and took root among American thinkers and educators such as communitarian Robert Owen, essayist Ralph Waldo Emerson, kindergarten advocate Elizabeth Peabody, and district superintendent Colonel Francis W. Parker. The ideas and practices of these early Progressives were picked up and reshaped to fit an industrial democracy by John Dewey and other educational reformers in the closing decades of the nineteenth century.[3]

If the above may be described as the time "before" Progressivism in schools flowered, then there are the Progressive ideas and practices in the opening decades of the twentieth century that permeated schools until the Progressive Education Association closed its doors in the 1950s.

Differences among historians, social scientists, reform-minded policy analysts, and latter-day Progressives in telling the decades- or century-long story of the Progressive movement in schools, including which individuals play leading or supporting roles, are echoed by differences in telling the story of the later movement of civil rights reformers in the 1950s to 1970s and those business-struck reformers behind the standards-based, testing, and accountability movement in the closing decades of the twentieth century.

PUBLIC SCHOOLING IN THE PROGRESSIVE ERA

In the late nineteenth and early twentieth centuries, Progressives worked hard to solve problems that plagued an emerging industrial democracy. Urban slums, filled with recent European immigrants, harbored diseases and crime. Easily bribed big-city political bosses appointed constituents to an array of city jobs ranging from municipal clerks to school board members. Meatpackers, to keep their products from rotting, sold consumers pork and beef containing poisonous formaldehyde. Prices for oil to heat homes rose and fell until John D. Rockefeller's Standard Oil monopolized the industry and set prices. Steel industrialist Andrew Carnegie refused to raise wages at US Steel and brought in private police to quell striking unionized workers. Muckraking newspapers, magazines, and books exposed these national ills year after year.[4]

Wealth and poverty were blocks apart in cities. Gilded mansions and epicurean restaurants were nestled not far away from grimy factories and packed tenements where immigrant families and boarders squeezed into tiny apartments—one single square block on the Lower East Side of New York City had three thousand people—and shared spare dinners of bread and soup.

And public schools? Child labor laws compelled families to send their sons and daughters to overcrowded urban schools that offered a traditional curriculum and straitlaced pedagogy to students speaking a medley of languages.[5]

Corrupt politicians and corporate industrialists gouged American citizens, consumers, and workers, while outdated and tradition-bound educators failed to prepare children for a different economy and world.

Growing unrest among a white middle class to do something, anything to rid the nation of these troubles morphed into a multifaceted Progressive movement, a good-government crusade, rooted in Christian evangelism to right wrongs and make America great again. One religious group, for example, wrote a Social Creed; others swore to end child labor and to fight for workers to be paid a living wage. Religious zeal did fuel the movement, as it remained largely a white-led reform. While there were Black Progressives, Jim Crow laws ruled the South and caste norms pervaded the non-South, keeping Progressivism a largely white movement (discussed below).

Eager to remove crooked politicos, end corporate rapaciousness, reduce urban poverty, and upend traditional schooling, a generation of Progressive reformers worked hard at improving core American institutions.

The Progressive Agenda

In the words of one historian, Progressives looked "backward to an older America . . . [they] sought to recapture and reaffirm the older individualistic values in all strata of political, economic, and social life. They wanted the public good to supersede private interests." Yet this mix of businessmen, good government reformers, mayors, US presidents, school superintendents and teachers, women's club members, and muckraking journalists calling themselves Progressives were hard to pigeonhole.[6]

For example, Republican President Teddy Roosevelt and Democratic President Woodrow Wilson called themselves Progressives. Philosopher John Dewey and measurement expert Edward Thorndike belonged to the movement. Settlement house founder Jane Addams and teacher union leader Margaret Haley saw themselves as Progressives. Efficiency expert Frederick Winslow Taylor and wealthy businessman and later Illinois Governor John Altgeld considered themselves Progressives. A polyglot bunch of reformers in government, business, community improvement, and education sheltered under the wide umbrella called Progressivism.

Even a century later, historians cannot yet agree on a definition of Progressivism, who led the movement, what areas of American life were substantively altered as a result of the movement, and how long the movement lasted. So if historians today differ on answers to such basic questions, readers may be disappointed that I cannot do better than my peers in answering these questions.[7]

What historians do agree on, however, are the impulses that drove those who called themselves Progressives to work hard for decades to improve American society. Moving from largely rural agriculture in the eighteenth and nineteenth centuries to an industrial and urban-based economy in the decades following the Civil War transformed the economy, society, and culture of the nation. Steel, beef, and oil trusts, as these monopolies were then called, paid low wages for workers and set high prices for consumers. Cities grew as manufacturing and transportation centers. Rural migrants and European immigrants flocked to these cities to get jobs that paid barely enough to cover rent and food.

Political machines oiled by bribery and nepotism governed these urban centers, caring little for the disease, crime, and poverty endemic to densely packed slums. Reform-minded mayors pledging to solve these problems came and went, but political machines endured. Worsening conditions even more were the unpredictable and periodic economic panics (1873 and 1893) that threw hundreds of thousands of workers out of jobs, overwhelmed city leaders, and frightened city-dwelling middle-class families, many of whom had moved into emerging suburbs.

Between the 1890s and 1914, then, white upper- and middle-class men and women joined a movement to solve problems growing out of the new industrial economy, such as monopolies, governmental corruption, urban poverty, and rigidly traditional schools that they believed undermined democratic institutions. They called themselves Progressives.

Yet there were Black Progressives as well. While the Progressive movement accepted segregation and Jim Crow reigned in the South and dominated many parts of the North, Midwest, and West, it affected reform efforts. There were Black Progressives who tirelessly worked to improve the economic, political, and social status of the race. And just as the white-led Progressive movement varied greatly among those who shared a general ideology of improvement, so too did Black Progressives vary in working to overturn the caste system. Educators Booker T. Washington at Tuskegee and Mary Church Terrell in Washington, DC, civil rights activist and scholar W. E. B. Du Bois, religious leader Reverend Reverdy Cassius Ransom, and antilynching journalist Ida B. Wells were Progressives in the late nineteenth and early twentieth centuries yet differed among themselves over how best to end the oppressive caste system pervading America.[8]

Fighting Corporate Monopolies and Cleansing Government Corruption

Beginning in the 1880s, good government reformers (or "goo-goos," as their critics called then) worked at the national, state, and city levels. Often failing but sometimes succeeding, these reformers swept out crooked politicians and dishonest businessmen in a rash of laws and crackdowns that were amply reported in the press.[9]

Trust-busting Theodore Roosevelt became president in 1901, followed by Progressives William Howard Taft in 1909 and Woodrow Wilson in 1912. Over decades, these Progressive leaders—both Republican and Democrat—initiated and signed legislation that broke apart monopolies like Standard Oil (e.g., the Sherman Antitrust Act of 1890). Reform-driven officials protected consumers from bogus products (e.g., the Pure Food and Drug Act of 1906). During these years, twenty-one Progressive state governors (e.g., Hiram Johnson in California) and legislators amplified voter voices through initiatives and referenda by allowing citizens to place measures on a ballot that would curb corporate capitalists and government inaction.[10]

Getting rid of federal, state, and local patronage systems took decades, but Progressives did precisely that by reorganizing governance at all levels, including schools, to make them more efficient in serving the public. For example, reform legislation aimed at reducing political appointees sorted out competent from incompetent applicants for government jobs through competitive civil service examinations. With the Pendleton Civil Service Reform Act (1883), by the early 1900s nearly two-thirds of federal employees were hired on merit. State governors such as California's Hiram Johnson signed the Civil Service Act in 1913. City mayors diminished powerful local political machines in different ways, including reorganized municipal governance by elected mayors and city councils and city manager systems that hired employees on the basis of credentials and civil service exams.[11]

Urban Progressives rooting out corrupt city officials also aimed at altering how school districts were governed. Ward-run schools in many big cities provided easy pickings for crooked officials to stuff their wallets by selling, for example, teaching positions to those who wanted jobs. No surprise, then, that municipal and school governance reforms (discussed below) were joined at the hip.[12]

Consider Progressive activists helping the urban poor. Getting relief for impoverished immigrants jammed tightly together in urban slums prompted both men and women reformers to establish settlement houses in major cities across the nation. Jane Addams's Hull House in Chicago, Lillian Wald's Henry Street Settlement in New York City, Reverend George Hodges's Kingsley House in Pittsburgh, and many other associations founded by white middle- and upper-middle-class men and women provided social and medical services, food, advice on employment, day care for children, kindergartens, and adult education. These services were restricted to whites.[13]

Impoverished Blacks in cities, many of whom had recently migrated from the South, had to be helped separately by their churches; there were also some white-funded settlement houses staffed by Blacks, and occasionally Black-led settlement houses. In Minneapolis, for example, wealthy whites funded the Phyllis Wheatley House in 1924. It provided recreational, educational, and cultural activities for middle- and working-class Blacks in a highly segregated city. The Wendell Phillips Settlement in Chicago and the Lincoln House in New York City were other examples of Black-staffed settlement houses funded and directed by upper-class whites.[14]

Born a slave, Victoria Earle Matthews in 1897 founded the White Rose Mission in New York City. The Mission provided Black women and girls basic literacy and training in how to help one's self and family. It was, as one researcher put it, "among the very few Black settlement houses that succeeded in providing services with an exclusively Black leadership."[15]

Settlement houses, of course, were not the only segregated institutions that Progressives maintained. From schools and churches to swimming pools and water fountains to trolleys and hotels—segregation both in the South and in the rest of the country white Progressives seldom challenged.

One prominent Progressive did. In 1905, Republican President Teddy Roosevelt invited Black leader Booker T. Washington to dinner at the White House. Not since Frederick Douglass had been invited to meet with President Lincoln in 1863 had a Black met with a president in the White House. It triggered headlines across the nation and efforts to get Roosevelt to rescind his invitation. He had dinner with Washington.[16]

Over a decade later, Democrat Woodrow Wilson, however, promoted Jim Crow rule in the federal civil service. When a delegation protested the Southern-born president's acceptance of downgrading federal jobs held by Blacks and even allowing their dismissal, he said, "If the colored people made a mistake in voting for me, they ought to correct it." Moreover, at a White House social event in 1915, he hosted a showing of the silent film *The Birth of a Nation*, a tale of the Ku Klux Klan terrorizing ex-slaves in the South following the Civil War. He called the film "writing history with lightning."[17]

So the Progressive movement aiming at cleansing corruption, ending monopolistic control of critical industries, and revitalizing democracy through restructuring governance mirrored the racial segregation that also was part of the America they sought to improve.

This was nowhere more true than in schooling, where separate schools for Blacks and whites were upheld as constitutional (*Plessy v. Ferguson*, 1896). While there were Black Progressive educators in these years, white Progressives did not challenge de jure segregation. What Progressives did successfully challenge was not only corrupt municipal governance but also crooked and inefficient school board governance at the state and local levels.

Inefficient and Shady School Governance

Consider that many big-city school systems, with scores of schools, thousands of teachers and administrators, and tens of thousands of students, were divided into districts or wards (created by city leaders), each with a "trustee" or unpaid school board member. These local trustees were expected to raise taxes for ward schools, contract to build and repair buildings, hire teachers, and supervise what occurred in schools. Affiliated with the political machine, these ward representatives also made policy for the system, since many also were members of large city-wide school boards. Detroit, for example, had seventeen members on its school board; Boston had twenty-four; Philadelphia, forty-two; and New York City, forty-six. Thus, most big cities in these years had large district school boards with little power to supervise local ward trustees who authorized and spent in their local schools.[18]

Opportunities for graft were rife in such a decentralized system. Teaching jobs in San Francisco, for example, allegedly sold for $200 a piece; in St. Louis, board member Edwin O'Connor sent the contract for supplying and installing furnaces in schools to his company and that of the school board president.[19]

Faced with such an inefficient and corrupt system of school governance, some mayors took matters into their own hands. In 1894, for example, reform-minded Detroit mayor Hazen Pingree, angry with school board members appointing friends to school posts and taking kickbacks from contractors hired to fix buildings, marched into one school board meeting. He said that unless the board resigned tonight, "there are quite a number of the members of this board who are going to jail." When some board members refused to resign, Pingree took out a list and instructed policemen to arrest those he named.[20]

Efficiency-driven Progressives, like their reform-minded municipal cousins, downsized school boards and promoted middle- and upper-middle-class business and civic-minded men and women like themselves to serve their communities. No more appointed cronies of political bosses. No more ward heelers with itchy palms. Additionally, educational reformers sought to professionalize the superintendency, bureaucratize the organization, and ensure that teachers had credentials showing a grasp of the subject knowledge they were expected to teach the young. It was a reform agenda aimed at divorcing school districts from city politics while increasing respect for teaching and administration.[21]

Progressives also worked at the state level. While funding of public schools continued to be drawn largely from local property taxes, state governors, as they had done in rooting out corrupt practices and expanding democratic participation, slowly exerted their authority through state boards of education and departments of education: they compelled parents to send their children to school, set standards for teachers and administrators, established minimum curriculum requirements, and provided some financial aid to districts. States slowly centralized their authority over school districts. But state departments of education had few employees to enforce state requirements. State education officials depended on local districts to put policies into practice. Inevitably, much variation occurred as local districts using their autonomy chose among state regulations.[22]

Reforming Traditional Curriculum and Instruction

In the decades before and after the twentieth century began, exposés of what students learned and how they were taught caught Progressives' attention. Pediatrician Joseph Rice, for example, visited schools in thirty-six cities, describing what he called "mechanical" instruction, teachers leading rote lessons and students reciting memorized answers, often in unison. He reported such lessons in New York City, Baltimore, Philadelphia, Buffalo, Chicago, and elsewhere. For example, while in Cincinnati, Rice sat in a third-grade reading lesson:

> The lesson was announced soon after I entered the room. When all children had placed their books upon the desks, the teacher said: "Position! Books in your left hands; right hands behind your backs!"
>
> The lesson was conducted as follows: one child was called upon to read a paragraph, then another pupil was told to read the same paragraph over again, and lastly, this paragraph was read by the class in concert. The same course was pursued in all the paragraphs read. Taken in all, this reading sounded like a piece of music consisting of a solo, an echo, and a chorus.

Following this description, Rice said, "How interesting the story must have been to the children!" Over a century later, I can reasonably say Rice was being sarcastic.[23]

Journalist Adele Shaw observed classrooms in twenty-five New York City schools filled with immigrant children. She marveled at how swiftly children arriving from Sicily, Greece, Cuba, Hungary, and Russia became Americanized: "Esther Obberhein in the entering class changes to Esther O'Brien in the next grade. Down in Marion Street a dark-eyed son of Naples who came last spring as Guiseppi Vagnotti appeared in September as Mike Jones."

Classes of sixty-five students sitting in rows of desks bolted to the floor listened to the teacher's directions and recited passages from the textbook one at a time as the teacher listened and judged responses. While Shaw was thoroughly impressed with the patience and skill of many lower-grade teachers managing sixty-plus students, she described short-tempered ones as well. In one school, a lower-grade teacher shouted at a student: "You—Are—Not—Still . . . You dirty little Russian Jew, what are you doing?"[24]

Teachers used commonly accepted teaching practices to transmit the traditional curriculum: students memorizing textbook paragraphs, daily recitation, written homework, tests, and strict behavioral discipline. Because these urban schools were age-graded, at the end of the school year, teachers and principals decided which students would be promoted to the next grade and which would be retained. Those retained for a few years often dropped out.

Rice and other Progressive educators wanted a "New Education." They wanted schools where a student was seen as more than a memory machine. They wanted lessons drawn from the latest scientific knowledge. They wanted lessons where students were actively engaged in learning both content and skills. They wanted lessons that took into account the student's physical, mental, emotional, and psychological development, or the "whole child."

Francis Wayland Parker's work in Quincy, Massachusetts, public schools as superintendent (1875–1880) inspired John Dewey and many others to experiment with alternative ways of educating the young beyond punitive discipline and rote instruction.

Dewey's Lab School at the University of Chicago (1896–1903)—a private school—built on Parker's ideas. These "pedagogical" Progressives, as historian Lawrence Cremin labeled them, wanted teachers to be less formal in their instruction and have children and youth grasp ideas through engaging in different classroom activities, working collaboratively in small groups, learning the arts and humanities, and being physically active. They wanted children and youth to work on projects that connected their outside lives to school lessons. They wanted students to learn by doing and not sit passively at desks or woodenly recite paragraphs from the text. The wanted a "child-centered" education.[25]

The rhetoric of pedagogical Progressives altered the vocabulary of academics, superintendents, principals, school board members, and teachers in these years. Phrases like "child-centered," "learning by doing," and "projects" dominated Progressive talk.

And there were other Progressive educators using the common patois who prized efficiency in operating schools, curriculum, and instruction. They differed sufficiently from fellow reformers to be recognizable to both their contemporaries and, later, historians. These efficiency-minded Progressives wanted to use scientific knowledge to rid traditional administrators and teachers of making gut-based decisions on how to manage schools, sort students by their abilities, and deliver the curriculum through one-size-fits-all programs.

Some historians have called Columbia's Edward Thorndike, Stanford's Ellwood Cubberley, and Chicago's Charles Hubbard Judd "administrative Progressives." The same has been said of superintendents William Wirt of Gary, Indiana; Frank Spaulding of Minneapolis, Minnesota; and Jesse Newlon of Denver, Colorado. These efficiency-driven educators infused the rhetoric of pedagogical Progressives into management practices borrowed from the corporate world to alter school governance, curriculum, and instruction.[26]

Consider the "platoon system" as an instance of such mix-and-match reforms. Initiated by Superintendent William Wirt in Gary, Indiana, in 1906, platoon schools, endorsed by Progressive doyens John and Evelyn Dewey in their best-selling book *Schools of To-morrow* (1915), rippled across the nation. The idea of fully using a school building to accommodate surging enrollment by having students on a schedule that divided the school day into work-play-study caught fire. Not only was it a way of saving money in erecting new schools, but it gave urban children experiences they seldom got in traditional elementary schools. District after district adopted this new way of organizing elementary schools.[27]

How did the platoon school work? A designated group of students—a "platoon"—would follow a daily school schedule of eight periods lasting thirty-five to forty minutes each. For half the day, students would attend academic periods covering reading, math, geography, civics, and nature study. In the other half of the day, that platoon would spend periods of the same length participating in special activities in the gym, library, music, manual arts workshops, and art rooms.[28]

Beyond William Wirt's innovation, these reformers also adopted fact-finding and quantitative ways of measuring school and student progress. Pushed by Thorndike and other efficiency-driven advocates, intelligence testing of students became prevalent. Progressive administrators used student test scores as scientific data to sort individual students by ability into different curricula and classrooms. They commissioned district surveys that assessed buildings and measured district practices down to how well teachers taught lessons. Altogether, these efficiency-driven Progressives increased access to tax-supported schooling for young and older children, established new curricula, and created business-like ways of managing that had become "best practices" by the 1940s to better educate the "whole child."[29]

These administrative Progressives blended the vocabulary and aspirations of pedagogical pioneers such as Parker and Dewey with corporate-inspired ideas of efficiency. Yet their ideas and practices far exceeded the influence of pedagogical Progressives on curricula and classroom instruction. Or as historian Ellen Lagemann put it: "[O]ne cannot understand the history of education in the United States during the twentieth century unless one realizes that Edward L. Thorndike won and John Dewey lost."[30]

Yet the victory wasn't as clear-cut as the clever maxim suggests when it came to superintendents and teachers. The quote overlooks the many variations in beliefs and practices among educators who created hybrids of Progressive practices in thousands of districts, schools, and classrooms. The umbrella of Progressivism sheltered many reformers.[31]

As historian David Gamson pointed out in his study of four western urban districts (Oakland, Denver, Portland, and Seattle) led by superintendents during the decades before and after World War I, these school chiefs saw themselves as Progressives combining the language, policies, and implementation of both pedagogical and administrative Progressives. They were practical men (there were only a handful of women superintendents before World War I), and they drew from an array of reformers as they worked on district governance, organization, and curriculum. Appointed by Progressive school boards, these pragmatic school leaders introduced both intelligence testing and kindergartens; differentiated curricula including vocational education and guidance counselors; organizational charts and the Project Method.

So when it came to daily practices in managing districts and schools and putting new school curricula into lessons, Progressive-minded superintendents drawing from pedagogical, administrative, and other reformers mixed and matched reforms in altering traditional schools and classrooms.

Yet while Progressive school boards and superintendents can notch victories onto their belts in altering how districts were governed and managed and in creating new curricula, the traditional age-graded school and classroom lessons were far harder nuts to crack.

Expanding the Age-Graded School: Kindergartens and Secondary Schools

Between 1900 and the present, few changes have occurred in the traditional organization of the age-graded school except for expanding access to it. And that exception of broadening entrée into public schools is highly significant, because the twentieth-century conversion from educating an elite few to schooling all Americans gave substance to the belief that education and democracy—however defined—are wrapped together.

Most educational Progressives wanted to make public schooling available to all. And "all" meant schooling for immigrant, poor, and middle-class families. So these reformers gradually embraced adding innovative kindergartens to the traditional grammar school. Begun as private ventures by civic-minded women toward the end of the nineteenth century, kindergartens were initially established in response to concerns about the many urban children left on their own as immigrant parents worked long hours in factories and sweatshops. Heavily influenced by the work of Friedrich Froebel in Germany and its child-centeredness, kindergartens also attracted the attention of middle-class families. By the 1890s, a few urban superintendents had adopted kindergartens. What were once eight-grade grammar schools became K–8 organizations.[32]

But what about all the children who exited schooling after the elementary school grades? Efficiency-driven Progressives wanted a new type of organization inserted between elementary and high school that would retain eleven- and twelve-year-olds who usually dropped out after the fifth or sixth grade. The Progressives envisioned extended education for Americans, not one that ended at puberty.

Enter the junior high school. Progressives saw this new organization as the next step in democratic schooling. Junior high curricula had newly created courses like woodworking, printing and metal shops, cooking, and sewing that provided opportunities for students to use their hands and heads to acquire skills. By the 1920s, there were nearly one thousand junior high schools (just fifty-five were stand-alone buildings); most junior high schools in that year were located in senior high school buildings. By 1938, there were just over 7,500 junior high schools, with about one-third located in separate buildings. Sixth graders would now transition to the junior high school and spend three years there before, reformers hoped, moving on to high school. That was the Progressive thinking of the day.[33]

By the Great Depression, the Progressive belief that in a democracy all American children deserved schooling from ages five through eighteen had become mainstream ideology among educators and most of the public. And it was in the 1930s, when widespread unemployment ravaged the nation, that youth facing few options for work chose to stay in school; students completed junior high school at increasing rates and entered the nearest high school. During the Depression, high school graduation rates soared from 17 percent (1920) to 51 percent (1938).[34]

The establishment of the junior high school and the conversion of the traditional college preparatory high school into a comprehensive one, with multiple curricula including vocational education, became the Progressive agenda for organizational reform before and after World War I. Instead of only one college prep curriculum in the traditional high school, Progressives made new courses of study available to students between the 1920s and 1940s. Using intelligence tests and past academic performance, teachers guided students through a differentiated curriculum. Students could choose from a menu of vocational, commercial, college preparatory, and, later, "life adjustment" curricula. Progressives added guidance counselors to help students and parents choose from curricular menus.[35]

The comprehensive high school where all students, helped by the newly created post of "guidance counselors," could choose college-prep courses, vocational and commercial classes, or blends of both along with an expanded afterschool extracurricular program was considered by all stripes of Progressives as their crowning achievement.

The Durability of Age-Graded Schools

Broadening access to public schooling by embracing kindergartens, junior high school, and comprehensive high school, however, did not disturb the age-graded school. Such additions to the existing organization, in fact, added steel rebar to the age-graded school. No longer a mid-nineteenth-century innovation, the age-graded organization spread in cities before World War I and by the 1930s had become institutionalized by Progressives as the only way to organize K–12 urban schools for ever-growing enrollments.

Twenty-first-century parents and grandparents attended such schools and accepted them as the best way—perhaps the only way—to organize a school. After all, in first grade children learned to read; in third grade teachers taught cursive writing; and in sixth grade ancient Egypt and mummies enthralled preteens.

Even with much criticism of the age-graded organization in the late nineteenth century, its growth and sustained support from parents and educators continued among nearly all Progressives as the correct way to organize schools. Yes, there were a few Progressives who sought individual learning and mastery of subject matter and skills regardless of grade level. Superintendent Carleton Washburne's Winnetka Plan in the

Chicago suburb and other programs such as the Dalton Plan blended Deweyan ideas with efficiency practices. Such scattered innovations enjoyed much positive acclaim initially and spread fitfully but hardly altered the primacy of the age-graded school. By 1940, the age-graded school had rebuffed efforts decade after decade to alter it.[36]

Changing Instruction

While the daily language of Progressive educators included phrases like "child-centered" and the "project method," converting these words into curricular and instructional policies, which, in turn, teachers converted into daily lessons, was much more difficult than reformers had expected in a country with thousands of school districts, tens of thousands of schools, and hundreds of thousands of classrooms. What did occur in these schools and classrooms was spotty, often mixes of the traditional and innovative, and paled next to the soaring rhetoric of Progressive reformers.

Too few historians have documented what teachers and students did in these classrooms. Those who have done so located actual lesson plans, classroom photos, teacher diaries, and observations of lessons by journalists and administrators. Their findings, given the fragments of evidence they collected, are that most teachers in these decades while calling themselves Progressives had actually worked out realistic ways of blending traditional and Progressive practices—under the most difficult conditions—into classroom lessons. What made putting Progressive ideas into classroom practice so hard?[37]

Begin with the traditional classroom furniture: student desks fastened to the floor. Consider that in New York City between the 1890s and 1920s the school board's architect developed the standard classroom for grades 1–4 with forty-eight bolted-down desks; for grades 5 and 6, classrooms had forty-five desks, and for grades 7 and 8, classrooms had forty stationary desks. Pedagogical Progressives called for much child movement in the classroom. Small groups of children and youth working together on projects or having activity centers in the classroom to which students would move displayed the clunkiness of nailed-down desks. Progressives called for movable desks, chairs, and tables to alter traditional instruction. But they were expensive.[38]

Even those teachers enamored of putting Progressive ideas into practice faced large class sizes and superiors' demands to cover prescribed courses of study to ensure their students would be prepared for the next grade. Many primary grade teachers incorporated Progressive ideas into their lessons by establishing play areas (e.g., sandboxes, painting corners, reading nooks), and upper grade teachers introduced individual projects. Such teacher and student work was enticing, but it often took multiple weeks to teach, forcing those few teachers who tried it to scramble to catch up with other teachers in the same grade. Moreover, even for new subjects like civics, problems of democracy, and business math, teachers, given the time for lessons, used textbooks, assigned homework, and often lectured.

What most reformers failed to fully grasp was that these Progressive ideas required teachers to create new curricular materials, reorganize classroom space, and develop activities that got students to participate in small groups and team up with classmates on projects. More to the point is that the reform ideology asked teachers to get to know their students psychologically, intellectually, socially, and emotionally. Likewise, giving students greater freedom to engage in discussions, make choices, and work closely with classmates was something that most teachers of the day had little experience with, much less the expertise to implement.

In these decades, the demands of covering required content and skills while seeking out different instructional materials (or creating them) to individualize lessons kept most teachers working double time. Given class sizes and having a life outside of school, that kind of effort signaled colleagues that such instruction was too much to do or expect over the course of a school year. As a result, most teachers focused on existing texts, tests, lecturing, and memorization. But a substantial fraction selected some of the new ideas and combined them with their routine classroom practices, creating mixes of classroom activities or hybrids of instruction.

And yet even with these constraints, there were some teachers who grasped Progressive rhetoric and tried hard to incorporate it into their daily teaching.

Consider a lesson taught in 1924 by Mrs. Spencer, a fourth-grade teacher in a New York City elementary school. Journalist and Progressive cheerleader Agnes De Lima admired what Progressive teachers did in private schools in the city. In going into a few public schools, she found shrunken versions of what she admired in the private schools. De Lima visited one public school where the principal selected Mrs. Spencer, "his very best teacher," for the journalist to observe.[39]

De Lima described the forty-two children engaged in small-group activities and the movement the teacher allowed in a very crowded room. The entire morning had back-to-back lessons covering arithmetic, reading, and geography, and then recess. Here is De Lima's account of the geography portion of the morning:

> "Take out your geographies and turn to the map of Asia. Page 185."
> "Henry, what is Asia?"
> "Asia—Asia," Henry grasped for an answer.
> "Class?"
> "Asia is a continent," they said as one.
> "Well, what is the meaning of a 'continent,' Elsie?"
> "A continent is the largest division of land."
> "Right, when I talk about a continent, what do I mean? I mean land...."
> Question followed question, with children occasionally summoned from their desks to pick up a pointer used by the teacher and identify a place on the map. Recess interrupted the recitation.

During the writing lesson that followed recess, Mrs. Spencer said to the class, "Do your very best. We have only a week or two before promotion day." "Three girls sighed and covered their faces," De Lima wrote. Following the writing lesson was the class reading "A Mad Tea-Party" from *Alice in Wonderland*. According to De Lima, students were eager to read the parts, and Mrs. Spencer chose four volunteers. "The playlet," DeLima said, went off admirably. And Mrs. Spencer said, "Fine, you were all good."[40]

Under the sway of pedagogical, administrative, and other strains of Progressive reformers, then, there were some modifications in classroom activities and routines. Rote recitation—as Joseph Rice described in his visits to city systems in the early 1890s—declined, as did unbending discipline and scowling teachers. Teachers who had learned about the psychology of children and learning became less formal in getting to know individual students. Many teachers in the early grades began teaching small groups of children while assigning the rest of the class desk-bound activities.

There were other teachers like Mrs. Spencer—my guess is about one out of four teachers in the 1920s and 1930s—who departed from the norm and tried different Progressive methods, such as teaching small groups, student-led discussions, and students working independently or in teams on projects. These teachers humanized the rigid recitation, were more flexible in managing the students, and created activities that allowed students to work in small groups and make independent decisions about what to study and how to carry it off.[41]

Through these decades, most teachers, however, slowly combined Progressive and traditional practices into lessons. In effect, they altered some routine classroom practices and created hybrids that fused traditional and Progressive ways of teaching. What happened in these classrooms was similar to what David Gamson describes for the superintendents in four western cities who combined both child-centered and efficiency-driven Progressive ideas that seemingly conflicted into a mix of policies and practices applied to school governance, organization, and curriculum.

Summing Up

The Progressive movement was fueled by a passion to improve civic and economic life in America for middle- and working-class citizens, consumers, and children. Zealous reformers cleansed municipal corruption, reorganized state and city governments, and reduced corporate predations on both workers and consumers.

The Progressive reform umbrella also sheltered educational reformers who took on inefficient and traditional schooling by downsizing and centralizing school board control to eliminate bribery and corruption and upgrade the competence of teachers and administrators. New curricula flowed across the nation's school districts. But when it came to altering substantially classroom instruction, the going got difficult.

What did appear in a substantial fraction of districts, schools, and classrooms in the early decades of the twentieth century were mixes of Progressive and traditional practices that gave some credence to the work of Progressive-minded superintendents, such as Ella Flagg Young, a former student of John Dewey, who led the Chicago schools (1909–1915); Teachers College graduate Jesse Newlon, who headed the Denver Public Schools (1920–1927); and William Davidson and Ben Graham, superintendents who headed the Pittsburgh Public Schools back-to-back (1913–1942).

Those two Pittsburgh superintendents, serving nearly thirty years, presided over major changes in a school system that had grown swiftly as immigrants from southern and eastern Europe and migrants from the southern US sought jobs in its sprawling steel industry.

The final part of this chapter turns to the Progressive movement, both municipal and educational, as it unfolded in Pittsburgh during these decades.

THE PROGRESSIVE MOVEMENT IN PITTSBURGH PUBLIC SCHOOLS

In May 1903, *McClure's Magazine* published "Pittsburgh: A City Ashamed." The muckraking journalist Lincoln Steffens had profiled many cities in the magazine, and now he turned to the western Pennsylvania smoke-filled city astride three rivers. By 1900, the city had grown to over 450,000, absorbing wave after wave of immigrants, many of whom worked in the mills lining the Monongahela River.[42]

Steffens's article began softly: "Two rivers flow past it to make a third, the Ohio . . . beneath it are natural gas and coal which feed a thousand furnaces that smoke all day and flame all night." Then he hammered home the punch line: "The city has been described physically as 'Hell with the lid off'; politically it is that same with the lid on." Steffens described the chokehold that steel and mining industry leaders, aligned with bankers and local business elites, had on the city in the late nineteenth century.[43]

As in other cities of the era, political machine bosses and business elites struck quiet agreements to run municipal decision-making and provide services without interference from outsiders, especially reform-minded activists. Conflicts with unions in the bloody railroad strike in 1877 and the pitched battle between strikers and hired private police at the US Steel Homestead plant in 1892, with subsequent skirmishes in later years, drew steel industry capitalists to support the existing political machine that had controlled those elected to office, often through rigged elections, for decades.

Since the 1880s, the Republican machine in Pittsburgh, run by Chris Magee and William Flinn, had controlled the mayor and decentralized ward and city council decision-making through patronage and boodle—a lovely but seldom-used word for bribery. The elected mayor had little authority, and most decisions were made by the city council, two chambers composed of over a hundred elected representatives from the wards.[44] Steffens recounts how Magee and Flinn created ghost voters in elections, thereby controlling local government:

> Boss Magee's idea was not to corrupt the city government, but to be it; not to hire votes in councils, but to own councilmen; and so, having seized control of his organization, he nominated cheap or dependent men for the select and common councils. Relatives and friends were his first recourse, then came bartenders, saloon-keepers, liquor dealers, and others allied to the vices, who were subject to police regulation and dependent in a business way upon the maladministration of law.[45]

Moreover, local bankers were in the thrall of the machine as well, since public funds had to be deposited. Magee and Flinn chose particular banks so that favors asked by machine politicians for loans seldom were turned down. Steffens minced no words about how local bankers were corrupted:

> This service [depositing public monies in certain banks] . . . not only kept them [the bankers] docile, but gave [Magee] and Flinn credit at their banks. Then, too, Flinn and Magee's operations soon developed on a scale which made their business attractive to the largest financial institutions for the profits on their loans, and thus enabled them to distribute and share in the golden opportunities of big deals.

"The manufacturers and the merchants were kept well in hand," Steffens wrote, "by many little municipal grants and privileges, such as switches, wharf rights, and street and alley vacations" (allowances to take over a public street when a business expanded).[46]

So it is no surprise that municipal contracts for trolley lines, road repair, bridges, and parks also went to machine leaders. Flinn's construction company, for example, received scores of contracts. Nor should readers be surprised that the Director of Public Works, who signed such contracts for the city, was a cousin of Chris Magee, boss of the Pittsburgh machine.[47]

Challenges to the Magee machine occurred periodically in the 1880s and 1890s. Good government reformers in Pittsburgh's Civic Club and the Voters' League, organizations made up of socially prominent men and women including business leaders, professionals, and activists, embraced Progressive ideas, particularly copying efficient practices displayed by corporate executives in steel, mining, banking, and transportation. They lobbied state legislators to alter city governance by pressing for more mayoral authority. They were largely unsuccessful until 1911.

These Progressives supported Democrat George Guthrie for mayor in 1906. A decade earlier, he had run for the post and lost as a result, he claimed, of the machine adding thousands of false names to voter registry lists. And a decade later, he beat the Republican machine.[48]

Guthrie introduced strict business and bookkeeping rules in city departments so that awarding contracts and depositing municipal funds were no longer Magee decisions. He got the powerful Pennsylvania Railroad to stop running trains through the heart of the downtown district. He ended "perpetual" contracts given to street railway companies. And for those middle- and working-class families who had for years pleaded with authorities for clean water, Mayor Guthrie established a city-owned water-treatment plant to reduce annual deaths that had made the city "the typhoid capital of the Western world." Further, Guthrie equalized taxes—getting industrialists to pay more—channeled public funds into schools and public services, especially in low-income wards, and, when the 1908 recession hit the city, hired the unemployed to work on city projects. However, Guthrie could only serve one term and left office in 1909.[49]

Progressives finally triumphed in 1911. Activists in Pittsburgh and Philadelphia finally got the state legislature to charter both cities with strong mayor-councils. The state altered the governance of both cities (and school boards, discussed below) by reducing the size of the Pittsburgh city council from twenty-seven members elected by the wards to nine members elected by a citywide vote. The charter law, then, abolished the ward-dominated, decentralized government that made it easy picking pockets for Republicans and Boss Magee.[50]

Just as municipal and school reform marched hand in hand in other cities, so too Pittsburgh. There were sixty-one ward-based school districts in the city that decided how to spend their allotted funds. As one newspaper article described:

> Many [of these] school boards . . . [were] made up of saloon keepers, proprietors of gambling houses and "joints," city employees, common loafers, and contractors who openly accepted contracts for school buildings in direct violation of the law. . . . Janitors were political powers in the wards and sometimes even responsible for placing principals in their jobs.[51]

Bribery for securing contracts and the city machine meting out school jobs to underlings was common in these ward-based boards.

As for the citywide board of education, each ward sent representatives. The hundreds of members of the central board had little authority, a situation often leading to ward-based decisions that, depending on the property tax base, created wide disparities in school buildings, staffing, and who got jobs and contracts. There was money to be made, and both the machine and school officials dipped into the public trough.

The 1911 state school code eliminated school district governance by wards by creating a central board of education of fifteen members appointed by local judges. This newly constituted board had authority over the entire district in levying taxes on property, appointing top school officials, and directing district staff in schooling nearly sixty thousand students, many of whom were from families of recent immigrants. Appointed by Common Pleas judges and serving six-year terms, the smaller board protected the district from the partisan political influence that was so evident in previous decades.

Within a few years, the smaller, reconstituted board of education—drawn from upper-middle-class business and professional men and women imbued with Progressive ideas of the day about efficiently governing schools—altered district organization and curriculum. It was led by businessman Marcus Aaron, who was appointed in 1911 as a member of the new board and served continuously between 1922 and 1942, often as its president, finally retiring from the post in 1947.

Under Aaron's leadership in that first decade, the board levied taxes; adopted corporate management approaches, especially developing an administrative hierarchy; and began a massive construction and renovation program. The system expanded in size, particularly with the arrival of immigrants to fill industrial jobs, and by merging with other districts in Allegheny County. By the time the US entered World War I, the district schooled nearly seventy thousand students. And as in other urban districts in the nation, the board of education appointed efficiency-minded superintendents, each serving six-year terms, to lead the districts.[52]

Between 1913 and 1942, two Progressive educators, William Davidson and Ben Graham, led the ever-growing district, providing continuity under the vigilant eyes of Marcus Aaron and other veteran board members as they grew the bureaucracy to administer an expanding school population, larger school staffs, and new buildings. For example, by 1916, below the superintendent there were eight associate superintendents and ten directors supervising academic and vocational subjects, kindergartens, special education, music, and art. Then below these supervisors were five departments directed to manage buildings, school supplies, legal matters, and budgeting. In 1928, an independent commission praised Davidson and his management of the district for its "efficiency."[53]

Davidson served nearly three terms as superintendent between 1913 and 1930, and subsequently Ben Graham, an insider in the district, was promoted to the top post, holding office until he died in 1942. Such leadership continuity meant that the board and superintendent shared the same goals and expected that the Progressive agenda would stay intact. And it did. Davidson not only expanded the bureaucracy, he also altered the organization, curriculum, and instruction to align with other reform-driven districts across the country while offering the Pittsburgh version of efficiency in action.

Organization, Curriculum, and Instruction

In these decades, industrialized Pittsburgh drew tens of thousands of immigrants from southern and eastern Europe eager to find jobs, work hard, raise families, and become American. Most of these men, women, and children could not speak English and were largely uneducated even in their native lands. Unfamiliar with the language and culture, these hard-working immigrants settled into low-income neighborhoods and sent their children to kindergartens and age-graded schools. As Superintendent Davidson pointed out:

> The fact that 45 per cent of the [kindergarten] children come from homes where the English language is slightly known makes this department of the school a very present help. . . . No better medium can be found for reaching the great body of alien races crowding into our city and making them a vital part of our civic, industrial, and social life than the little child in whom all the interests of life and labor and love find a common center.[54]

Given the influx of immigrants and strong Progressive beliefs in learning by doing, working on projects, and blending the head and the hand, elementary and secondary school subjects taught boys how to make wood and metal products using the machinery of the day—staffs called them "shops"—while girls learned how to cook, sew, and make clothes. Also, the board established separate vocational schools for boys and girls.

When the innovative Larimer Junior High School opened its doors to students in 1916, it was one of only three junior high schools in the nation; vocational subjects were part of the required curriculum. At the high school level, by the end of the 1920s, students could choose to take a vocational course of study or leave for separate vocational schools elsewhere in the city.[55]

Under Superintendent Davidson, the traditional K–6 or K–8 school continued to dominate elementary school organization, except he promoted, as did fellow Progressive educators, the junior high school and separate vocational high schools. Further, he advocated a six-year secondary school where students attended grades 7–9 in the same building that housed the high school. This six-six arrangement continued under his successor. In 1939, for example, out of twenty-one secondary schools, thirteen had both junior high and senior high school grades in the same building. Also, by the end of both Davidson's and Graham's terms in office, there were eight separate vocational high schools in the city.[56]

Davidson's signature reform was the board's approval of his recommendation in 1916 to adopt the platoon school, or work-study-play plan, that had originated in Gary, Indiana, a decade earlier. Like other industrial cities where immigrant families settled to find work, Gary schools soon became overcrowded. Many districts had to have double sessions—that is, shorter hours—so that all students could attend school during the day.

Progressive educator William Wirt, a former student of John Dewey at the University of Chicago, wanted to solve two problems when he assumed the position in Gary: how to use a school building to its full capacity, while also giving children access to a complete education in the arts, with special subjects like music, woodworking, and physical exercise. The answer was the Gary Plan, and the school board provided Wirt with resources to add auditoriums, gymnasiums, and music and drawing rooms to existing buildings. Unheard of at the time.

With a constantly growing enrollment common to industrialized cities in the early twentieth century, Davidson saw the advantages of this innovation imported to the Steel City. Christened the Pittsburgh Platoon Schools, the innovation altered the traditional curriculum, adding subjects (music, art, health) that many students had seldom experienced. Of equal importance, it doubled the capacity of schools, particularly the larger elementary ones, to accommodate large numbers of students. The plan had substantial financial benefits insofar as funding new school construction as enrollments grew each year. Platoon schools spread throughout the district under Davidson and Graham's tenures, although the plan was not mandated for every Pittsburgh school.

In 1916, three elementary schools piloted the work-study-play plan. Over a decade later, the innovation had spread to eighty-six schools, making Pittsburgh the second largest city in the nation operating platoon schools. By 1939, the plan was in 94 of 125 elementary schools, or 75 percent of all elementary schools.[57]

In 1939, the board of education (Marcus Aaron was president and Ben Graham was superintendent) asked a leading Progressive, Professor George Strayer of Teachers College, Columbia University, to study district schools. Strayer and staff did an exhaustive survey of the system, including the ninety-four platoon schools.

This independent 1940 survey of Pittsburgh Public Schools described the operation of these platoon schools. Typically, these schools' daily schedules called for eight periods of thirty-five to forty minutes each, or forty instructional lessons a week. Administrators standardized this arrangement by supplying each school with a chart listing the number of periods a week to be spent in each subject. In the sixth grade, for example, platoon schools divided those forty periods of instruction among eleven subjects, thus allowing two to seven periods for each subject per week.

The report laid out an average day in these schools:

> A pupil may spend the first two periods of the forenoon in the home-room studying academic subjects and the second two periods in such special rooms as the gymnasium, library, art or music rooms. In the afternoon two more periods are usually devoted to academic work and two more to special subjects. In some schools all academic subjects may be taught by one teacher, while in others, a departmental plan divides the academic work among two or more teachers who specialize in such subjects as reading or arithmetic.[58]

The survey found much variation across platoon schools. Among the ninety-four schools, over a third omitted the first grade from the platoon; other schools omitted primary grades, leaving only the upper grades in the program. In twelve of the schools, there were multiage primary units designed to omit grades completely, and in fourteen schools there were "activity" programs geared to projects. There were also programs for gifted children and for those students who needed remedial work.

While the survey documented fully the entire curricular and instructional program, condition of the buildings, and financial situation—it was still in the midst of the Great Depression—the platoon school had fallen in disfavor among Pittsburgh's Progressive educators. Staff noted that top administrators were moving away from the work-study-play plan that had been in operation across most district schools over two decades. These academic survey authors encouraged such movement as they politely criticized platoon schooling in key sections of the report. And the Pittsburgh Public Schools did eventually divorce itself from the plan after Ben Graham died in office (1942) and World War II came to dominate district affairs.

Here is where I enter this analysis of Progressivism across the country and in Pittsburgh. In 1939, when I was five years old, my mother marched me from our apartment at 2829 Centre Avenue across the street to Minersville Elementary School, where I took a seat in a first-grade classroom. I attended two elementary schools and one junior-senior high school, experiencing remnants of the platoon system until I graduated in 1951. In the next chapter, I describe my experiences as a student in the Pittsburgh Public Schools.

CHAPTER 2

A Student in the Pittsburgh Public Schools (1939–1951)

I HAVE OFTEN ADMIRED THOSE ADULTS WHO RECALL in great detail and with affection (or hatred) elementary school teachers they had. They describe what she looked like (nearly 90 percent of all elementary teachers are—and have been—women), activities they engaged in, and incidents that seemingly have been imprinted on them forever.[1]

Here is 2016 Democratic presidential nominee Hillary Clinton recalling some of her teachers:

> It's funny what school memories have stuck with me over the years: Miss Taylor reading to my first-grade class from Winnie-the-Pooh every morning. Miss Cappuccio, my second-grade teacher, challenging us to write from one to one thousand. It was an impossible task for our tiny hands, but the exercise taught me what it meant to follow through on big projects.[2]

Or writer and former teacher Kate Haas, who recalled her fourth-grade teacher:

> Yelling, intimidation and threats were a daily practice with her. She humiliated students regularly, as on the morning she forced my fourth grade best friend to stand in front of the class, hectoring her to tears over a multiplication problem. Still vivid is my teacher's furious tirade against another girl, who had dared use purple in a drawing of the sky. Didn't we all know, she raged, that the sky was blue?[3]

My memories of elementary school teachers and classrooms, however, fall far short. What I do remember is sketchy, at best. So while my long-term memory is intact for many experiences, I cannot join Clinton and Haas in remembering my grade-school teachers. I do better, though, with a few of my junior and senior high school teachers.

Mottled memories follow of being a student in three Pittsburgh public schools during the closing years of the Progressive education movement. To reconstruct those years as a student, I used a major district survey conducted by outside researchers and school board reports to get information about the schools I attended. For my direct experiences, I had only one official document, a transcript of grades, photos of me as a young boy with my parents and brothers, and yes, my Swiss cheese memory.

Beware then, readers, in my recounting experiences in Minersville and Roosevelt Elementary Schools and Taylor Allderdice secondary school.

Bits and pieces of being in school come back to me, albeit in blurred, inexact ways. But those memories persist. In alerting readers to the inherent flaws of trying to remember what occurred decades ago, Italian writer Primo Levi put the act of remembering best:

> Human memory is a marvelous but fallacious instrument. The memories which lie within us are not carved in stone; not only do they tend to become erased as the years go by, but often they change, or even increase by incorporating extraneous features.[4]

The second warning to readers is to reinforce the obvious fact that going to school is only one part of a child's life—albeit an important one. Multiply 180 days (the average number of days the fifty states have required school to be in session over the past few decades) by the hours that most US students spend in school (6.5 hours), and the total is nearly 1,200 hours a year in school.

Consider further that in such a year the child is awake nearly six thousand hours (subtracting eight hours of nightly sleep). In other words, in each year, about 80 percent of a student's life is spent *outside* of school. This is indirectly saying that while tax-supported schooling in a market-driven democracy is essential if for no other reason than granting credentials that are required to complete high school, finish college, and enter the workplace with the proper pieces of parchment, it takes up about one-fifth of a five-year-old's life or a high school student's last year prior to donning robes for graduation.[5]

With these two cautions in mind, what do I remember of those years in school?

FAMILY BACKGROUND

Jewish immigrants from the Kiev area in Czarist Russia, my parents, who spoke Russian, Yiddish, and later English, had come to Pittsburgh (where my mother had family) and New York City (where my father had relatives).[6] My mother met my father in New York City. They got married in 1919 and started a family. My two brothers were born in the 1920s, and I came along in the mid-1930s.

My father initially worked in New York City as a restaurant waiter. Like most immigrants, he worked from dawn to dusk to bring home enough money to cover rent, put food on the table, and clothe the family. He spoke Russian and Yiddish at home and in the workplace. But he learned English slowly. What today would be called "broken English" was what I remember at home growing up. When my mother and father spoke either Russian or Yiddish, that was a clear signal to all of us that the subject was something serious like money, work troubles, or events that parents did not want children to know about.

My mother was the "homemaker," watching the nickels and dimes, cooking, cleaning, and caring for the children. She had attended junior high school in Pittsburgh for a year or so and her English, while accented, was clear to all of us. She was ambitious for her husband and for each of her sons. She dominated our family when big decisions had to be made, like moving from one neighborhood to another or when crises occurred. She was clear in her dreams for what her husband and children could achieve.

After working at different restaurants and grocery stores for over a decade, my parents had saved enough to buy a mom-and-pop grocery store in Passaic, New Jersey. They moved from New York City when my father was forty and my mother, thirty-six. I was born in Passaic in 1934 and was the youngest of three sons. My brothers, Norty and Marty, were then nine and fifteen.

Within two years of their buying the grocery store, however, the German-American Bund—a group that had grown quickly in the wake of Adolph Hitler's becoming Germany's chancellor in 1933—boycotted Jewish-owned grocery stores in the city. Customers stopped shopping at our store. We went broke. So in 1936, my family of five moved to Pittsburgh.

My parents chose Pittsburgh because my mother had lived there after immigrating from Russia. She had three sisters and a brother there. Though we arrived in the midst of the Great Depression, we found housing in what then was called the Hill District, a neighborhood inhabited by a mix of mostly Black working- and middle-class families and Jewish immigrants.

My father, like so many other unemployed, could not find any work until he landed a job with the federally funded Works Progress Administration. Eventually he found work with a food distributor selling meats, pickles, and dairy products off of a rented truck to mom-and-pop grocery stores in Pittsburgh and nearby towns. By this time, my two older brothers were teenagers attending nearby junior and senior high schools and working at odd jobs after school to contribute to the family income.

MINERSVILLE ELEMENTARY SCHOOL

In 1939, at age five, I entered first grade at Minersville Elementary School just across the street from where we lived in a second-floor apartment. The school had been in operation since 1859. It had been renovated in 1873 and rebuilt in 1893. As to its physical condition when I entered the school, external researchers had rated each of the 140 district schools on a five-point scale going from "superior" to "inferior." They rated Minersville "inferior." The old, dilapidated building was torn down a few years after I transferred to Roosevelt in 1941.[7]

I can only guess why I skipped kindergarten. Either my mother convinced the principal that I was capable of doing first-grade work or the administrator put me there because the kindergarten already had over sixty children. Whatever the reason, I joined thirty-plus first graders.[8]

The year I entered the first grade, Minersville Elementary had 462 students dispersed across thirteen classrooms—each built to hold forty students sitting in rows of bolted-down desks. It was largely Black in enrollment—I remember one white girl in the school—and racial encounters occurred outside of school. Class size was around thirty-five students. Minersville had one kindergarten class with sixty-three children and a room for "special" students.[9]

Nearly all of the other first-grade children, who were a year or two older than me, had been in kindergarten—a Progressive reform adopted and expanded by the Pittsburgh Board of Education. But I had not attended kindergarten.

I entered the first grade uninitiated in school and classroom routines that most of my classmates had already absorbed a year earlier. They had been taught to obey the teacher, told when they could talk and when to be quiet. They knew how to ask permission of the teacher to get up from their desk to sharpen their pencils.

They had already picked up what schooling teaches the young—what academics call "socialization" or the "hidden curriculum"—that is absent from teachers' lesson plans. Moreover, my classmates already knew the colors of the spectrum; they could count to ten and add numbers; and some were actually reading. I was way behind my peers socially and academically.

The first-grade teacher's major task was to get students to read through phonics. I finally learned to read with understanding by the second grade. Then my family moved, and I began third grade at Roosevelt Elementary School in Greenfield. There, I grasped reading like a life preserver. As I got older, I took the trolley or walked to the Carnegie Library in Oakland, which became my second home.

My memory fails me in recovering experiences from those early years at Minersville. I can recall no particular teacher or lessons. This is not to say that I wasn't exposed to or did not absorb parts of the Progressive curriculum, since I slowly grasped reading and arithmetic basics. But my memory fails me in remembering who taught me, what I was taught, and how.

Progressive reform in Pittsburgh, as noted in the previous chapter, differed from other urban districts such as New York City, Denver, Colorado, and Seattle, for the simple reason that the Pittsburgh Board of Education and its superintendents in these years embraced the organizational reform called the "platoon school."[10]

Was Minersville a platoon school? Because many district platoon schools excluded first and second graders from the work-study-play organization, and since only one of four elementary schools was designated as a platoon school, I don't think Minersville was one. Bolstering the guess is that platoon schools, for the most part, had large enrollments, and Minersville enrolled only 462 students in grades K–6 (1939). Finally, the building was one of the oldest in the district and in disrepair.

What I can recall most vividly from being thrust into Minersville's first-grade classroom at age five is my fear and anxiety over not knowing all of the informal rules that my peers practiced without thinking. Walking single-file in hallways, lining up at the classroom door to go to the bathroom, and sitting with hands folded at the desk until the teacher told us what to do were habits that my classmates had absorbed. I do remember sitting a lot. Specifically, I recall carefully scrawling the shapes of individual letters pictured above the black slate boards as an introduction to cursive writing, but mostly I can remember sitting at a desk until the teacher directed us to the next activity.

I also remember looking around the classroom constantly to make sure that I was doing what other six-year-olds were doing. Was I anxious? Must have been, since even writing down these fragments of memory dredges up feelings of unease, of worrying over being out of sync with others. Desperately wanting the approval of the teacher, I tried doing everything she requested. I quickly picked up the alphabet and putting words together and adding numbers. But I never learned to tie my shoelaces into bows, something my classmates had picked up in kindergarten or at home.

It was a world apart from living with my parents and brothers. The informal social rules of the classroom and fear of the teacher got to me from time to time. I was often scared, a feeling that swept over me every morning that I crossed the street to go to school. Once I was sent home for soiling my pants. Other times, classmates broke into laughter when I misunderstood the teacher's request. This is what I remember.

Outside of school, on upper Centre Avenue, where Black working-class and middle-class families had moved out of the poorer lower Hill District, I recall vividly certain incidents. I was bitten on the thigh by the German shepherd of our next-door neighbor—a minister in a nearby Black church. I also recall being hit by a department store truck making a delivery while I was playing next to the curb and my mother taking me to the nearby hospital for a damaged ankle.

ROOSEVELT ELEMENTARY SCHOOL

I was seven when the US entered World War II—I remember that Sunday in early December and the hushed conversations in our second-floor apartment—and President Roosevelt announced on the radio that Japan had bombed Pearl Harbor. A few months later, we moved to Greenfield, a largely Italian and Irish Catholic neighborhood with few Jewish families. The US Army and Navy had drafted my brothers, and I was the only child at home.

I entered the third grade at Roosevelt Elementary School. Whether it was because I was new to the school, Jewish, or some other reason, I heard lots of nasty epithets going to school, during recess, and while sprinting home two blocks once the last bell had rung. When I got into fights, I was usually on the losing end.

Was Roosevelt Elementary School a Progressive-era platoon school? Perhaps. It was larger—over 750 students—and in better physical condition than Minersville. There might have been eight thirty-five- to forty-minute periods alternating between academic subjects and special activities during the school day. Sadly, I have no recollection, so I cannot say for sure.

Whether Roosevelt teachers taught in Progressive ways—encouraging play and curiosity, exploring literature, math, and other academic and nonacademic subjects—I neither remember nor could put into words the few vague wisps of memory I have. I do remember an art teacher who encouraged my drawing sufficiently for me to enter radio-sponsored art contests for young children. I didn't win but enjoyed drawing nonetheless. By third grade, I knew all of the informal and formal rules of how to behave in the classroom and on the playground during recess. While there are adults who look back fondly at their early years in school, calling up the very names of their teachers, as much as I ransack my mind, I cannot call up any names or classroom incidents that are memorable.[11]

What I do recall are events that occurred outside of school. Since I went to Roosevelt during World War II, rationing of essentials (e.g., milk, meat, sugar, fuel), frequent anti-Semitic taunts, and neighborhood fights remain unforgettable. What eventually saved me from bullying and getting beaten up was coming down with polio.

I well remember rationing. Sacrificing for the war effort was a lesson I learned in and out of school. Priority goods went to soldiers and sailors—like my brothers. My parents received monthly ration coupons for meat, sugar, gasoline, tires, and other items. When our monthly coupons ran out, that was it. I do remember my parents speaking in Russian and Yiddish, worrying about what they could and could not get in the remaining days of each month.

I joined other students, teachers, and parents in collecting tinfoil from discarded gum and cigarette wrappers. We rolled them into balls that we turned in to collection centers. I gathered chicken fat from my mother's kitchen and neighbors as well. My parents gave me a dime weekly to buy savings stamps and later defense bonds at school.

Then, in the summer of 1944, a polio epidemic hit Pittsburgh, and I caught it. But I was lucky. While other children were put into "iron lungs" to stay alive or youngsters had to wear leg braces—as President Roosevelt did—I was lucky and only lost the calf muscle in my left leg. I have walked with a limp since then.

Because polio was a scourge that devastated the young and no one knew how children contracted it, fear of getting it, like a latter-day fear of AIDS in the early 1980s and the coronavirus in the 2020s, was omnipresent on Loretta Street. When I returned from the hospital, no one came near me. No more playground fights, no more anti-Jewish epithets. I was in sixth grade, preparing to enter Taylor Allderdice, a nearby junior-senior high school. I had missed a month of school—and I could barely stand when I returned home in early June. That is what I remember from those wartime years living in Greenfield and going to Roosevelt Elementary School.

TAYLOR ALLDERDICE (1945–1951)

Under my mother's prodding and my father's hard work, enough money was saved to buy a small home in Squirrel Hill, a largely Jewish neighborhood and the pinnacle of my mother's ambition for her family. At age eleven, I entered the seventh grade a couple of years younger than my Taylor Allderdice classmates.

Taylor Allderdice was a six-year secondary school. We lived about a mile away, and I walked to school daily—but not in the seventh grade. Because of polio, I missed twenty-seven days, according to my high school transcript. When I returned to school, my Dad drove me in his truck. Breakfast was drinking down a raw egg each morning—doctors said it would strengthen me—and eating a bowl of oatmeal. Then my Dad would drop me off.

Overall, during the six years I spent at Allderdice, I was an average student, racking up Cs galore. Only in history and science courses did I receive scattered A's and Bs. In English and math, mostly Cs and Ds. I do remember particular teachers and classes. Seemingly, the rhetoric of Progressive policies, curriculum, and pedagogy had trickled down to inhabit the daily schedule. I recall the school day starting with homeroom period, a time set aside for a teacher who would stay with a group of students for four years, offering guidance, encouraging self-government, listening to teenager bragging and woes, and giving advice when asked.

Sam Blitz, a most amiable gentleman with a wry sense of humor, was my homeroom teacher between the ninth and twelfth grades. For those high school years, we elected homeroom officers (a Progressive practice of civic participation), but it was largely a joke, since these officers had no practical responsibility. During homeroom period, I remember joking with friends, doing assignments, and sneaking glances at girls on whom I had a crush.

Then the bell would clang, and I would go through my daily schedule of forty-five-minute periods taking academic subjects, breaking for lunch, going to physical education, and ending up in my homeroom for the final minutes of the school day. In academic classes, I recall frequent lectures and occasional whole-group discussions, students making oral reports, reading texts, and doing homework in class. Looking back, I can remember my teachers using a mix of Progressive and traditional pedagogies in academic courses.

Except for the vocational shop classes I took in the seventh and eighth grades. A clear Progressive innovation in the early twentieth century, every junior high boy had to take vocational subjects such as printing, wood, and electric shop classes. Every girl attended sewing and cooking classes called "home economics."

Unlike the academic courses where I would sit at a desk for forty-five-minute periods, occasionally raise my hand to answer a teacher question, daydream about the girl two rows over from me, and read from the textbook, in this Progressive curricular innovation, I learned how to set type for school documents on what was even then an old printing press. Mr. Block was the teacher and a veteran of commercial print shops. For woodworking, I learned how to use clamps, vises, and electric saws. No surprise to parents of woodshop students, then and now, I made towel racks and my crowning achievement, an end table, both of which I brought home. Electric shop, however, was not my strong suit. I had to learn how to make electric circuits boards, and for reasons unknown I just had a terrible time completing projects and making anything work beyond wiring a battery to light a 60-watt bulb.

But memories of those hands-on, learning-by-doing courses stay with me. While I cannot recall the names of the wood- and electric shop teachers, I do remember the experiences of making real-life objects. Progressive-minded reformers were right, at least in my case, that working with both head and hands would be motivating to early teenagers. Less so for the required academic subjects.

My eighth-grade English teacher, Miss Bowlin, was strict in keeping the class orderly and attentive to what she taught. We diagrammed sentences and read novels and poems. For one assignment, every student had to memorize a poem and recite it in front of the class. I recall being assigned the poem "Abou Ben Adhem" and how frightened I was to stand up, slowly walk down the row toward the teacher's desk in front of the blackboard, turn around to face my classmates, and deliver the poem rhythmically and slowly. When it was my turn, Miss Bowlin signaled me to begin. I recited the poem speedily before hurriedly returning to my seat. I did not understand what I recited as I dashed through it. Did Miss Bowlin say anything? I don't remember or even whether there were any student comments. Relief is all I recall.

To refresh my memory, I looked up Leigh Hunt's "Abou Ben Adhem" before writing these paragraphs. As soon as I saw the first line saying his name with the addition "(may his tribe increase)," fear of Miss Bowlin, the ordeal of reciting the poem, and immense relief all came back to me anew.

I also remember Dorothy Albert, who taught English. I was never in her class but often saw her in the hallways and heard about her from friends who were in her classes. When I was an eleventh grader, I remember teachers and students whispering that she was a Communist—a word I could not then define. In 1950, she left Taylor Allderdice. When I began writing this chapter, I found out that Albert had been fired for being a member of the Communist Party.[12]

My tenth-grade world history teacher, Miss Bertha Mitchell, opened doors to the past that I relished. Like most of the other teachers at Allderdice, she taught from the textbook, lectured, held periodic whole-group discussions, and gave quizzes. Much of what we took in was chronological and factual. She encouraged us to get extra points to boost our grades. One option I grabbed: drawing maps of Egypt, Greece, and imperial Rome. Why I liked cartography—didn't know the word at the time—I cannot explain. Perhaps it was Miss Mitchell's positive comments that spurred me. But copying and then embellishing maps I saw in atlases and the text enthralled me. Doing them after I got home and finished my chores was something I looked forward to. For the first time in a high school course, I got an A.

Another A was in biology. I cannot remember the teacher's name but was entranced by the study of the human body and animals—less so for paramecia and amoebas (it was also the first time I had ever used a microscope). I remember learning the Latinate names for flora and fauna and, yes, memorizing them for quizzes. Dissecting frogs remains vivid in my mind. Actually doing something by hand and exploring the innards of a once-living animal captured my curiosity and drove me to stay abreast of the text and homework and be prepared for end-of-chapter tests.

Fast-forward: Based on this experience, I chose biology as my college minor. That helped me considerably after graduating in 1955, because teaching biology was the only job I could find. I interviewed for a social studies job in the Pittsburgh schools, but the interviewer said I needed to teach in the suburbs for a few years before the Pittsburgh district would consider me. So I found a job teaching biology and general science at

McKeesport Technical High School, about twenty miles from where I lived in Pittsburgh.

Rewind: Lon Colburn was my chemistry teacher in eleventh grade. I earned Cs in his class although I worked so hard in completing the homework, memorizing the periodic chart, and doing experiments with my lab mates. He was very demanding, and I wanted very much to master the content and meet course requirements. Lectures and labs commanded my attention, but, truth be told, even after following the lab manual I could not grasp or understand the chemical reactions I engineered. What I did was memorize the text and as much as I could of Colburn's lectures and imperfectly spill them back on quizzes and tests. By far, it was the hardest academic course I took in high school—apart from algebra and trigonometry, both of which I did poorly in, grade-wise.

And then there was the eleventh-grade US history teacher who lectured almost every day. We had to read the textbook closely, and she tested us frequently. I was enraptured by her voice and the content that she supplied beyond the text. Anna Quattrochi had a doctorate and required students to call her "Dr. Quattrochi." We did. I got a B in her class.

Fast-forward: I did major in history in college and graduate school. Bertha Mitchell and Anna Quattrochi had stimulated my thinking about both my personal and national past. I taught history for fourteen years in Cleveland and Washington, DC, high schools.[13]

Rewind: These memories of teachers and classes are surely fragmentary, as is the sketchy recall I have of what social interactions occurred outside of classes in the hallways and during lunchtime. One memory, however, remains vivid even now. As a senior, I tried out for the class play, *Out of the Frying Pan*, a comedy about unemployed actors in New York City trying desperately to get paid parts in a Broadway play.

In writing this section, I had to look up the plot since I had no recall of the story line. The play's director was a theater major at Carnegie Tech (now Carnegie Mellon) who held afterschool auditions. I was cast in a small role as one of two policemen who spoke a total of three lines at the very end of the play. On opening night, my three lines brought down the house. I had never been on a stage before, and to hear the audience roar with laughter made my skin tingle. For the last few weeks of school, students I hardly knew (there were three thousand in Allderdice at the time) came up to me slapping me on the back and elbowing me for my "great" performance.

᠊᠊

Allderdice drew students from two neighborhoods: Greenfield, where I used to live, and Squirrel Hill. The former was largely Italian and Irish with occasional Black families. Squirrel Hill contained mostly Jewish families. Social class divided the population, with many business and professional families living "north of Forbes" and middle- and lower-middle-class families living along Murray Avenue (south of Forbes) and its connecting streets—where my family lived.

Class differences showed up in the presence of Allderdice fraternities and sororities, the clothes that students wore, and what tables they occupied in the cafeteria. Teenage girls "north of Forbes," for example, often wore cashmere sweaters and two-colored saddle shoes; boys primarily wore khakis and white buck shoes. The groups that met at "The Wall" outside of the building to smoke, exchange gossip, and connect for Saturday night dates were segregated by ethnicity, religion, race, and social class. I seldom joined any (nor was I asked to).

While I recall far more about high school classes than my years in lower grades, both pale in comparison to what I remember about my life outside of school.

LIFE OUTSIDE OF SCHOOL

Looking back on those six years at Taylor Allderdice, I remember fragments of social interactions I had with classmates, some of my teachers, subjects that motivated me, and snatches here and there of what occurred between 8:30 a.m. and 3 p.m. I did pass all of my academic subjects and received a diploma. What I remember clearly, however, are the events that occurred outside of school after I recovered from polio, growing involvement in sports, and the boys I came to know and love in a nonschool club that I joined in the tenth grade.

In the late 1940s, my father earned enough as a jobber selling deli products from a panel truck to mom-and-pop grocery stores in the Pittsburgh area to meet the monthly mortgage payment on our small Squirrel Hill home and put enough food on the table to feed his family. My mother rented out an attic room to a college student, and my brothers, one married and the other unmarried and working at different jobs, also contributed monthly. Still, money was short every month. I do not remember getting a weekly allowance, so as a twelve-year-old recovering from polio, I worried about attending a large secondary school with an empty wallet.

There was a nearby bowling alley on Murray Ave. Not the popular large tenpins requiring three finger holes in fourteen-pound bowling balls. This bowling establishment trafficked in small rubber-band duckpins. Ten wooden pins arranged in a triangle ready to be knocked down by grapefruit-sized balls weighing about three pounds, with no finger holes in them. Bowlers stayed behind a foul line as they rolled these balls down a sixty-foot-long polished wooden lane to knock down all of the pins for a strike. If unsuccessful, they used a second ball to whack the remaining pins for a spare. I was entranced by the game, the skilled bowlers throwing balls that curved from the lip of the gutter and smashed the headpin. Watching pins scatter as they were hit and getting high scores at the end of ten frames became a goal of mine right then and there.

At first, the owner let me bowl free in exchange for occasionally setting pins for other bowlers. What that meant was to sit atop a pit at the end of the sixty-foot alley and wait for the two balls that a bowler laid down for each of the ten frames in a game. After both balls were thrown, I would drop down into the pit and step on a pedal, and a triangle of spikes would pop up, upon which I set the pins that had been knocked down. When all ten pins were set, I would release the pedal, jump back up on the ledge, and wait for the next bowler to send a ball down the highly waxed lane. I became a quick and reliable pinsetter.

The owner of the alley eventually asked me if I wanted to set pins in the afternoons and early evenings and during weekends. He would pay me a few pennies for every game (bowlers then paid a dime for every game). He let me set two alleys—one adjacent to the other—at a time, so a few hours of work would earn me a dollar or more. After school and after dinner, I would bowl and then earn money. In time, I became quite skillful, cocky enough to gamble against older bowlers winning more times than losing.

I also delivered the afternoon newspaper on my street. Sam, the previous newsboy on our street, got a higher-paying job, and he asked me if I would take the route. I did. Between setting pins, betting on my bowling, and delivering newspapers, I had coins jingling in my pockets.

Although I still walked with a limp, I also played baseball and basketball and became a better-than-average athlete for a fourteen-year-old. I sprouted to over six feet and, while lean, I could hit the ball well and play center in pickup basketball games. Yet I was a slow base runner and a tough but sluggish center in basketball.

My connection to former newsboy Sam, skilled bowling, and being athletic brought me into a boys' club that left an imprint on the rest of my teenage years and whose influence has continued until the present day with the friendships I made then.

Youth Club

In the late 1940s, Sam belonged to a local chapter of B'nai Brith youth called Victory AZA. He asked me if I wanted to become a member. A passion for sports, growing interest in girls, driving cars, and being accepted by the "guys" stirred me. For some of us, practicing Judaism was also a crucial part; for others, less so. The boys voted me in to Victory.

High school and Victory were intertwined in our daily lives. While we spent more seat time in high school classrooms and corridors than in those weekly Victory meetings in a synagogue basement, much of our intellectual, social, and athletic life revolved around the club, not high school. As part of Victory's activities, we played each sport in its season, attended weekly meetings, and double-dated while gnawing nails over how to carry off a goodnight kiss. In the four years I belonged to Victory, what we probably did most was talk.

And did we talk! Over hot dogs at the local deli after club meetings or at one of our homes after a pickup football game or in cars late at night after dates were dropped off, we would talk about everything—rarely, however, about school. For some of us, this club served as family; for others it was just another activity in an already rich and busy life; and even for others it eased the stormy passage through difficult years. No matter which purpose Victory served in our lives, the club glued us together.

And we learned from one another. I remember one meeting vividly, when Sam was president of Victory. On the agenda—we knew well *Robert's Rules of Order*—was an item to vote on new members. Because you aged out of the club at eighteen, there was constant turnover in this group of about thirty members. New members were recruited, and sometimes teenagers simply wanted to join because of the full array of sports teams that we fielded over the course of a year, the B'nai Brith sports tournaments we went to in western Pennsylvania and West Virginia, and the many social activities. We often voted unanimously to accept the handful up for membership because they brought athletic skills, social skills, and smarts from which we felt the club would benefit. Except for one teenager, whose nomination for membership triggered a vigorous discussion that I remember to this day.

There was a split in our group over whether Merle should become part of Victory. Those who argued for him saw his speaking skills—we also had a debate team that went to B'nai Brith regional and state tournaments—being useful to the club. Those who argued against him pointed out that his argumentative skills went too far, and he was constantly talking and trying to win his point. Moreover, his talk was too self-absorbed; he didn't respond to what others were saying. So that evening there was a deadlock over admitting Merle, a highly unusual situation, one that in my experience had never occurred.

Presiding over the discussion was Sam. He listened carefully to each point made by advocates and opponents of Merle's entry into Victory. At one point, one of us asked Sam what his opinion was of Merle. Sam answered by saying that when he considered each nominee for membership, he asked himself not only what the boy could do for Victory but also what Victory could do for the boy. He felt that Merle would surely help the club given his verbal skills, but more important, Sam felt, we could help Merle become a better person.

Up to that point, I had asked only one question: How would the nominee contribute to our athletic, social, intellectual, and religious activities? I had never considered Sam's additional question. I then thought of how the club's culture and activities had a significant influence on how I thought and what I did. After Sam's response, someone called for the vote, and we agreed that the discussion was over and it was time to decide. Merle became a member of Victory.

As commonly happens with teenagers, such intense club life was put aside after high school graduation. Nearly all of us aged out of Victory after starting at the University of Pittsburgh, a short trolley ride from our homes in Squirrel Hill. Those in our group who didn't go to college eventually drifted away into jobs. About a half-dozen former club members, however, continued to see each other before and after college classes, on occasional double dates, during weekend pickup football and softball games, and at the summer jobs we needed to earn money for the next semester of school. Four of that group, Yus, Dave, Sam, and I, saw each other a great deal during college and after we graduated.

To pay for tuition and out-of-pocket expenses while living at home, I worked after classes for four years at various jobs. After trying pre-med—organic chemistry was my downfall—I ended up majoring in history with a minor in biology. In my junior year, I decided to become a teacher, got admitted to the School of Education, did my student teaching, and in 1955 graduated. I then became a biology teacher. No longer an object of Progressive-era reforms as a student, I approached my career, initially as a teacher, then later as an administrator, and finally as a professor, always with an eye to improve what happened in classrooms, schools, and districts, for the next six decades.

Even after we graduated college, entered careers, married, had children, and moved away from Pittsburgh (as Dave and I did), at least four of us (Yus, Dave, Sam, and I) remained close friends for the rest of our lives.

REFLECTIONS

In the years I attended three Pittsburgh public schools, I was in a district that had undergone Progressive innovations. A smaller board of education, professional superintendents, and a large bureaucracy were all signposts of governance changes that had occurred decades earlier in the district. None of that impinged directly on me, though I did take courses in secondary school that were imprinted with Progressive ideas. Instruction insofar as projects and small-group work—well, I cannot recall much, which is not to say it didn't occur in various classes I attended.

There is little drama in my story either inside or outside of school. No family abuse. No addictions. No violence (beyond a few street fistfights). When such recollections reveal personal trials, even dark secrets, as often occurs, they become excuses for self-therapy and generate sympathy for the author. I doubt that my account will meet that common standard for this genre. Perhaps my account may well even put readers to sleep. I hope not, but from my imperfect memory, this is what I recall.

Most important, looking back on my years in the Pittsburgh Public Schools (1939–1951), when Progressive school reforms dominated the talk and policies of district educators, I found few traces of that talk penetrating schoolroom routines. While these schools with their age-graded organization, academic curriculum, teacher-centered instruction, and cultural socializing surely shaped what I came to know and feel, the fact is what I recall most vividly and believe to have touched me more than what I took away from schooling are the external events that occurred (e.g., Great Depression, World War II, moving into different racially and religiously divided neighborhoods, getting polio) and enduring relationships with family and friends. My education was split between formal schooling and life education.

Of course, it is possible that those remembrances that stick in my mind were not the most significant in shaping who I am. Elementary and secondary schooling may have played a far larger role than I ascribe to it now as an octogenarian.

Yet the inescapable fact remains that over 80 percent of children's and teenagers' waking time is spent outside of school, in the family, the neighborhood, the company of friends, religious settings, and the workplace. Too often, I believe, formal schooling in those 1,200 hours a year, important as they are socially in acculturating the young, politically in cultivating civic participation, and economically in accumulating diplomas and degrees for jobs and careers, all of that is given far more weight than it deserves in assessing how children and teenagers become adults. Family, friends, and larger events go well beyond formal schooling in shaping character and behavior over a lifetime. Life educates.[14]

CHAPTER 3

The Civil Rights Movement (1950s–1970s)

W ERE THERE PROGRESSIVE-MINDED EDUCATORS who contin- ued their activism in the civil rights movement in the 1950s and 1960s? The answer is an unqualified yes. Many teachers, for example, chose content and skills fitted to the children they taught, encouraged learning by doing, and connected the classroom to the outside world. They used approaches with children and adults that would have brought smiles to the faces of turn-of-the-century school reformers. Inside and outside the classroom, these Progressive educators also were civil rights activists decades later. They bridged both reform movements.

One South Carolina teacher taught in segregated schools for much of her career while at the same time creating evening classes for adults who wanted to learn to read, write, and vote. This teacher's "citizen- ship schools" eventually became part of the civil rights movement in the 1950s and 1960s.

Eighteen-year-old Septima Clark began teaching at Promise Land School on Johns Island, near Charleston, South Carolina, in 1916. She was in charge of a two-teacher school with 132 Black children coming from tenant farm families working on island plantations. Clark taught fourth through eighth graders, while the other teacher took the younger children. The nearby white school had three children.[1]

The school was made of logs with clay grout layered in to keep win- ter wind and rain from entering. A big chimney stood in the middle of the room, and there was no glass in the windows, just shutters. The girls, according to Clark, would get grass to sweep the floor, while the boys cut wood to feed the stove on cold mornings.

As the teacher-principal of this school, Clark earned $35 dollars a month; the white teacher at the nearby school earned $85 a month for the three children she taught. Clark recalled how she taught at Promise Land School:

> We had no blackboards at the time. . . . [M]ost of the time we would bring from the city a dry cleaner's bag and write on the bag things they could copy. For reading we had to make up stories about the things around them—the trees, foliage, the animals. They learned to read these words first. . . .
>
> I wrote their stories on the dry cleaner's bags, stories of their country right around them, where they walked to come to school, the things that grew around them, what they see in the skies. They told them to me, and I wrote them on the dry cleaner's bag, and tacked it to the wall. . . .
>
> After they learned the stories of their own island, I was able to get some books through the county system . . . I was never able to get enough books so that each child could have one. That's the way I taught all the time.[2]

After the school day ended, Clark returned to the house where she boarded with a Black family. On weekends, she would walk all over the island and get to meet the families of her students:

> There were very few people over there who could read. They wanted to speak in church or at a large meeting and they did not know how to read at all. So for my own pleasure at nights I would teach the adults how to read and write. It was really a kind of recreation for me to work with them at nights after they got out of the field.[3]

Interviewed in 1981, Clark described how she began with children and adults by asking what they wanted:

> I found out that you don't tell people what to do. You let them tell you what they want done and then you have to have in your mind certain things that you feel they need to do. And so you get their thoughts and wind your thoughts around. . . . But if you have a cut-and-dry program for them, you'll lose out every time.[4]

So Clark used tenant farmers' experiences on land and water, including available materials such as the Sears catalog, to teach illiterate adults. In 1919, she returned to Charleston but came back to Johns Island often in the following decades.

In the Charleston schools, where only white teachers were hired in the district, Clark joined the National Association for the Advancement of Colored People (NAACP). She and a cadre of volunteers got twenty thousand Blacks to sign petitions demanding the state legislature allow the school district to hire Black teachers and appoint Blacks as principals. The legislature voted to do both in 1920 and 1921. She also continuously fought for Charleston Black teachers to be paid salaries equal to those of white teachers. To Clark, civil rights, education, and economic justice were one and the same. Her entire career as a teacher and active member of the NAACP was devoted to all three.[5]

In 1956, the state legislature mandated that no state employee could be a member of the NAACP, so the Charleston City Board of Education fired Clark and took away her pension. She needed a job. After attending interracial workshops at the Highlander Folk School in Tennessee, Myles Horton, knowing of Clark's work as a teacher, especially her work with illiterate adults in the Sea Islands, hired the jobless teacher to direct Highlander workshops and teach adult literacy courses.[6]

Clark recruited her Charleston cousin Bernice Robinson, who had experience as a seamstress, office clerk, and beautician, to teach a two-month class on Johns Island. The students told Robinson that they wanted to learn to read the Bible, make out checks, order from catalogs, fill out voter registration forms, and take driver's license exams. Robinson described her methods:

> I started off with things that were familiar with them. They were working in the fields and I'd have them tell me stories about what they did out in the fields and what they had in their homes. I'd write these stories out and work with them on the words. I'd say now, "This is your story. We're going to learn how to read your story."[7]

While there were many stumbles along the way, those who stayed in the classes did become literate. Clark captured the joy of teaching adults:

Can you ask for a greater reward than this one? Seeing Mr. Hamilton, a man of 75 years of age, demonstrating his ability to read a newspaper and the Bible as well as holding a registration certificate to vote. He had to read a part of the South Carolina Constitution and write his name in cursive writing to get that certificate.[8]

Clark brought this expertise in teaching adult literacy to the Highlander Folk School, where literacy classes, or "workshops," were renamed "citizenship schools." She directed the program, led workshops, and recruited and trained teachers for these schools. One Highlander workshop participant recalled Clark:

> I am always respectful and very much in awe of the presence of Septima Clark because her life story makes the effort that I have made very minute. I only hope there is a possible chance that some of her great courage and dignity and wisdom has rubbed off on me.
>
> When I first met her in 1955 at Highlander, when I saw how well she could organize and hold things together in this very informal setting of interracial living, I had to admire this great woman. She just moved through the different workshops and groups as though it was just what she was made to do, in spite of the fact that she had to face so much opposition in her home state and lost her job. . . . She seemed to be a beautiful person and it didn't seem to shake her.[9]

This description of Clark came from Rosa Parks of Montgomery, Alabama, who attended Highlander workshops. After those workshops, Parks, a longtime member of the Montgomery NAACP and veteran critic of segregated city buses, went on to spark the yearlong city boycott against separate white and "colored" seating. Parks, a seamstress at a local department store and secretary to the city's NAACP chapter, was arrested for civil disobedience, eventually losing her job. The national NAACP took her case through the court system, challenging the state law that allowed segregated seating in public buses. The US Supreme Court in 1956 ruled that the Alabama law was unconstitutional.[10]

Highlander Folk School, however, harassed by state authorities for their interracial and political activities, ran into financial difficulties. In 1961, Horton persuaded Martin Luther King Jr. of the Southern Christian Leadership Conference (SCLC) to adopt citizenship schools.

Septima Clark then worked for SCLC in training over ten thousand adults—mostly women—to be citizenship school teachers across the South, who in turn taught more than twenty-five thousand adults. She eventually became the only female member of the SCLC Board.[11]

Beginning in 1916 as an eighteen-year-old Progressive teacher in a two-room schoolhouse on Johns Island to actively working a half-century with children and adults to get southern Blacks full civil rights, better schooling, and economic justice, Septima Clark spanned both national reform movements.

PUBLIC SCHOOLING IN THE CIVIL RIGHTS ERA

As with the Progressive movement, there is a "short" and "long" story to the civil rights movement. Septima Clark's life points to the roots of the civil rights movement in one part of coastal South Carolina going back to the early twentieth century. That is part of the long story of the movement. I return to where Clark fits into the long story below, but for now, I offer the more popular and well-known short version.

The "Short" Story

The abbreviated account of the civil rights movement centers on the period spanning two decades between the 1954 *Brown* decision, the passage of the Voting Rights Act of 1965, and the first term of President Richard Nixon ending in 1969. For activists, the federal government was the go-to source of political and financial support for equal rights and better schooling in this momentous period.

John F. Kennedy and Lyndon B. Johnson, Rosa Parks, Martin Luther King Jr., Thurgood Marshall, Ralph Abernathy, Stokely Carmichael, and many others loom large in that plotline for these years. The civil rights movement combined registering voters, lobbying federal officials, and outlawing segregated buses, toilets, and schools. Lingering on the edges of this familiar account are Black nationalists such as Malcolm X and others who sought Black economic and social independence rather than integration with whites.

The civil rights agenda included not only desegregating southern schools but also academically improving schools in deep southern states like Mississippi (e.g., the Freedom Schools of 1964) and urban districts in the North, Midwest, and West that were populated by mostly students of color. Equal schooling would level the playing field—a favorite metaphor of political activists—for Blacks and other minorities to attain the American Dream. As the decade unfolded, however, cascading events altered that agenda.[12]

In the late 1960s through early 1970s, a potpourri of protests erupted against government actions such as the Vietnam War, court-ordered busing to desegregate schools, and laws requiring affirmative action in hiring practices. Anger over police brutality in handling protesting minorities also prompted outbursts of urban violence. Add into the medley of events college student uprisings for ethnic studies, the growth of militant feminism, and the emergence of Black power ideology. All of these ingredients boiled over into a political backlash that put "law and order" Republican Richard Nixon in the White House. The short story line of the civil rights movement ends with wiretaps, a bugle call saying goodbye to that glorious decade.[13]

The "Long" Story

To those who subscribe to the long version, as I do, the civil rights story and its embrace of schools go back over two centuries to the principles embedded in the Declaration of Independence, the framing of the Constitution, the antislavery movement prior to the Civil War, the First Reconstruction (1865–1877), the emergence of Jim Crow laws (1890–1954), and a legal strategy focusing on upending segregated facilities and separate and unequal treatment of Blacks (1920–1960s). It is a story of fits and starts, uprisings and squelched hopes that weaves in and out of the past two centuries.[14]

The major weakness of the short story line of the civil rights movement is its striking omission of the earlier struggles and achievements of ex-slaves who started their own schools and led those set up by the Freedmen's Bureau throughout the First Reconstruction. Furthermore, it leaves out Booker T. Washington's work at Tuskegee, W. E. B. Du Bois's studies of schooling during Reconstruction, the antilynching work of Ida B. Wells, and, yes, men and women like Myles Horton, Septima Clark, and hundreds of others who worked decades earlier for civil rights, better schooling, and economic justice. All of that is missing from the short story line that fills so many post–World War II histories.[15]

The First Reconstruction (1865–1877). After the Civil War and passage of the constitutional amendments freeing slaves, making them citizens and voters, the issue of economic independence for ex-slaves—that is, to own land, harvest crops, and earn a living—was foremost in the minds of freedmen. For ex-slaves, it was achieving the American Dream.

One newly freed slave told a Northern journalist, "But widout land, de ole massas can hire or starve is as they please." Virginia freedman Bayley Wyat spoke up at a meeting about the lack of land turned over to ex-slaves:

> We has a right to the land where we are located. For why? I tell you. Our wives, our children, our husbands, has been sold over and over again to purchase the lands we now located upon; for that reason we have a divine right to the land. . . . And den didn't we cleare the land, and raise de crops ob corn, ob cotton, ob tobacco, ob rice, ob sugar, ob everything. And den didn't dem large cities in de North grow up on de cotton and de sugars and de rice dat we made? . . . I say dey has grown rich, and my people is po.

For a short period of time, many ex-slaves became landowners for the first time as the Union Army confiscated hundreds of thousands of acres on abandoned properties and distributed the land under General William Sherman's Special Field Order No. 15 in 1865. The order was fought vigorously by ex-planters, and eventually the land was returned to them by newly installed President Andrew Johnson after the assassination of Abraham Lincoln.[16]

Schooling. Next to owning land, becoming literate was immensely important to freed slaves. That ex-slaves wanted to learn to read and write was clear during the Civil War. Ad hoc schools staffed by both Black and white northern teachers began soon after the Union Army took control of individual Southern states. The US Congress established a federal agency called the Freedmen's Bureau that fed, housed, and provided medical aid and schooling to recently freed families.[17]

Also, along with thousands of Black churches that had started literacy classes, the Freedmen's Bureau built schools and hired teachers to work with largely illiterate former slaves. What is less known is that many literate ex-slaves not only founded schools but also were elected to state legislatures. Black legislators sought tax-supported public schools for both whites and Blacks. Consider the words of former slave George Washington Albright, an elected delegate to Mississippi's constitutional convention in 1868, who told an interviewer decades later: "Before the Civil War there wasn't a free school in the state, but under the Reconstruction government, we built them in every county. . . . We paid to have every child, white and Negro, schooled equally."[18]

While Black churches and the Freedmen's Bureau did supply teachers and build schoolhouses, it was Black and white legislators in Southern states who established universal schooling during the First Reconstruction. As historian W. E. B. Du Bois concluded in 1910 after his study of Southern governments in the decade following the Civil War:

> [W]hile it is possible to find some vestiges of free schools in some of the Southern States before the war . . . a universal, well-established system dates from the day that the black man got political power. Common-school instruction in the South, in the modern sense of the term, was begun for negroes [sic] by the Freedmen's Bureau and missionary societies, and the state public-school systems for all children were formed mainly by negro [sic] Reconstruction governments.[19]

With Black elected officials at all rungs of state government during Reconstruction, Black landowners, and the emergence of tax-supported public schools for both whites and ex-slaves, it seemed as if the South had been upended. But in terms of wealth and power, it hadn't. According to historian James Anderson, the "wealth and power in the postwar South continued to rest in the . . . hands of its prewar owners."[20]

President Andrew Johnson, a Southern Democrat who succeeded the assassinated Abraham Lincoln, put forth a set of conciliatory Reconstruction proposals that permitted ex-Confederate leaders and plantation owners to continue governing states. Opposed to Johnson were Congressional Republicans who controlled both houses of Congress. They wanted military control of the defeated South until Black and white elected officials politically and economically rebuilt each Southern state. Congressional Republicans fought Johnson's policies, even impeaching him in 1868 but falling one vote short of removing him from office.[21]

A conservative reaction to these Reconstruction amendments occurred soon after the failure to remove Johnson from office. The sharp increase in numbers of Black county, state, and federal legislators and the establishment of public schools for both white and Black children prompted some white Southerners to use homegrown militias and night riders (early versions of the Ku Klux Klan) to terrorize Black landowners and schoolteachers with hangings, whippings, burning churches, and closing schools, even with federal troops stationed across the ex-Confederate states.[22]

What advanced reconciliation of white Southern leaders with their Northern counterparts was the growing opposition among both Democrats and Republicans to keeping federal troops in the South. The conflict reached an intense level in the disputed election of 1876. The outcome of the election between Democrat Samuel Tilden—whom Southern leaders supported—and Republican Rutherford B. Hayes was clouded by accusations of voting fraud and confusion in the Electoral College over who would enter office in 1877.

A private agreement between Congressional Republicans and Southern Democrats—the "Compromise of 1877"—was worked out that removed federal troops from the South, put Republican Rutherford B. Hayes in the White House, and returned governance to Southern leaders.[23]

In subsequent decades, southern state legislators, with the support of planters and business leaders, placed restrictions on Blacks through the tenant system of sharecropping and intimidated voters through mandatory literacy tests and poll taxes. They passed Jim Crow laws segregating contacts between the races. They used terror through the Ku Klux Klan and frequent lynchings to reinforce the subservience of Blacks as the lower caste in a hierarchical system based on skin color. Slavery had ended, but subordination continued.[24]

Black schools in the rural and urban South were separate but grossly unequal to white schools in funding, condition of buildings, teacher quality, and available materials. Recall Septima Clark's teaching in a two-room schoolhouse on Johns Island in South Carolina between 1916 and

1919. Detailed descriptions of these segregated schools abound in both academic studies and in lawsuits that Black lawyers brought to state and federal courts beginning in the early decades of the twentieth century. This legal strategy of documenting separate but unequal schools secured a series of victories that slowly chipped away at the US Supreme Court's precedent, established in *Plessy v. Ferguson* (1896), of "separate but equal."[25]

Of course, the *Brown* decision in 1954 toppled that half-century-old precedent. In the ensuing decade the emerging civil rights movement, using nonviolent protests, gained federal legislation and court decisions backed up by the Kennedy and Johnson administrations, overturning legal segregation in nearly every facet of southern life while expanding Black rights and opportunities across the nation.

This abbreviated account of the First Reconstruction is often missing from the short story of the civil rights movement. Absent that explanation, readers miss the simple fact that the struggle for equality, waged by both Blacks and whites, has stretched back well over a century. I now turn to the familiar story of the civil rights movement that some historians call the Second Reconstruction.

The Second Reconstruction (1948–1970s). The First Reconstruction, led by Congressional Republicans, sought to alter completely the slave-owning system and admit ex-slaves to full citizenship with the right to vote and access to tax-supported public schools. That effort lasted just over a decade before the conservative political backlash turned back the clock. Beginning in the 1880s, the establishment of Black Codes, racial segregation, and whites' economic control of rural and urban southern Blacks spread throughout the South. These Jim Crow laws, as historian C. Vann Woodward wrote, "put the authority of the state or city in the voice of the street-car conductor, the railway brakeman, the bus driver, the theater usher, and also into the voice of the hoodlum of the public parks and playgrounds."[26]

Times, however, changed. After the national experience with the Great Depression and winning World War II, when Blacks served throughout the military (yes, in segregated units), President Harry Truman ordered the US military to desegregate in 1948. A few years later, the *Brown* decision launched the Second Reconstruction and another civil rights movement.

The Black-led bus boycott in Montgomery, Alabama, in 1955 inscribed the names of Rosa Parks and Martin Luther King Jr. in the American consciousness. President Eisenhower sent the 101st Airborne Division to Little Rock, Arkansas, in 1957 to ensure that nine Black students would enter the previously segregated Central High School. In 1960, Black college students at North Carolina Agricultural and Technical State University, inspired by Martin Luther King Jr., sat in segregated Greensboro, North Carolina, restaurants in order to buy hamburgers and french fries. Young Freedom Riders like nineteen-year-old Stokely Carmichael challenged interstate segregation on buses in 1961. Then 250,000 Blacks and whites marched on Washington for jobs and freedom in 1963, hearing Student Nonviolent Coordinating Committee (SNCC) activist John Lewis, Martin Luther King Jr., and others call for jobs and equal rights for all Americans.[27]

Although President Lyndon B. Johnson had signed the Civil Rights Act in 1964, making the law apply to both Blacks and whites on a daily basis in southern towns and cities, customary behavior seldom changed overnight. SNCC and SCLC sent waves of young white and Black volunteers into the South to register voters and end segregated practices.

Swift and constant media attention to murders of civil rights workers, police brute force used to stop civil rights marches from happening, and beatings of jailed protesters stung the nation. Martin Luther King Jr. became the face and voice of the Second Reconstruction. He and other organizational leaders, such as SNCC chairman John Lewis and Congress of Racial Equality (CORE) director James Farmer and his successor Floyd McKissick, pressed Washington officials to send federal marshals to dangerous venues where local officials allowed, if not encouraged, violence against civil rights workers registering voters and teaching in rural schools.

As in many social movements, divisions among leaders over direction, strategy, and tactics emerged in the push for Blacks to become full citizens. By 1965, King's nonviolent, direct action approach dominated the movement. Some activists, however, disagreed with that strategy.

Those disagreements became evident in 1966 over Mississippian James Meredith.

Overcoming enormous resistance from Mississippi authorities including the governor, notching victories in state and federal court cases, and with direct intervention from President Kennedy and Attorney General Robert Kennedy, James Meredith, a US Air Force veteran, became the first Black to enroll in the University of Mississippi in 1962. Although campus riots occurred initially, order was restored, and other Blacks entered Ole Miss.

Meredith completed his degree, studied abroad, and returned to his home state in 1966. He then proposed a Black Man's march of 220 miles from Memphis, Tennessee, to Jackson, Mississippi, to highlight continuing Black fear of violence and economic and social oppression in the state even after landmark federal laws had been passed in the past two years. He began his march alone. On the second day, a white man ambushed Meredith, who was then rushed to a hospital.[28]

The attack mobilized King, Carmichael, and other Black leaders to continue the Meredith March to Jackson. They attracted over ten thousand Black and white protesters, including Meredith, who rejoined the march. Along the route, SNCC and SCLC workers registered Black voters.

During this protest, marchers arrived in Greenwood, Mississippi, to camp at a Black elementary school. City officials said protesters were trespassing and refused to let them stay. The police arrested Carmichael. The city then gave the marchers permission to camp in a nearby park. A rally was held that evening, and Carmichael, released from jail, spoke. Historian David Garrow described the scene:

> When he [Carmichael] mounted the speaker platform, he gave free vent to his emotions, telling the audience that black people had to take charge and that "every courthouse in Mississippi should be burnt down tomorrow so we can get rid of the dirt." Black sheriffs ought to preside over the Delta counties, and black citizens ought to demand "black power." . . . Carmichaels' words struck a chord among his listeners. "We want black power," he shouted, and the crowd took up the chant: "We want black power. We want black power."[29]

King wrote later that after hearing what occurred in Greenwood that evening, "I had reservations about 'black power' and how it might widen internal divisions while also conveying hostile connotations to white onlookers both near and far."[30]

The thirty-seven-year-old King and the twenty-four-year-old Carmichael enjoyed a warm relationship in private. It even deepened into a friendship to the point that King hosted dinners for Carmichael at his home in Atlanta. After the Meredith March, however, Carmichael became a national icon for Black nationalism (Malcolm X, who advocated the idea, had left the Nation of Islam in 1964 and shortly thereafter had been assassinated).[31]

What had been brewing for some time beneath the surface among civil rights leaders divided over direction (integration or separation) and strategy (nonviolence or violence) broke out openly. Stokely Carmichael, for example, replaced King supporter John Lewis as chair of the SNCC in 1966. Movement leadership split.

What else was occurring in America, of course, drew attention away from voter registration and improved schooling, familiar targets of the civil rights movement. Consider the following brew of events occurring about the same time as the above took place:

- In the summer of 1965, the Watts neighborhood in Los Angeles exploded with urban riots, with similar disturbances occurring in the following summers.
- Anti–Vietnam War protests escalated across the nation.
- President Lyndon B. Johnson announced in 1967 that he would not seek office the next year.
- The murder of Martin Luther King Jr. in 1968 was followed again by urban violence and destruction.
- The bitter, contentious 1968 campaign for the White House between Republican Richard Nixon and Democrat Hubert Humphrey ended in razor-thin victory for Nixon.

The century-plus story of civil rights efforts is the "long" story of a movement's successes and failures, popular support and white pushback. It is a story of lunges forward and backward shuffles.

And the long story continues into the twenty-first century with many protests over police shootings of Blacks, resegregated city schools, emerging organizations such as Black Lives Matter, and the contested role of the federal government in both stifling and supporting the quest for equal treatment.[32]

Seventy-nine-year-old retired schoolteacher Rutha Mae Harris sees the long story also. Harris had been jailed with Martin Luther King Jr. when they marched in Albany, Georgia, against segregated public facilities in the 1960s. She watched TV news reports of protests in 2020 after George Floyd, a Minneapolis Black man, was killed by the police. With teary eyes, when she saw both whites and Blacks marching together, she said: "I love it . . . It has surprised me, and it gives me hope. I thought what I had done was in vain."[33]

REFLECTIONS ON THE CIVIL RIGHTS MOVEMENTS IN CLEVELAND AND WASHINGTON, DC

The second part of this chapter deals with civil rights movements in Cleveland and Washington, DC, where I served as a teacher and an administrator in 1956–1963 and 1963–1972, respectively.

Cleveland, Ohio

Patterns of ethnic and racial segregation in Cleveland had developed early in the twentieth century, when neighborhoods became easily identifiable as Italian, German, Polish, Jewish, and Black. In the late nineteenth and early twentieth centuries, upwardly striving immigrant Jewish families clustered in the Central, Scovill, and Woodland Avenue neighborhoods close to downtown.

With the end of World War I, an influx of southern Black migrant families seeking jobs, better housing, and access to schools settled in along those avenues, pushing many of the Jewish families there to move eastward into Glenville. A Black ghetto emerged.

Hostility to having Blacks as neighbors showed up in deeds carrying racial covenants that led to residential segregation, a norm seldom broken in Cleveland. Houses in the Central neighborhood were subdivided into apartments; families living in apartments rented out rooms to lodgers, and open prejudice against both recent Black middle-class and migrant families created a densely populated Black ghetto. Schools mirrored neighborhood demographics. Yet Black and white city leaders raised few objections to the common practice of residential segregation. And the reason was that Cleveland had a reputation in these decades for being racially moderate and hospitable to immigrants while accepting segregated schools as part of the bargain.

Before, during, and after the Civil War, Blacks had been lynched in Philadelphia, Cincinnati, and New York, yet no lynching had ever taken place in the Forest City. As caste lines hardened in the north in the early years of the twentieth century, Black leader John P. Green, an Ohio state legislator, called Cleveland a "haven of rest to the persecuted and forlorn." When twenty-five race riots swept across the nation in the wake of World War I, no racial violence occurred in the city. Times and conditions, however, change.[34]

Before and after World War I, George Myers, an entrepreneurial Black businessman, along with other Black businessmen, had worked closely with white leaders to maintain traditions of equality and integration that the Cleveland community had advertised and prided itself on for decades. Myers owned a large barbershop housed in a downtown hotel popular with white businessmen and tourists. In-migration of southern Blacks after World War I and race riots in Chicago and other cities in 1919, however, altered that sentiment in both Myers and white business and civic leaders. Demographic shifts plus long-standing racial attitudes changed behavior.

Consider that between 1910 and 1920, the Black population in Cleveland more than tripled. Schools in largely Black neighborhoods reflected that increase. Nearly 90 percent of the city's junior high school Black students, for example, were enrolled in only four of its twenty-three schools; over 60 percent of Black senior high school students attended only one, Central High School. By 1931, white students were only 3 percent of Central High School's enrollment. By that time, district administrators had assigned Black students to Central even though Black families lived closer to other high schools.[35]

As for teachers, in 1919 the district employed sixty-eight Black teachers, most of whom graduated from Central High School. A decade later, there were eighty-four Black teachers working in forty-one schools (only one taught in high school) housing 87 percent of all Black students. Those demographic changes in neighborhoods and schools brought to the surface racist attitudes that touched Myers and other middle- and upper-middle-class Blacks.[36]

In 1923, Myers planned to retire, and the hotel landlord informed him that the fifteen Black barbers he employed would be replaced by whites. Three years later, Myers condemned the Chamber of Commerce for ignoring the influx of southern migrants into the Scovill and Central Avenue neighborhoods. He told the white business leaders:

> Denounce and discourage all forms of segregation, and in all public affairs give the race recognition. . . . [G]ive them decent habitation at a reasonable rental . . . coupled with Police protection instead of Police persecution. . . . Teach them how to live, acquaint them with Northern customs and the requisites of good citizenship. Much good will thus be accomplished, as well as a better feeling between the races and we will indeed have a better and greater Cleveland to live in.[37]

Few business and civic leaders took note of his appeal. By the end of the decade, Myers—along with other high-profile Black leaders—openly struggled with the blatant discriminatory policies of City Hospital. He publicly condemned the city's director of welfare as a racist. The carefully scrubbed veneer of equal treatment and integration that both white and Black leaders had taken pride in hid the harsh realities of residential and school segregation, job discrimination, and second-class treatment in receiving city services.[38]

By the 1930s, the out-migration of Jewish businesses, synagogues, hospitals, and charitable institutions' services from the Central and Woodland neighborhoods into Glenville resulted in 105th Street, a main thoroughfare, being dotted with synagogues, retail businesses, and theaters. Glenville High School became nearly 90 percent Jewish in that decade.[39]

Residential segregation and another wave of Black southerners after World War II again created overcrowded housing in the already racially separated Central, Scovill, and Woodland neighborhoods. Upwardly mobile black families slowly moved into the Glenville area in the late 1940s and early 1950s. Neighborhood schools shifted from nearly all Jewish to mostly Black enrollments. By 1956, when I arrived at Glenville

High School as a teacher, it and the adjacent junior highs and elementary schools were already over 90 percent black.[40]

In the years I taught at Glenville (1956–1963), Cleveland's neighborhoods remained segregated, with a nearly all-white West Side and a mostly Black East Side. I learned much from my students and colleagues about Cleveland's segregated East Side housing and schooling during these years. In 1963, for example, 93 percent of elementary school students, 78 percent in junior high schools, and 83 percent in high schools were attending de facto segregated schools. In 1963–1964, a few months after I had left Cleveland, the racial tensions brewing from overcrowded housing, police incidents with Black residents, and inaction from a school board and administration to alter segregated schools boiled over into a year of continuous protests.

In the early 1960s, moderate Black civic leadership challenged by newly created activist organizations (e.g., the United Freedom Movement) coalesced in favor of desegregating the city's schools and, for the first time, used the multiple and targeted tactics that southern civil rights leaders used: private negotiations with the city's civic and business leaders, peaceful picketing of schools, mass demonstrations, nonviolent sit-ins, school boycotts, and legal action against the city's school board and mayor.[41]

Wanting to end crowded segregated schools and tired of official promises for action that never materialized, Black parents planned a one-day school boycott in 1964. Ninety-two percent of Black students attended eighty "Freedom Schools." The upshot of all of these efforts was a small busing program transporting some Black elementary students from overcrowded segregated schools to all-white ones but without any mixing of bused students with the rest of the school. Anger over such paltry outcomes from the boycott grew within the Black community.[42]

The US Commission on Civil Rights held a series of hearings in 1966 that revealed to attendees and readers of the report long-standing problems of racist employment practices, congested and dilapidated housing, police brutality, and segregated schools. Shortly thereafter, those long-standing problems detonated.

A dispute at a local white-owned tavern in the all-Black Hough area adjacent to Glenville led to a large rock-throwing crowd and eventually the burning of the bar. Police could not control the crowd, and six days of rioting erupted, resulting in four Blacks being killed and millions of dollars in property damage. Not unlike what had occurred in other American cities earlier that summer and in the next two years, the Hough riots—or synonyms that appeared afterward, such as "uprisings," "rebellions" or "civil unrest"—grew out of the simmering, then boiling tensions around racist laws and practices.[43]

The 1964 school boycott, the 1966 Hough riots, and foot-dragging by white business and civic leaders, coincident with the rise of Black Power ideology among civil rights activists, led to a growing sense among Cleveland Black leaders that directly acquiring political power was a better way of ending racist practices and improving conditions that had been neglected for decades. Lawyer and state legislator Carl Stokes ran for mayor in 1965 and was narrowly defeated, but two years later he became the first Black mayor of one the ten biggest cities in the US.[44]

By the time Carl Stokes became mayor, I had already left Cleveland for Washington, DC, and had been teaching for four years at Cardozo High School while directing the returned Peace Corps teacher-training program.

Washington, DC

Three facts dominate the history of civil rights and schooling in Washington, DC:

Since the US Congress assumed control of the capital along the Potomac River in 1790, Congress has governed, taxed, and financed the District of Columbia. Congress required residents of the city to pay taxes while at the same time they stripped those taxpayers of their right to vote for local officials in 1801. Nor did Congress allow the capital city to elect a representative or two senators to Congress as states did. Not until 1964, when the Twenty-Third Amendment was adopted, were DC residents allowed to vote for president of the US. Subsequently, Congress allowed District residents to have one non-voting representative in the House and finally, in 1973, elect their mayor and city council. Yet complete home rule still remains out of reach, since both houses of Congress continue to approve the city's budget.[45]

From its earliest years, freed Blacks and slaves lived in the capital and after the Civil War created a political, social, and cultural life, including education, that attracted Black people through the twenty-first century. Or as one historian put it in describing the 1880s in the District of Columbia: "[T]he three factors, despite manifold discouragements, made Washington a center of Negro civilization were government employment, Howard University, and the Bethel Literary and Historical Association." By 1960, Blacks had become the majority in the city's population.[46]

Between the early 1800s and the 1950s, the District of Columbia was a southern city. Its laws and customs duplicated race relations that branded Richmond, Virginia, Charleston, South Carolina, and Atlanta, Georgia, as southern cities. In short, Jim Crow dominated life in the nation's capital.[47]

On these three facts, the political, economic, and social character of the District of Columbia pivoted for a century and a half. As did the episodic civil rights movements during these years.

Following the Civil War, the Black community expanded greatly with the extension of citizenship and voting to freed slaves. Rural Blacks moved to DC throughout the closing decades of the nineteenth and early years of the twentieth century. Economically, some highly educated and skilled Blacks did find a few low-level jobs in the federal government (in 1891, out of 23,000 federal employees in DC, almost 2,400 were "colored"). Other educated Blacks taught in the public schools, practiced law, and led churches in the segregated community. The majority of Washington Blacks, however, worked as domestic servants and unskilled labor as they did in other southern cities.[48]

Deeds containing racial covenants prohibited sales of white-owned homes to middle- and upper-middle-income Blacks. Most low-income Blacks, however, lived in the maze of alleys that ran between streets in largely Black neighborhoods. Nonetheless, middle-income Black families established businesses, churches, and cultural clubs and began schools. Dunbar, the first high school for Blacks in both DC and the US, opened its doors in 1870.[49]

While middle- and upper-class Blacks created a separate business and cultural life within the confines of a segregated city, they did not escape police mistreatment in disproportional arrests and sheer brutality. As one historian pointed out, both persisted throughout the closing decades of the nineteenth century and through the 1960s. Between 1889 and 1960, District of Columbia police arrested more Blacks than whites even though they were a minority of the population. Nor did DC escape the wave of race riots that swept across the nation in 1919 or the unrelenting burden of Black residents being treated as second-class citizens. [50]

By the end of World War II, the nation's capital remained a segregated city little different from neighboring Richmond, Virginia, and Baltimore, Maryland. In 1947, for example, when Blacks were nearly a third of the city's population, President Harry Truman's Committee on Civil Rights reported:

> If he [a Negro] stops in Washington . . . with very few exceptions, he is refused service at downtown restaurants, he may not attend a downtown movie or play, and he has to go into the poorer sections of the city to find a night's lodging. The Negro who decides to settle in the District must often take a job below the level of his ability. He must send his children to the inferior public schools set aside for Negroes and entrust his family's health to medical agencies which give inferior service. In addition, he must endure the countless daily humiliations that the system of segregation imposes upon the one-third of Washington that is Negro.[51]

Segregated practices remained the rule in the following decades even as federal courts struck down Jim Crow practices. In 1948, for example, the US Supreme Court declared that using racial covenants to bar Blacks from buying homes in white neighborhoods was unconstitutional. While that opened a few DC neighborhoods to middle- and upper-middle-class Black families, two-price housing—one for whites and one for Blacks—emerged, ensuring that overcrowded Black neighborhoods remained densely packed. Not until 1953, three years after longtime resident and esteemed educator Mary Church Terrell filed suit against Thompson's

Restaurant, a few blocks from the White House, for refusing to serve her, did the US Supreme Court decide that barring of Black patrons by DC restaurants was unconstitutional. Segregation remained intact in the capital city. No surprise, then, that a central and salient community institution was also legally segregated: public schools. In the years following the 1954 *Brown* decision (one of the consolidated cases challenging segregated schools was *Bolling v. Sharpe*, which involved the DC system), the unraveling of de jure segregation occurred swiftly in DC.[52]

Events cascaded in the years following the March on Washington in 1963 when SCLC, SNCC, and other Black leaders lobbied the White House and Congress as a political path to end segregation in the capital city. Under federal pressure from Presidents John F. Kennedy and Lyndon B. Johnson, Congress expanded civil rights and worked toward ending segregated practices in southern states. So too did the District slowly dismantle the dual systems that had existed in municipal agencies, public facilities such as hospitals and parks, and, of course, schools.

Erasing segregation was one thing, but Black and white Washingtonians having representation in Congress, voting for president, and electing city officials to run District affairs was another thing that remained out of reach. The main reason for DC being treated like a colony was that in these decades, southern Democrats controlled both the House and Senate Committees overseeing the District of Columbia's government and budget. Every year District officials, including Board of Education members, would meet with the Democratic chairs of the Senate and House committees (e.g., Representative John McMillan from South Carolina, 1948–1972) to review the DC budget.

Often these chairs, hostile to the majority-Black city ever gaining control of their local government or representation in Congress, raised questions about crime, poor school performance, increased numbers of families on welfare, or any local issue that white District residents brought to the all-powerful chairs. Not until 1972 did McMillan end his quarter-century rule over the House District Committee.[53]

Over these decades, District residents continued to be disenfranchised when it came to electing their local officials. In 1970, Congress permitted Washingtonians to elect one nonvoting delegate to the House of Representatives. But DC in 2021 has no representation in the Senate. As for local government, no city official was elected; they were all appointed. "Home rule," as every city across the nation already had, still lay beyond the reach of DC residents.

Washingtonians had a long way to go before they were permitted to run their own affairs. President Lyndon B. Johnson, like his predecessor John F. Kennedy, urged Congress to let District residents elect city officials. In 1968, DC was allowed to elect their Board of Education. In 1967, for the first time, President Johnson appointed a mayor and city council. Not until 1974 were District voters allowed to elect their local government. Even then, however, officials made the annual trek to Capitol Hill to gain approval for their budget. No surprise, then, that since 2000, DC license plates have read "End Taxation Without Representation."[54]

With the demise of de jure segregation across the city's institutions, the civil rights struggle morphed into securing "home rule," especially after the rise of Black power ideology and its fracturing of the civil rights coalition. That split in leadership spread to DC as SCLC's Martin Luther King Jr. and SNCC's Stokely Carmichael worked together sporadically to advance efforts of Washingtonians to gain a voice in both local and federal government. In the severe turbulence in the District of Columbia that followed the death of King in 1968, the split in moderate-to-militant leadership became obvious, spreading to local leaders such as longtime activist Julius Hobson, SNCC's Marion Barry, and Reverend Walter Fauntroy.

Consider Marion Barry, a Fisk University graduate who was active in the Nashville sit-ins and the SNCC and moved to DC in 1965. Shortly thereafter, he became the local activist for "home rule." In 1966, after the privately owned DC Transit bus company proposed a large increase in fares, he mobilized over seventy-five thousand Washingtonians to boycott buses for one day.[55]

Following the successful bus boycott, Barry founded "Free DC," an organization that pressed for home rule. He corralled other Black city leaders to join him in seeking the self-rule that had been denied for over a century and a half. Flanked by ministers at the launch of the organization, Barry said, "We want to free DC from our enemies: the people who make it impossible for us to do anything about lousy schools, brutal cops, slumlords, welfare investigators who go on midnight raids, employers who discriminate in hiring, and a host of other ills that run rampant through our city."[56]

After the president and Congress authorized local elections, including the board of Education, DC voters elected Barry to serve on the board of education in 1971. Three years later, he ran for city council, serving one term. He then campaigned successfully for mayor in 1977 and ran the District until 1991. By that time, DC public school administrators, teachers, and students, judges, police chiefs and officers, and those who led and staffed multiple local agencies had become majority Black or were in the process of becoming so.

Similar to what happened in other cities such as Cleveland, Black leaders in DC sought political power to then legislate improvements that would better the lives of their constituents. In DC, however, it was a constant struggle with Congress for self-rule and voting representation in the House of Representatives and Senate. In June 2020, the House of Representatives voted to create the "State of Washington." The Senate refused to take up the bill. The struggle continues.[57]

Since the founding of the capital city, the US president and Congress have shaped the political and economic lives of Washingtonians. Moreover, daily lives were largely segregated for a century and a half. Since then, challenges to the lack of representation in Congress continue in 2021 with attempts to make the District of Columbia the fifty-first state, with two Senators representing Washington.[58]

I began teaching at Cardozo in 1963 and stayed nearly a decade as a teacher and an administrator. While the fight to completely end "taxation without representation" in the District has seen occasional successes, much remains to be done in achieving both self-rule and full congressional representation. Schools are no longer de jure racially segregated, but since the 1960s they have been de facto segregated. Mayoral control in 2006 brought new superintendents—now called chancellors—to run DC schools. Both the mayor and chancellors since then have encouraged parental choice by allowing charter schools to flourish, with nearly half of all students enrolled in these schools. District leaders for the past decade have increased choice, encouraged public schools to compete with charters for students, and pressed teachers to lift students' academic performance and narrow the yawning achievement gap. Whether mayoral control, another slice of self-rule, has improved District schools remains contested insofar as students' academic performance, graduation rates, and admission to colleges.[59]

CHAPTER 4

High School History Teacher in Cleveland and Washington (1956–1972)

As a teacher, I was not a civil rights activist. While I did participate in a few marches, I was never arrested at a demonstration. Nor did I join any organizations at the forefront of the movement. While my wife Barbara and I contributed to civil rights groups and moved our family into an integrated Washington, DC, neighborhood, my involvement in civil rights activities was close to nil.

But not so in schools. For the most part, where and when I was involved in civil rights grew directly out of whom I taught and what I did in my classes at Cleveland's Glenville High School and Washington, DC's, Cardozo and Roosevelt High Schools.

I was a classroom teacher who worked in de facto segregated Black schools in two cities. As a white teacher teaching history to Black middle- and working-class students who already had experienced segregated schools, racial discrimination, and institutionalized racism on a daily basis—preparing uncommon lessons about the American past and helping students finish high school was the civil rights road that I traveled in the years I taught at Glenville.

Later, at Cardozo High School, I continued on that path, but my activities expanded as I began to connect what I was doing inside school with events occurring outside of school, ranging from sponsoring teacher conferences about new curriculum materials to joining protest marches and even working for a short time at the US Commission on Civil Rights, a federal agency committed to integrating schools.

BECOMING A TEACHER

After graduating Taylor Allderdice High School, I attended the University of Pittsburgh (hereafter, Pitt) for four years while living at home. The first in my family to attend college, I tried premed, but organic chemistry proved my undoing. I drifted into other preprofessional courses and eventually entered Pitt's School of Education.

In the early 1950s, the School of Education had professors imbued with Progressive ideas of teaching and learning that had dominated the field for decades. I took courses in which I read John Dewey, absorbing the ideology of Progressivism. I cannot remember if I had read his *My Pedagogic Creed* (1897) at the time, yet his words "education is the fundamental method of social progress and reform" I believed when I entered the classroom.[1] In courses on teaching social studies, I developed lessons organized around topics consistent with the unit plan laid out in Henry Morrison's textbook, *The Practice of Teaching in the Secondary School*. Progressive vocabulary and ideology were in the air that we breathed. And I inhaled a lot.[2]

My final semester in the School of Education required me to student teach two high school history classes. When I showed up at Peabody High School, I listened for about a half-hour to the two middle-aged white teachers assigned to supervise me. They then gave me their copies of the required textbooks and student attendance rolls. I seldom saw them after that.

I discovered that teaching is part performance. That wowed me. What I remember is that every day was a dramatic show and I had to be ready. My lines had to be memorized. I had to get audience participation. Before each class, I could feel my stomach muscles tense. I was wired for action.

I could write that I entered teaching to improve the lot of undereducated children, to serve the community, or a similar noble sentiment. While such motives may have been buried within my psyche—and I believe they were—what really appealed to me initially was performing in front of a captive audience and the challenge of conveying to others what I believed to be crucial information, ideas, and skills.

I graduated in 1955 with a major in history and a minor in biology. That summer, I applied for a dozen jobs in social studies and was turned down for each one. One month after school started, I found a one-year job teaching biology and general science in McKeesport, an industrial city twenty miles from home. The students I was expected to teach had had a series of substitutes, and when they saw me in early October, their eyes glazed over. They believed me to be yet another teacher who would leave shortly.

I stayed until June. My rookie year of teaching was hard, but I did survive.

From collecting animal specimens for biology class in Schenley Park's Panther Hollow to preparing late-night lessons on mass and volume, I barely made it. McKeesport Tech had no wet labs, no microscopes, and few instructional materials. Thus, I gathered salamanders in nearby creeks. I built pulleys and simple machines at home.

None of my Pitt education courses coated with Progressive ideology and dressed up with student-centered lessons applied to my flailing efforts to do a journeyman job teaching biology and general science. What did help me survive was Gene Surmacz, the chemistry teacher who had been there for three years. He saw my floundering and asked if I needed help in teaching biology. He gave me lessons that he had used when he taught the course and set aside time for coaching me. He was my life preserver that year.

But I wanted very much to teach history and social studies. Every week I looked for newspaper postings of vacancies across western Pennsylvania and Ohio, applying for any social studies spot I could find. Just before school opened in 1956, I heard from the Cleveland public schools (signaling to me that I was at the bottom of their last barrel of newbies) that I should report to Glenville High School immediately to teach social studies. At twenty-one, I left home to start a career in teaching.

GLENVILLE HIGH SCHOOL (1956–1963)

My memory of teaching over a half-century ago is filled with holes. In thinking back to the time when I began teaching at Glenville High School in Cleveland, Ohio, I can remember some events, some students, some teachers, and my first principal, but there is much I cannot recall. Slivers of memory remind me of what I did daily in my five US and world history classes over the seven years. And even those fragments are disconnected. What helps me keep from sentimentalizing my memories are yellowed copies of actual lessons I taught, wrinkled student papers with my comments on them, old spiral-ringed gradebooks listing students and their marks, occasional articles about one or more classes of mine in the student newspaper, and photos of me teaching in the annual yearbook. That's it.

I do recall my shock when I had lunch with Glenville principal Oliver Deex just before I had to report for teaching in September 1956. I was startled to find out that Glenville's student body was over 90 percent Black—the word then was "Negro." He gave me a once-over-lightly account of segregated schools in Cleveland and the differences between the increasingly Black East Side and the all-white West Side, separated by the Cuyahoga River. He began my education in Cleveland's residential segregation and the growth of ethnic and racial ghettos.[3]

SEGREGATED CLEVELAND

As I pointed out in the previous chapter, patterns of ethnic and racial segregation in Cleveland had developed early in the twentieth century. Upward mobility among ethnic and racial minorities changed neighborhoods as the city became a magnet for southern migrants and European immigrants. By the 1930s, for example, Jewish families had moved into the Glenville area, so that the high school became nearly 90 percent Jewish in that decade.[4]

In the late 1940s and early 1950s, as middle-class Black families moved eastward into the Glenville area, Jewish families moved into the eastern suburbs of Shaker Heights, Cleveland Heights, South Euclid, and Beachwood. By the time I settled into Room 235 at Glenville High School, it and adjacent junior highs and elementary schools were already over 90 percent Black.[5]

Classroom Teaching

Although my teacher preparation at the University of Pittsburgh was steeped in the Progressive tradition of student-centered instruction, any observer entering my high school history classes in those initial years would have easily categorized my instruction as wholly teacher-centered.

Students sat in rows of movable desks facing the front blackboard and my desk.

I planned detailed lessons for the five classes. In my written lessons, which I followed religiously in the early years, I would carefully list the questions I would ask for whole-group discussions, lecture on the text and additional readings I had assigned to the class, and all the while orchestrate a sequence of activities aligned to the questions. Ever performing in front of the class, I spent over 90 percent of instructional time teaching the whole group.

Toward the end of my first year at Glenville, I realized, albeit slowly, that teaching five classes a day in two subjects (world history and US history), grading homework from over 150 students, and learning the ropes of managing groups of students a few years younger than me not only wore me out—I was also taking late-afternoon and evening graduate history courses at Western Reserve University—but drove me to rely on lectures and the textbook.

Slowly, I became dissatisfied with how I was teaching. I routinely lectured, saw half of the students take notes and the other half stare into the distance or try to look attentive. Some fell asleep. I brought in artifacts and told stories. I asked students questions drawn from their textbook. One-word answers came back. Occasionally, a student would ask a question and I would improvise an answer that would trigger a few more students to enter into what would become a full-blown, back-and-forth discussion. It was unplanned and brief but mysteriously disappeared at the snap of a finger. Periodic quizzes and current events topics one day a week gave my routines an adrenaline shot, but student disengagement persisted.

After six months, I realized that I did not want to teach history mechanically, drowning students in forgettable facts that left me drained and dissatisfied at the end of a long day. I wanted to break out of that pattern. But I did not yet know how to do that.

These were the years before the civil rights movement had traveled northward. Rosa Parks had just triggered the boycott of Jim Crow buses in Montgomery, Alabama; Martin Luther King Jr. was ministering to his Dexter Avenue Baptist Church congregation in that city. After nearly a year of teaching, I became more aware of how Cleveland's racially segregated neighborhoods created schools like Glenville, blanketing them with malignant neglect. But it was slow going for a white teacher who gradually learned from his students and Black colleagues what was happening outside of school. Slow as it was, I began to see glimmers of my work inside the classroom, where students took notes and participated in discussions connected to their lives outside of school.[6]

I also grew intellectually. My principal, Oliver Deex, midwifed the expansion of my mind. A voracious reader and charming conversationalist, Deex introduced me to books and magazines I had never read: *Saturday Review of Literature, Harper's, The Atlantic, The Nation,* and dozens of others.

He often invited to his home a small group of teachers committed to seeing Glenville students enter college. When we were in his wood-paneled library, a room that looked as if it were a movie set, he would urge me to take this or that book. In his office after school, we would talk about what I had read. I have no idea why he took an interest in the intellectual development of a gangly, fresh-faced, ambitious novice, but his insistent questioning of my beliefs and gentle guidance whetted my appetite for ideas and their application to daily life and teaching.

The next year, I decided to experiment with different content to break out of those instructional routines that numbed me by the end of the day. For two of my five classes, I began to design lessons that differed from the assigned US history text (David S. Muzzey's *History of Our Country* published in 1955 had no entry for "Negro" in the index). Drawing from my evening university graduate history courses, I began to type up excerpts from primary sources, duplicate them on the department's one ditto machine, add questions, and assign them to those two classes. (The thought of doing this for all five classes overwhelmed me; two seemed doable.)[7]

For example, Muzzey's chapter on the thirteen colonies dismissed the origins of slavery as unimportant. I would copy descriptions of the transatlantic slave trade, slave auctions, and bills of sale in addition to historians' accounts that spelled out issues surrounding the introduction of Africans into the colonies. I would add questions to these readings that called for students to analyze both primary and secondary sources. In addition, I asked the librarian to gather the few books on Negro history that we had in our school and nearby libraries and put them aside in a special section for my two classes.

By my third year at Glenville, I had found that gaining students' interest in US history was only half the struggle. I was now using these materials in all five classes. Student response to non-textbook racial and multiethnic materials, however, was mixed. The novelty of studying Black figures and broader issues of race, ethnicity, and class triggered deep interest in maybe half of the students in my classes. But many students felt that such content was substandard because their textbooks didn't mention the information contained in the readings I handed out. Moreover, they complained openly that other history teachers didn't use readings and relied on the textbook more than I did. Some students even asked me to return to the text. I was surprised at first that some students wanted me to return to the deadening routine that left me and most students anesthetized. Then I realized that using textbooks in high school was all that they had experienced.

Overall, however, I judged student response as sufficiently positive for me to continue, and truth be told, I was excited about the readings and ways of getting students to think about the past. I saw that students studying a past in which racial content and inquiry practices were important enabled both students and me to make connections between then and now that had been missing when I began teaching. Sure, I was weary at 3:30 p.m., but now I looked forward to the next day of teaching.

Within four years, I had expanded my repertoire beyond weekly use of ethnic and racial subject matter. I slowly introduced new content and direct instruction in skills into my US history classes. As I learned the methodology of the historian in my graduate courses, I designed lessons on analyzing evidence, determining which sources of information were more or less reliable, and assessing what makes one opinion more informed than another. A later generation of scholars and practitioners might have labeled my uncertain baby steps as "teaching historical thinking."[8]

Anyone coming into my classroom, let's say a visiting Pitt educator imbued with Progressive ideas, would characterize what I did as clearly subject-driven and wholly teacher-centered. I write that with no embarrassment or apology. But I was trying out different ways of getting content across and developing inquiry skills that slowly changed the mix of activities I included in lessons.

I experimented with not only historical content but classroom tasks as well. I began using activities that increased students' interactions with me and among themselves. In one class, for example, I had students create a historical newspaper with student-written articles on the assassination of Julius Caesar or had students put Napoleon on trial after Waterloo. Sure, I tried small-group work on a few occasions for particular reading assignments, students leading discussions, and, of course, films and filmstrips followed by worksheets and discussion. Student participation grew.

It was not all as smooth as the above words might suggest. Sometimes I had ill-planned activities, gave fuzzy directions to students, or lacked key materials (sometimes all three in a disastrous trifecta of failure), and the class fell apart before my eyes. Many students dug in their heels over my asking them to participate in class discussions, panels, and tasks I assigned. And student interest would ebb and flow. Some students transferred to other classes. Other students objected to some of the activities—saying, "Mr. Cuban, why don't you teach like the other social studies teachers?"—but stayed in the class.

Consider my effort to directly teach my students to be critical thinkers. Still imbued with Progressive ideas (recall that John Dewey wrote *How We Think*), in my fifth year of teaching at Glenville I began teaching my US history courses with a two-week unit on thinking skills.

I had already introduced materials to my classes on what was then called "Negro history" (see above). I now began experimenting with the direct teaching of critical thinking skills. I believed that such skills were crucial in understanding history but of even greater importance in negotiating one's way through life. So I added the unit on thinking skills to the first semester. I figured that students learning these skills early could then apply them when I began teaching later units on the American Revolution, the Civil War, and the Industrial Revolution. I assumed incorrectly.

In this two-week unit, I selected skills I believed were important for understanding the past, such as judging the reliability of sources, understanding the difference between fact and opinion, making hunches about what happened and sorting evidence that would support or contradict those opinions, and distinguishing between relevant and irrelevant information in reaching a conclusion.

For each of these skills, I chose a contemporary event—a criminal case in the local newspaper, a national scandal that was on television, and occurrences in the school—and I wrote a one-page story that would require each student to apply the particular skill we were discussing, such as making an informed guess, collecting evidence to support their hunch, and reaching a judgment. I also gave the class additional sources, some reliable that they could use and some crippled by bias, to select information to support their conclusion.

Each forty-five-minute period—I was teaching five classes a day— was filled with engaged students participating in flurries of discussion, debates over evidence, student questioning of each other's conclusions, and similar excitement. I was elated by the apparent success of my critical thinking skills unit.

After the two weeks of direct instruction in skills, I plunged into the coming of the American Revolution and subsequent historical eras. From time to time, over the course of the semester, I would ask students some questions that I felt would prompt use of those thinking skills, often about the bias and reliability of sources, that we had worked on earlier in the year. Blank stares greeted me, with the occasional "Oh, yeah" from a few students.

I came to realize that my assumption of students applying thinking skills they had learned to a different setting—vetting the quality of sources and evaluating arguments about the American Revolution—was mistaken. Transfer of learning, as the psychologists put it, wasn't automatic, as I had assumed. It was a lesson that I had to relearn again and again. Many policy makers, practitioners, and parents believe that skills learned in one context can be easily applied to a different context. Ain't so.

Most nonteachers also forget a fact of life. Teaching five classes a day is tiring. Creating new instructional materials takes enormous swathes of time to organize, present, and then redo when they belly flop. No surprise, then, that at the end of each day, I was bushed. I would see students before school, midday when I began eating bag lunches in my classroom, and after school. When I became faculty adviser for student activities, even more students would stop by. I was also continually running down materials and films and scrounging paper for the ravenous ditto machine. And taking night classes in history to get a master's degree at a nearby university.[9]

Then I got married in 1958. Evenings that I had used for grading homework and preparing lessons and weekends for completing graduate papers were no longer as available as when I was single. Fatigue and the joyous awareness that I could have a life outside of Glenville brought me face-to-face with managing the dilemma of how to combine work demands and being with Barbara and eventually my two daughters, Sondra and Janice. Threading that needle was never easy for me as a teacher or later as an administrator.

In seven years of teaching, I had created in fits and starts, with many stumbles, a homemade history course. I was a classroom reformer in fashioning a different American history course in a de facto segregated school.

I came to believe that all teachers could adopt and adapt lessons tailored to their students, especially economically disadvantaged students in segregated schools. My belief in engaging classroom materials in turning around low performing students and schools grew out of those lessons I had created. If more teachers and schools did what I did, then, I believed, urban schools would improve. (My reform-driven belief turned out to be too narrow, perhaps even inaccurate, in confusing student engagement with learning, and too demanding of teachers given the working conditions they faced.) The ideas I put into classroom practice of getting students to connect the racially inflected American past to the present, I thought, would help my students understand what was happening in the south with Freedom Riders and student sit-ins in segregated restaurants. Without fully knowing it myself, my belief in the power of education to reform society, as Dewey put it, lay behind the materials I developed and the classroom activities I managed. That was the small part in the civil rights movement that I played.

In the next decade, my family and I would move to Washington, DC, and my work as a classroom reformer developing practical curriculum materials and lessons to engage minority students would continue. Current events, however, spilled over into public schools. Civil rights leaders led mass marches and engineered boycotts against segregated facilities, biased employers, and blatant housing discrimination. President Lyndon B. Johnson signed the Civil Rights Act of 1964 and the Voting Rights Act of 1965. His "War on Poverty" lost traction, however, as US involvement in Vietnam escalated American casualties, swallowed billions of dollars, and generated massive protests.

Moreover, a generational and organizational split over Black Power reshaped the civil rights movement at the time that riots in Los Angeles, Newark, Detroit, and other cities over police brutality, inadequate housing, lack of jobs, and segregated schools broke out year after year. Martin Luther King Jr.'s vision expanded beyond fighting segregation as he came slowly to see that the Vietnam War, continuing poverty among both white and Black Americans, and the economic system were intimately tied together. Then he was shot dead by a white sniper. Civil unrest—looting and fires—in over a hundred cities erupted across the nation. Governors and mayors called in the National Guard to quell disturbances and bring order to cities.[10]

All of these events seeped into school lessons and activities. In these years, I began to see a much larger picture of the nexus between the worlds outside and inside schools and how the complexities of school reform stretched far beyond my students in one classroom or an entire school.

CARDOZO HIGH SCHOOL (1963–1967)

In 1963, after seven years at Glenville and going part-time for a doctorate in American history at Western Reserve, and having written chapters for a dissertation on Black leadership in Cleveland, two job offers came to me. One was to teach US history at a Connecticut college with the understanding that I would complete my dissertation, and another was to move to Washington, DC, and work in a federally funded teacher-training project located in an all-Black high school. The job was to be a "master teacher." That is, I would teach two history classes and supervise four Peace Corps volunteers, who had just returned from two years abroad, in the craft of teaching social studies. My previous work in developing racial content in instructional materials at Glenville, I would guess, helped the director offer me the job. Yes, I was ambitious, I wanted to be noticed, recognized, and approved, but I had a family now and was uncertain what to do with these competing offers.

In retrospect, I can see now more clearly that I was lucky when I entered the job market in 1963. Born during the Great Depression, my generation was one of the smallest cohorts ever. As a young white man in the decades following World War II—I did not have to serve in the

Korean War because of my bout with polio—discriminatory hiring practices against Blacks and women gave me many opportunities in a growing labor market that, were I born a generation later, I would not have had. When I got jobs I sought later in my career, I attributed my success to a combination of aggressive ambition and talent and forgot the importance of luck.[11]

In 1963, then, faced with two job offers, I was at a fork in my career. I had to choose. I took the one-year job in 1963 at Cardozo High School in Washington, DC. It was a big risk to move Barbara and toddler Sondra for only a year to DC, but I was eager (and pushy) to join like-minded educators drawn to Washington in the Kennedy years. Career ambition, not family concerns, drove my decision-making.

Federal policy makers in those Kennedy-Johnson years (John F. Kennedy was assassinated a few months after the project began, and Vice President Lyndon B. Johnson became president) framed the problem of low performing urban students dropping out of school as having too few skilled and knowledgeable teachers who could create engaging lessons to motivate teenagers to stay in school and go to college. The solution to the problem of poverty and poorly performing urban schools was neither added funding nor more jobs for the unemployed nor inexpensive housing. The solution was: prepare better teachers.[12]

Setting

Readers can be forgiven for forgetting that until the late 1950s, the District of Columbia, the seat of government for the United States, was a segregated city. Water fountains, parks, public toilets, restaurants, hotels, and, of course, schools were separate by law.

After the US Supreme Court's decision in *Bolling v. Sharpe* in 1954 that segregated schools in DC were unconstitutional, the schools slowly desegregated. Keep in mind that whites constituted 43 percent of school enrollment in the 1950s, a figure that fell year after year. White families departed DC for the emerging suburbs in Maryland and Virginia. By 1966, Black students were 91 percent of district enrollment. Desegregation had become a pipe dream by the end of the decade.[13]

Set on a hilltop at 13th and Clifton Streets, the castle-like Central High School building had been a whites-only school until after World

War II. But as Black middle-class families moved into the neighborhood and white families left, the school was nearly empty. The all-Black Cardozo High School located in the nearby Shaw neighborhood was overcrowded and shabby. In 1950, the board of education transferred Cardozo students to the much larger, but also deteriorating, Central High School building. Thus, Central became Cardozo.

The view from the school was majestic. Students looked out of large windows and saw both the US Capitol and the Washington Monument. The neighborhood at that time had a mix of middle- and working-class and poor Black families.[14]

Within a decade, however, the neighborhood had changed. Percentages of families on public assistance, unemployment, and students not living with both parents had grown. Crime escalated. While mostly white- and blue-collar families sent their sons and daughters to Cardozo, the neighborhood had acquired a reputation of being poor and neglected. Local media labeled the neighborhood as a Black ghetto and "slum," terms that students, teachers, and parents bitterly resented.[15]

In the early 1960s, the school had over two thousand students, of whom fewer than ten were white. Nearly all faculty were Black and ranged from a core of dedicated, well-qualified teachers to time servers who counted the weeks until retirement. As in all DC high schools at the time, the track system sorted students on the basis of IQ test scores and academic performance into the honors, college preparatory, general, and basic tracks. At Cardozo there were very few honors and college preparatory classes when the Cardozo Project in Urban Teaching settled into Room 111 in the fall of 1963.[16]

The Cardozo Project in Urban Teaching

The federally funded, one-year pilot project was a teacher-driven, school-based, neighborhood-oriented solution to the problem of low performing students and dropouts. It created a different, school-based model of preparing sharp, skilled teachers involved in the local community who could turn around a low performing de facto segregated school. This school-based reform model rejected traditional university-based teacher education programs wholly separated from impoverished neighborhoods.[17]

Master teachers in academic subjects trained returned Peace Corps volunteers to teach and develop new curriculum materials while drawing from neighborhood resources. Once trained, these ex–Peace Corps volunteers would become crackerjack teachers who could hook listless students through creative lessons, drawing from their knowledge of ghetto neighborhoods and personal relationships with students and their families. As a result, fewer students would drop out and more would go on to college. That was the theory of action driving the reform model.

As luck would have it, the project got funded and expanded each year. I continued to teach at Cardozo High School, eventually directing the program that had grown to encompass neighborhood junior highs and one elementary school. Given the expansion and a need for more experienced teachers, I recruited veteran Cardozo teachers—we called them "affiliates"—to train interns.

By 1965–1966, applicants included Peace Corps returnees, civil rights activists who had lived in southern communities, and veterans of VISTA (Volunteers in Service to America) who had jobs fighting poverty. It was a feisty mix of teachers and community activists who were active in DC civil rights actions and growing anti–Vietnam War protests.

In early 1965, the project sponsored a conference for DC teachers on improving instruction and connections between schooling and civil rights. Held on Howard University's campus, it attracted nearly one hundred DC teachers and activists. For the keynote address, I got Staughton Lynd, a Spelman College professor who had directed the Mississippi Freedom Summer in 1964, when more than forty summer schools were set up in Black communities. Following the keynote address, there were workshops on teaching basic-track students, analyzing links between poverty and schooling, teaching social studies during civil rights protests, and developing actual lessons.

That was a high for me, to bring together District teachers (including current and former project teachers) for a conference on curriculum and instruction tailored to DC students at a time when civil right activists pressed for multiethnic materials and murmurings of Black Power began to emerge. My civil rights involvement had continued its focus on classroom teaching but now probed at the deplorable conditions of DC schools and how to improve them.

If the conference was a high, the low I experienced was the continual coping with uncertain funding each year. Tortuous conversations with federal and DC agencies opened my eyes to how politically and bureaucratically thorny it is to engage students and involve parents and residents while negotiating with top-level local and federal administrators. The complex network of social relationships inside and outside of the district and the intersection between school, students, community, and organizational bureaucracies became hurdles to leap in order to get teachers to spend afternoons and evenings working with families in federally funded neighborhood centers near Cardozo.

It took four long years for me and other advocates to convince the DC superintendent and school board that recruiting and training Peace Corps returnees and recent college graduates benefited the District, not only because these efforts contributed to student learning, but also because the program lessened the annual scramble to staff all of its classrooms. The superintendent finally agreed to take over the program in 1967, renaming it the Urban Teacher Corps and expanding it from recruiting and training fifty new teachers a year to over a hundred.[18]

Now that I saw my job of getting the teacher education program incorporated into the regular DC school budget completed, I returned to teaching US history half-days at Roosevelt High School, another DC high school farther north on 13th Street.

ROOSEVELT HIGH SCHOOL

Why return to teaching? Why not look for posts that offered higher salaries and more status? After all, I was ambitious, seeking bigger and better positions that would stretch me and give me the recognition, if not approval, that I sought.

The answer is many-sided. One part is simply that I was drained. Recruiting and selecting interns, directing a project, negotiating with school and District agencies in addition to teaching two classes daily, well, that wore me out.

A second part is that I wanted to spend more time with my wife and two school-age daughters. Career had clearly come before family in the past four years, with long hours at work, little time at home, and nagging guilt over neglecting Barbara and the girls. Moreover, we had moved into DC's Shepherd Park, an integrated neighborhood, in the fall of 1967, and both Barbara and I wanted to be part of that community.

Started by civil rights activist Marvin Caplan, Neighbors Inc. worked hard to avoid realtor-driven blockbusting, where agents got white home-owners to sell cheaply by stoking fears of Blacks moving into the neigh-borhood and then turned around and sold those homes whites had just left at high prices to incoming Blacks seeking homes outside of ghetto neighborhoods. Such realtor practices had turned many neighborhoods into cash cows as they quickly went from a few Black families to swift white flight from DC.

Working closely with realtors of both races, Neighbors Inc. devel-oped an infrastructure of social and political events and networks of like-minded families who wanted to have a stable integrated neighborhood. After we moved into 1436 Holly Street, Barbara became deeply involved in Neighbors Inc. and wanted me to participate in the organization.[19]

A third part of the answer is that I wanted to write about my expe-riences at Cardozo and also pull together for the educational publisher Scott Foresman a paperback US history textbook based on what I and history interns had created over the years.

So I had a full agenda, but external events in the civil rights move-ment overwhelmed it. The rise of Black Power activists in the movement and their presence in DC, the assassination of Martin Luther King Jr. fol-lowed by violence a few blocks away from Roosevelt High School, and taking on part-time a job at the US Commission on Civil Rights (CCR) upended that school year.

I did teach two US history classes the first semester. They were small classes of about fifteen or so general- and basic-track students. I aban-doned the textbook and instead used materials drawn from units used at Cardozo. That worked out reasonably well.

Teaching two classes in the morning and spending afternoons writ-ing gave me time with Barbara and my daughters after they returned home from school. I also could help out around the house.

A few months after returning to teaching, I got a call from the CCR that David Cohen, the director of the commission's Race and Educa-tion Project, was leaving the post and had recommended me for the job. The CCR had just published a multivolume national study called *Racial*

Isolation in the Public Schools, which Cohen had directed. The director of the commission wanted the Race and Education Project to do further studies.

I was startled and pleased. My career drive to be noticed, recognized, and approved was unabated, and the thought of having a high-profile national position in charge of research on race and education grabbed me.

Because I was teaching part-time at Roosevelt, the CCR staff member proposed I continue teaching in the mornings and work at the commission in the afternoons. I discussed the possibility of another job with Barbara, and we both agreed that it was worth exploring.

Over the next few weeks, I went downtown for interviews with CCR staff and the director. He offered me the job, and we agreed I would begin the first week in January 1968. The tradeoff of losing the precious time I had sought at home with the family, neighborhood involvement, and writing was evident to me, but the burning desire to do work that excited me while gaining recognition won out. What it meant on a daily basis to work at a desk job within a federal agency, as a midlevel manager, never crossed my mind.

I taught in the mornings and drove to CCR's downtown offices at 19th and M. My initial task as Director of Race and Education was to develop a research agenda aimed at both desegregated and segregated schools in the country. For the first few months, I read widely about the history of the CCR and its reports over the past decade. Every day I was handed a thick sheaf of media articles describing what was going on in the country concerning civil rights and especially school desegregation. I was responsible for a multiracial staff of five, three of whom were professionals who had worked on the *Racial Isolation* report and were now working on other studies. I learned slowly, very slowly, the rituals and protocols of working in a federal bureaucracy. And I felt the muted racial antagonism among CCR staff that had existed prior to my taking the post. What became clear to me within a month was that I was in a high-conflict situation and way in over my head.

At Roosevelt High School, my friend and assistant principal Reggie Williams asked me to give up one of my US history courses and start a Negro History course at the beginning of the new semester. She rounded up twelve students, and I pulled together a series of units from Cardozo,

Glenville, and what I had published in *The Negro in America* a few years earlier. So I had a new course to teach in addition to the new part-time job I had taken on. I became a proficient, if often tired, juggler.

Discussions of readings on slavery as an institution, the Civil War, and Reconstruction formed the core of the small Negro History class. A few of the students had contacts in the Students Nonviolent Coordinating Committee (SNCC), and that organization's tilt toward building racial solidarity—the rallying cry then was "Black Power!"—entered our discussions. A few students raised the question of whether a white teacher could or even should teach such a course. Emotions rose and fell as we tackled these questions.

A month after the class began, former SNCC chair Stokely Carmichael came to Roosevelt. A graduate of Howard University and one of the early Freedom Riders, he had also been deeply involved in Mississippi's Freedom Summer schools in 1964. He was in Washington organizing Howard University students then in conflict with the university administration. The charismatic Carmichael's actions and speeches galvanized both Blacks and whites.[20]

Worried about security, school administrators asked the local precinct to assign police officers both inside and outside the building. Over five hundred students came to the auditorium after school to hear Carmichael talk. There were many students who had read about Carmichael and admired both his rhetoric and actions, especially about Black pride, respect for one another, the importance of African heritage, and racial unity, particularly mending social class divisions within the Black community. There were a few references to the upcoming Poor People's March on Washington sponsored by Martin Luther King Jr.'s organization, a protest where King had gotten Carmichael to agree to the nonviolent principles behind the campaign.[21]

There were also many students who questioned these ideas of Black unity, dropping integration, and joining the poor to improve their lot. In forceful questions, some students expressed their belief in individualism as being more important than community. "You got to make it on your own," a few said aloud. Others agreed with the importance of Black pride and supporting local businesses but still held onto the importance of integration.

I admired how Carmichael handled student questions respectfully, listening and answering each one but seldom retreating from the positions he laid out. Here were students listening to a veteran activist and skilled speaker whose ideas challenged what they and their parents believed. Often the assembly devolved into raucous exchanges and then it was over.

In days following Carmichael's talk, the Negro History class had a string of volatile discussions on the pros and cons of what he advocated for Black people. Divisions along social class lines—students from middle-class families supporting poor people's demands—that were mirrored during the student assembly reappeared in our small group. I tried, often ineffectually, to channel the high-pitched emotions into academic tasks (e.g., book reports, research topics). Then April 4 occurred.

THE KING ASSASSINATION

The murder of Martin Luther King Jr. in Memphis, Tennessee, where he was supporting sanitation workers' demands for higher wages and better working conditions triggered explosive anger across the country. Civil unrest broke out in over one hundred cities across the US. Protests, looting, and fires swept the nation.

In Washington, DC, the 14th Street business corridor, a few blocks from Roosevelt High School, was picked clean and burned. A news article described the scene:

> As night fell, angry people began to pour from their houses into the streets. Headed by the black activist Stokely Carmichael, crowds surged along 14th Street, ordering businesses to close. Carmichael tried to keep control, but things quickly got out of hand. A rock was thrown through a store window. Then a trash can was hurled. Someone used lighter fluid to start a small fire in a tree. As firefighters doused it, someone in the crowd yelled, "We'll just light it again!"[22]

Over four days of violence and fire, thirteen people died and damages or destruction occurred to nearly 1,200 residential and commercial buildings. The president called in the National Guard. Barbara, Sondra, Janice, and I stood at the corner of Holly Street to watch troop-filled trucks and tanks roll down 16th Street toward heavily damaged areas in the city.[23]

Like so many other families in DC, we were distraught. Schools closed. Businesses shuttered their windows. TV reports of shootings shook all of us. Since grocery stores in the damaged areas were either wiped out or picked clean, many families in those areas needed food. St. Stephen's Church organized food drives and volunteers to take bags of groceries to families near 14th Street. For two days, these volunteers, including me, drove to apartment buildings and residences to drop off groceries.

King's assassination altered dramatically what happened in my Roosevelt classes and what occurred at CCR. At school, there was much absenteeism, and when even smaller classes convened, feelings were raw and silence was common during lessons. The school held a memorial service for Dr. King. Ever so slowly, my students re-entered discussions. In the Negro History class, where there had been many freewheeling discussions of racism in American society, three students displayed their anger at whites, including their teacher, over the next few weeks. Sullen aggressiveness was the order of the day from many (but not all) students.

At CCR, divisions among the multiracial staff grew worse. Hateful looks and whispered comments about whites were frequent and often went unanswered. The sadness and anger over the loss of an exceptional leader whose views of race had broadened to encompass poverty, capitalism, and the Vietnam War were evident in the weeks to come.

My own inexperience within a bureaucracy and working half-days increased my uncertainty over what exactly should be the unit's agenda for school desegregation. My shaken beliefs in what the US could ever do to rid itself of racist structures and behaviors ricocheted in my mind. My uncertainty and stumbling efforts to ease the racial antagonisms shaped the following months of work at CCR. My inability to come up with a viable agenda of research and, more important, heal the open racial divide that had erupted within our unit led, after many discussions with Barbara, to my quitting a few months later. No other job awaited me.

TREADING WATER

I was now unemployed. With no more salary checks from either the DC schools or CCR, Barbara found a job as an administrative aide to a Rabbi at a nearby congregation. I stayed home with Sondra and Janice, walking them to school in the mornings, writing, doing household chores, and making occasional dinners. I thought that with my name as an urban educator, an expert on multiethnic instructional materials, and an author I could drum up sufficient business as a consultant to provide enough cash to cover monthly mortgage payments and expenses. I was wrong.

I sent out many letters advertising my talents and experiences, but few requests dribbled in. Of those that came in, most asked me to speak or consult for free. My work on Scott Foresman textbooks brought in advances from the publisher. Between my paltry earnings and Barbara's job, we eked out our monthly expenses. Apart from worrying about money, I was thoroughly enjoying the time I spent with Barbara and my daughters.

Then in December, DC Associate Superintendent of Instruction Norman Nickens asked me to meet with him. When I directed the Cardozo Project and Nickens headed the Model School Division in 1964, a subsystem within the District aimed at reforming schools in the Cardozo area, he was my boss.

With the release of the Passow Report in 1967, a devastating evaluation of the entire school system by a cadre of professors from Teachers College, Columbia University, the acting superintendent deputized Nickens to oversee the implementation of the report's recommendations. Within a few years, Nickens had become the go-to person for reforming Washington public schools.[24]

As a respected insider, Nickens was politically smart and knew what buttons to push and levers to pull to get things done within the ever-growing District bureaucracy. Even though I was an outsider—I had been in District schools only six years—and white, we had developed a mutual respect for one another. He understood the importance of bringing in a new generation of teachers prepared to work in urban classrooms.[25]

A new superintendent had arrived just after Nickens created a districtwide Office of Staff Development. Nickens asked me to apply. Interviews went well, and in January 1969, I became the first Director of Staff Development. I now had an office at district headquarters.

Going from classroom history teacher at Roosevelt High School to bureaucrat at the federal CCR to central office administrator responsible for the professional development of thousands of new and experienced teachers was jarring. No longer a classroom reformer who believed that new multiethnic lessons would make a difference in teaching and learning, and no longer a schoolwide reformer concentrating on recruiting and training new teachers for an urban district, now I was in a district position poised to strengthen the entire teacher corps of a large urban district. The fundamental unit for change had shifted in my mind as I journeyed from Glenville to Cardozo to Roosevelt, from the classroom to the school and now to the district.[26]

OFFICE OF STAFF DEVELOPMENT

The two years in the District office fully opened my eyes to how the splintered governance of the city both complicated and obstructed the already difficult tasks of schooling Black and poor students. Moreover, add to the mix eye-openers in seeing fierce racial politics in administrative appointments and how bureaucracies clogged the arterial flow of resources into schools and classrooms. The District of Columbia schools were a textbook case of fragmented governance and stubborn bureaucracy.

My responsibilities as director brought me in close touch with the members of the board of education, superintendents, and an array of both innovative and foot-dragging central office administrators. I learned firsthand how the bureaucracy worked amid the fractured governance of presidentially appointed DC commissioners choosing board of education members giving way to an elected board of education and mayor and city council—all of whom had to go to the US Congress each year, hat in hand, to get funded. In doing so, the superintendent and his retinue had to swallow hard the guff that all-white Congressional representatives dished out.

From my journal, December 16, 1969:

Another example of how difficult it is to run the D.C. schools . . . is the calculated crap that eats up time, energy, and resolve. Consider that [Congresswoman from Oregon] Edith Green, chairing the subcommittee on education investigating higher education asked Ben [Acting Superintendent Benjamin Henley] to testify on the teacher training needs of the 1970s. I wrote up Ben's statement emphasizing that urban school systems will have to assume more responsibility for training and re-training. We [superintendent, associate superintendent, director of personnel, and I] go over to Rayburn Building for hearings. Green convened session with [Al] Quie [from Minnesota] and [Albert] Steiger [from Wisconsin]. Questions were rambling, unconnected, and strangely vacuous for a Committee dealing with higher education.

Then, a pattern emerged. Questions on violence in schools were asked by Green. Then Green asked Ben to stay for the testimony of Bolling Air Force Base parents who were complaining about the terrible time their children were having in Southeast [DC] schools. Apparently . . . the parents had gotten to Green who scheduled Ben to be a witness, making the point that violence is in the schools and satisfying the military parents. An arrogant use of power.

Then Congressman Steiger questioned Ben on Georgetown schools [a largely white neighborhood in DC] to which Black kids were being bussed [sic]. He tsk-tsk the "deterioration" of education and had great "sympathy for the white parents" who withdrew their children from these schools. It was a snotty, arrogant remark that could easily be labeled racist. Ben, as vigorously as he could, disagreed with the Congressman.

This divided authority for the DC schools was also a recipe for continual conflict within the system. The splintered authority crippled both the board of education and its appointed superintendents. I learned how things got done officially and unofficially, and the importance of informal and prior relationships inside and outside the bureaucracy. That racial politics was in this stew goes without saying. I also learned how the annual trek to the Hill was crucial for maintaining (but not necessarily improving) District finances and, of equal importance, how divorced the board of education and administration at the Presidential Building were from what happened in schools and classrooms.[27]

From my journal, July 7, 1969:

> After six months in the system at the level I am, I can see all of the difficulties I had barely perceived and wrote about but they are now more sharply in focus and more complicated which means, I guess, less open to quick, simple changes. My belief that good people working in concert could effect the "right" changes (sounds so much like Lincoln Steffens' prescription for corrupt-ridden municipal government at the turn of the century) is much more open to question. Not that good people aren't around but that the distrust and the inertia that is its by-product is so damn pervasive. Good-will, good ideas, energy, and vigor create the froth of reform but don't seem to get to the substance, i.e., change in behavior. It's so frustrating.[28]

Within a year of my arrival, however, a newly elected city council and an elected board of education—dependent upon funding from the council and ultimately from Congress—clashed over the budget. As the Office of Staff Development (OSD) budget grew and the budgets of a dozen or more District curriculum supervisors shrank, the social networks between school administrators offended by the reduction of their budgets and newly elected city council members blossomed into racial politics. These downsized supervisors quietly lobbied city council members to get rid of the OSD.

In negotiations between the board and city council for the 1971–1972 budget, one of the casualties was a deep cut in the OSD's budget. I saw the cuts as aimed at me. After many conversations with my wife and a politically astute deputy whom I had appointed, I decided to resign in order to maintain the OSD. The following year the city council restored full funding to the OSD. By then I had returned to teaching history at Roosevelt High School.

ROOSEVELT HIGH SCHOOL REDUX

On appearing on the first day at school, the first surprise I got was to discover that one of my colleagues in social studies would be Carol Carstensen. A former Glenville student and academic star would be teaching next door to me. She had gone to college, graduated and earned her license to teach, gotten married, and moved to DC. We became friends and colleagues, ending up planning lessons jointly for our US history classes.[29]

The second surprise I got was a phone call from former Cardozo High School teacher Maxine Daly, who had become director of the Urban Teacher Corps (UTC). She asked me if I would like to be team leader of a group of UTC English and history teachers assigned to Roosevelt. My full load of five classes would be gone, and all I would do was observe, confer, and supervise the five-person UTC team. I wanted to teach, so I retained one class and spent the rest of my time with team members during and after the school day. I thoroughly enjoyed the time with the young teachers who were eager to teach and learn while teaching.

As the year of teaching and supervising a team unfolded, I knew that this would be my last year as a teacher. I had learned a lot about a big urban district with minority and poor students. I wanted to do more to improve teaching and schooling. Ambition still burned in me. I wanted a larger stage for putting my ideas about how to reform class-rooms, schools, and a district system into practice. Many conversations with Barbara and close friends forced me to think concretely about what I wanted to do next.

As a teacher and district office administrator seeing up close how a superintendent and top deputies worked daily, I came to realize that I could run a district. I began to look at newspaper and magazine ads for principals and superintendents. Nearly all required a PhD.

A principalship opened up at my daughters' elementary school. I applied. Got interviewed, but the interviewing committee of parents and District administrators wanted someone who had experience as a school principal and, yes, also a doctorate. Rejected.

It became clear to Barbara and me that if I wanted to work either at the school or district level, I would need a doctorate. So we looked at our savings and figured out that we could go to a university outside of DC, rent our home, perhaps get a stipend from the university, and get through two years of coursework and writing a dissertation (I already had a master's in history and had almost finished a doctorate in his-tory when I was at Glenville). So I applied to two universities. Stanford accepted me and offered two tuition-free years and a stipend. In the summer of 1972, the four Cubans packed up their Chevrolet Impala and drove cross-country to Palo Alto, California.

REFLECTIONS

In looking back on those years of teaching (1956–1972) in three urban high schools, I was filled with a passion to teach history and help students find their niche in the world while working toward making a better society. That confident Deweyan belief in the power of schools (and, yes, teachers too) to reform society brought me to Washington, DC, in 1963 to teach returned Peace Corps volunteers how to become teachers at Cardozo High School. I stayed nearly a decade in Washington teaching and administering school-site and district programs aimed at turning around schools in a largely Black city, a virtual billboard for severe inequalities.

Looking back, I see far more clearly now than I did then that national political, economic, and social occurrences (e.g., recession, war, presidential changes) rippled across districts and schools, further weakening my initial beliefs that better schools could make a better society. Instead, I learned that societal effects flowed over districts, schools, and classrooms. I had the causal direction wrong: societal changes alter schools far more than schools remake society.

Thus, those years as a teacher and administrator coincided with frequent national and local protests. The nonviolent civil rights movement supplied the initial fuel energizing many of the school reforms that spilled over school districts before and after the federal Civil Rights Act became law in 1964. But ideological splits in the movement and subsequent urban turmoil that erupted, especially after the assassination of Martin Luther King Jr., strongly affected students, parents, teachers, and administrators. As an educator in two cities, my personal involvement in civil rights was, at best, low profile. No links to mainstream civil rights organizations beyond contributions, joining occasional marches, and active involvement in an integrated community marked the years I spent in classrooms and schools.

The reform-driven belief that a teacher developing curriculum materials could connect with disengaged students sufficiently to get students to learn and achieve I brought from Glenville to Cardozo. That belief became more complex as I discovered what reform looked like inside a school, especially at a time when the civil rights movement tackled resegregated urban schools outside the South. And as I spent time in one large district, my beliefs about the best unit of reform upon which to concentrate shifted from the classroom to the school and, after a decade in the District of Columbia schools, morphed into a more complicated cluster of beliefs about the district being the optimal unit of reform. My thinking had changed.

Now I believed that reform encompassed a teacher-led classroom and a revitalized school but also the essential task of mastering the organizational realities of a large district in the constant vortex of significant political, social, and economic events. While schools cannot end poverty, they surely can help children from poor families get into college and climb higher rungs on the socioeconomic ladder.

The unit of reform, depending upon the context, I discovered, can be the classroom, school, or district. All matter. Where the most influence over students, teachers, administrators, parents, and the community can be exerted, I concluded, was the district. I needed a PhD to become a superintendent, so we set out for Stanford University.

I have few regrets for what I and many other like-minded individuals who taught and administered in largely minority and poor schools did during the 1950s and 1960s. I take pride in the many students who participated in these reforms, who were rescued from deadly, mismanaged schools and ill-taught classrooms. But the fact remains that by the mid-1970s, the civil rights movement to desegregate and improve urban schools, with a few notable exceptions, had become no more than graffiti written in snow. And the social inequalities that we hoped to reduce, persisted.[30]

Although over the years, I experienced surges of pessimism about improving classrooms, schools, and districts, hopelessness did not triumph. As I describe in the next chapter about my years as a superintendent in a middle-sized urban district, I would come to believe that more and better ways of schooling could be achieved when school boards and superintendents worked in unison toward common goals. The best way to turn around classroom and school practices that nurtured student disengagement, I concluded, was to have district leadership engage principals and teachers in improving their practices. I believed that in the mid-1970s, during an economic recession and the Watergate crisis that led to President Nixon's resigning office. The civil rights movement seeking to bring America's ideals closer to their promise had lost steam by the end of the 1970s. Urban and suburban schools became even more racially segregated as Latinos and other immigrants flocked to schools.

By the late 1970s, as the civil rights movement receded, voices of worried business leaders deeply concerned about recessions, global competition, and the academic skills of high school graduates saw schools as producers of human capital (read: workers), but ones slipping in quality. Those fears prompted political leaders and policy makers to pay renewed attention to public schools not only as providing equal opportunity but also as incubators of economic growth. To corporate and civic leaders, schools and the economy were always helpmates, but direct action had to be taken to make them so. And another reform movement emerged just as I, with doctorate in hand, moved my family to Arlington, Virginia, to direct a school district of fifteen thousand students across the Potomac River from Washington, DC. Chapters 5 and 6 pick up that story.

CHAPTER 5

Standards-Based Reform Movement (1970s–Present)

A contracting firm in New York City employed 4,900 skilled mechanics direct from Europe, paying them fifty cents per day above the union rate, because it was impossible to secure such valuable workmen in our greatest industrial center. We must not depend on Europe for our skill; *we must educate our own boys.*

—REPORT OF THE COMMITTEE ON INDUSTRIAL EDUCATION,
NATIONAL ASSOCIATION OF MANUFACTURERS, 1905[1]

Education isn't just a social concern; it's a major economic issue. If our students can't compete today, how will our companies compete tomorrow? In an age when a knowledgeable workforce is a nation's most important resource, American students rank last internationally in calculus and next to last in algebra.

—JOHN AKERS, CHAIRMAN OF IBM, IN AN ADVERTISEMENT
IN THE *NEW YORK TIMES MAGAZINE* (1991)[2]

As THE 1970s UNFOLDED INTO THE 1980s, strong pressures from weak economic growth, recessions, and global competitors surpassing US companies took up the foreground of public attention. The civil rights movement continued but slid into the background of national and local affairs. A conservative white backlash against civil rights occurred with a shifting of focus to economic-driven events. As had occurred in the past, corporate leaders concerned about the state of the economy turned their attention to the quality of American schools.[3]

Consider the economic changes that occurred in these years. After the longest stretch of prosperity in the history of the nation in the quarter-century following World War II, the economic downturn of the early 1970s and the winding down of the national civil rights movement caused great turmoil among US opinion leaders, the corporate community, and growing numbers of disillusioned Black and white workers.

Between 1974 and 1981, annual growth of the gross national product (GNP) averaged only 2.2 percent, down from the annual average of nearly 5 percent between 1964 and 1972. Inflation, averaging just below 5 percent in the late 1960s, rose to an annual rate of 9.3 percent between 1974 and 1981. Unemployment had risen to 5.2 percent in the recession of 1974 (with the figure for out-of-work youth more than double that and rising to three times higher among minorities), growing to 7.5 percent in 1981 and finally plateauing at 9.5 percent during the recession in the following two years. Again, youth unemployment, especially among poor minorities, spiked at double these rates. Labor productivity, which had grown at an average annual rate of 3 percent between 1947 and 1973, grew at just 1 percent after 1973. The US share of the world market for manufactured goods fell by 23 percent in the 1970s. By then, Japanese and German automakers had captured 22 percent of American car buyers.[4]

By 1980, one economist said that the US had the "highest percentage of obsolete plants, the lowest percentage of capital investment, and lowest growth in productivity of any major industrial society other than Great Britain." One pollster tried to sum up the national mood: "The state of mind of the public is worried sick and in a panic . . . people know that there is something wrong." In the summer of 1980, *Business Week* editors concluded, "the decline in the U.S. economy has advanced so far that the public as a whole has begun to sense a need for change."[5]

But what should change? A search for causes of slow economic growth, low worker productivity, high unemployment, and escalating inflation in the 1970s triggered intense examination of national social, cultural, and educational trends. Corporations looked internally at management and improvement of their bottom lines. Many businesses pursued "organizational restructuring." Others sought mergers and downsized their organizations. They streamlined management, outsourced work to places where labor was cheaper, and laid off employees.

Looking elsewhere for ways to shake free of limited economic growth, CEOs, economists, and policy makers saw the production of human capital as a primary responsibility of tax-supported public schools and a surefire way of revving up the economic growth engine. More effective schools, policy elite thinking went, would turn out well-prepared graduates, spurring economic growth, higher standards of living, social stability, and global competitiveness. As had occurred in earlier economic downturns, corporate leaders, economists, and public officials turned their attention to the quality of public schooling.[6]

Employer criticism of high school graduates unprepared for the workplace, violence in urban schools, and the flight of white middle-class families from decaying and racially volatile cities to suburbs made it easy for faultfinders from both the political left and right to blame American public schools as a key source of larger economic and social problems. A sampling of typical one-liners pointed again and again to schools inadequately preparing the next generation of workers and citizens:

"A semi-literate population cannot support a productive economy." (Chester Finn, Assistant US Secretary of Education, 1987)

"Poverty and ignorance cause shortages of qualified workers and threaten America's stance in a global economy." (Committee for Economic Development, 1987)

"If we don't keep them in school and do a better job of educating them, who will do the work that enables the US to compete successfully in the global marketplace?" (Business Roundtable, 1988)[7]

Business and civic elites and academic critics used falling test scores repeatedly to confirm that public schools were failing. Data from international achievement exams such as the Second International Math Study (SIMS) and Trends in International Mathematics and Science Study (TIMSS), the National Assessment of Educational Progress (NAEP), the Scholastic Aptitude Test (SAT), and, finally, tests cited in *A Nation at Risk* (1983) appeared time and again to show that faulty schooling left American youth unprepared for an altered workplace no longer filled with manufacturing jobs.

Continued criticism of schools turning out insufficiently prepared graduates got the White House's attention. In 1989, President George H. W. Bush summoned all state governors to the first education summit in Charlottesville, Virginia, to draft six national goals for US public schools. Shortly thereafter, the Business Roundtable, the US Chamber of Commerce, the National Alliance of Business, and civic leaders, worried over students' low scores on standardized tests, pushed for better preparation of graduates to enter the workforce. Concerns about growing automation of jobs and higher-skilled workers being needed for twenty-first century jobs drove various business groups to lobby states to legislate curricular, organizational, and instructional changes ranging from expanding parental choice of schools, letting principals and teachers run their own schools, and enlarging work experiences of students.[8]

Thus, a coalition of civic and business leaders equating test scores with the quality of schooling actively identified deficient schooling as a national problem that had to be solved. Amplified by the media, other political and social constituencies voiced their dissatisfaction and joined the chorus of school critics.[9]

But to look at only these closing decades of the twentieth century, when economic turmoil turned the spotlight on schools, would be myopic. Just as the Progressive and civil right movements had their "short" and "long" stories, so too do the economic-driven reforms.

PUBLIC SCHOOLING AND THE STANDARDS-BASED REFORM MOVEMENT

The "Short" Story

The bookends of the standards-based movement are the report *A Nation at Risk* from the National Commission on Excellence in Education in 1983 and the No Child Left Behind Act in 2001. In those two decades, prodded by business leaders, US public schools toughened academic standards, increased standardized testing, and established accountability measures anchored in the belief that effective and efficient management of schools—as restructured corporations had accomplished—would increase the quality of high school graduates entering the workplace. Such improved "human capital" would sharpen corporate performance in making and selling products superior to those of their international competitors.

Imbued with the spirit of the civil rights movement, policy elites also declared that better-quality schools anchored in test data would raise the dreadfully poor academic performance of minority children and youth. Avoiding "the soft bigotry of low expectations" and reducing the "achievement gap" between Blacks and whites rallied US presidents, CEOs, and business groups to press for equal opportunity for those who had been ignored and neglected.[10]

A Nation at Risk. After President Ronald Reagan took office in 1981, he asked Terrell Bell, US Secretary of Education, to examine US public schools. Bell appointed a national commission that turned in a report in 1983. *A Nation at Risk* minced few words about the poor quality of US schools, recommending a new direction to achieve a competitive workforce. Responsibility for mediocre test scores and by inference responsibility for a weak economy and a noncompetitive workforce was laid upon schools. "We conclude," the report said, "that declines in educational performance are in large part the result of disturbing inadequacies in the way the educational process itself is often conducted."[11]

Schools, therefore, must change to produce excellent graduates ready to work in an information-driven economy. Not pervasive economic and social structures but better schools are the pathway to economic prosperity. Unless there was widespread school reform immediately, policy elites claimed, then weak economic growth and inequalities would worsen.

A Nation at Risk answered the question of which direction the US should take its public schools to become again a globally competitive nation. Thus began the standards-based movement.

Coalitions of elite reformers, including presidents Ronald Reagan, George H. W. Bush, and Bill Clinton, and corporate leaders, such as Electronic Data Systems' CEO Ross Perot in Texas and Louis Gerstner from IBM, promoted new state and federal educational policies. Throughout the 1980s and 1990s, state after state increased their graduation requirements, mandated tests that all high school students had to pass to get their diplomas, and put into place rewards and sanctions for high and low performing students, schools, and districts.[12]

With the bipartisan passage of the No Child Left Behind Act (NCLB) in 2001, President George W. Bush and the US Congress converted the "Texas Miracle" that Bush had presided over as governor into a national policy directive that shaped the next fifteen years of US schools under both Republican and Democratic administrations.[13]

With the renewal of NCLB, now called the Every Student Succeeds Act (2015), US schools have continued their focus on getting more students to graduate high school fully equipped with the necessary knowledge and skills to enter higher education and the workplace. The coronavirus pandemic of 2020–2021 that shoved schools into remote instruction before slowly returning to in-person schooling only hit the pause button for the standards-based movement. Extending over nearly forty years, then, public schooling has become the handmaiden of the economy.

That's the "short story" of the standards-based reform movement.

The "Long" Story

Education and the economy have been linked in the minds of reformers since the invention of tax-supported public schools. In 1842, intrepid reformer Horace Mann saw the linkage between tax-supported public schools and creation of both individual and national wealth:

> [E]ducation is not only a moral renovator, and a multiplier of intellectual power, but . . . it is also the most prolific parent of material riches. It has a right, therefore, not only to be included in the grand inventory of a nation's resources, but also to be placed at the very head of the inventory. It is not only the most honest and honorable, but also the surest means of amassing property.[14]

While the moral and social aims of public schooling have been far more often expressed than economic ones, reformers and employers since the mid-nineteenth century saw the linkage between economic returns from schooling as both natural and good. Since then, business and civic leaders have forged connections between a growing economy and education—or as economists, then and now, would put it, producing "human capital" for the workplace.[15]

Enhancing those linkages even further during the nineteenth century was school reformers' admiration for newly organized factories and booming employment for both Americans and arriving European immigrants. Moreover, an innovative way to organize schools modeled after the system in Prussia spread in the middle of that century. Called the age-graded school, it resembled the efficiency and effectiveness of the factories. These newly constructed eight-grade grammar school buildings sorted students by age, placed one teacher in each classroom, and sliced the curriculum into year-by-year segments. The age-graded organization tried to copy the efficiency of assembly-line factories producing merchandise. The slow-motion abandoning of the dominant model of elementary school organization—the one-room schoolhouse—occurred in the decades following the Civil War, especially in cities.[16]

By the early twentieth century, the school-as-factory metaphor was not only accepted but became an upbeat, even optimistic phrasing in efficiency-minded Progressives' vocabulary. Stanford University professor Ellwood Cubberley, a leading efficiency-minded Progressive, wrote in 1916:

> Our schools are, in a sense, factories, in which the raw products (children) are to be shaped and fashioned into products to meet the various demands of life. The specifications for manufacturing come from the demands of twentieth-century civilization, and it is the business of the school to build its pupils according to the specifications laid down. This demands good tools, specialized machinery, and continuous measurement of production to see if it is according to specifications, the elimination of waste in manufacture, and a large variety in the output.

A partisan of the then immensely popular "scientific management" movement in the growing corporate sector, Cubberley echoed the prevailing preoccupation with the age-graded school and the positive mindset reformers had for the model of the factory.[17]

While it is easy to quote members of the policy elites of the day about the virtues of assembly-line factories transforming traditional schools, it is still hard to capture the angst that seized business and civic leaders in these decades. Many had traveled to Germany and saw firsthand the connection between the economy and schooling. Industrial leaders saw the spread of European products across the globe as a result of government investment in a vocational education that prepared their youth for factory-dominated workplaces. To restore America's competitiveness, these business and industrial leaders pressed traditional educators of the day to add vocational experiences to the wholly academic course of study established in the age-graded high school. So over a century ago, policy elites hitched the economy to school reform.[18]

The rise, fall, and renewal of vocational education. In these years of Progressive reform, the idea of public schools taking on the function of preparing children and youth for the industrial workplace, thereby tying more closely schooling to the economy, became a reality as changes in the nature of work and the workplace, especially in the need for skilled and semiskilled workers such as machinists and assembly-line workers in factories, became apparent.

As the workplace changed, reform-minded groups such as the National Association of Manufacturers, the National Society for the Promotion of Industrial Education, union leaders, and educators boosted the goal of tax-supported schools preparing future workers. They pressed for adding vocational subjects to the curriculum and even creating separate vocational schools in districts (e.g., Lane Tech in Chicago, 1911; Manhattan Trade School for Girls, 1902).[19]

These varied interest groups succeeded in convincing educators as well as President Woodrow Wilson and the US Congress to not only endorse vocational education but also subsidize new courses in "agriculture, trade and industry, and home economics." The Smith-Hughes Act (1917), the first federal legislation funding vocational education, established the Federal Board of Vocational Education to oversee the implementation of the law. The aim of such schooling "shall be to fit for useful employment public school students fourteen years of age or older." The subjects to be taught, the number of hours of instruction, and the time to be spent on supervised work in the field were all set forth in the law. The board provided teacher salaries and stipulated which courses would be funded and what occupational skills students were to acquire.[20]

As vocational education spread across the nation in subsequent decades, most students in comprehensive high schools took at least one vocational course (e.g., typing, business math, auto repair). But those enrolled in the vocational curriculum or those who went to separate trade schools remained a small fraction of the student body. By the late 1920s, a decade after the law was enacted, enrollment in subjects specified by the law (e.g., industrial, agricultural, and home economics) ranged from 5 to just over 15 percent of high school students.[21]

What the Smith-Hughes Act and subsequent vocational state legislation pushed by a powerful coalition of industrial and commercial leaders, educators, and unionists accomplished, however, was including the goal of workplace preparation among the traditional social, political, and moral aims of tax-supported public school in the early decades of the twentieth century. Reformers then and now see schools and the health of the economy as inextricably bound to one another.

But vocational education lost its glow by the mid-twentieth century. Most students in comprehensive high schools—an innovation of the 1920s that incorporated vocational programs into the secondary curriculum—continued to take academic courses that prepared them for college. Federal efforts to renew the vocational education gloss failed as urban districts increasingly channeled potential dropouts and students alienated from the academic high school into vocational programs within the school or into separate trade schools.

By the late twentieth century, vocational schools were seen as dumping grounds for minorities, students with disabilities, and loners who could not fit into the comprehensive high school. But vocational education did not disappear. As the late twentieth-century economy shifted from industrial and manufacturing jobs to information- and service-driven employment, the century-old goal of workplace preparation found a new generation of large and small firms calling for schools to retool and prepare children and youth for different high-skilled jobs. Spurred by subsequent shifts in the economy and the *A Nation at Risk* report, the emerging standards-based testing and accountability movement sought to prepare all students for college. Vocational education was then reinvented into career and technical education (CTE).

Efforts to shift the focus of education from preparing youth for industrial and commercial jobs to preparing them for careers in professional, business, and high-tech sectors of the economy surged throughout US schools in the 1990s. In response to demand for high-skilled graduates who could think through problems and communicate clearly and swiftly in word and on-screen, educators combined academic and vocational subjects to equip students for both college and entry-level high-skilled occupations. CTE educators created curricula that drew from tough academic courses (e.g., advanced math, chemistry, biology) as well as workplace skills for students who sought entry in the health sciences, finance, manufacturing, business, and high-tech firms. CTE curricula blended academic work and on-site experiences.[22]

As in the past, influential business groups lobbied the federal government to fund programs. The US Congress passed the School-To-Work Opportunities Act in 1994 authorizing state grants to lay the groundwork for expansion of CTE in school districts. Subsequent renewals of the law and the Carl D. Perkins Career and Technical Education Act have aided the spread of CTE academies in rural, suburban, and urban districts.[23]

Support for CTE continues today, especially in high-tech industries. The explosion of information technology since the 1990s has spilled over to public schools, with CEOs, political leaders, and educators calling for computer science to be added to the curriculum (it was one of the recommendations in *A Nation at Risk*). Beyond cheerleading for computer science courses in secondary schools, policy makers, high-tech executives, and parents have pressed for all students to learn to code since, they believe, future jobs will require such skills.[24]

Where once vocational education was defined by separate subjects in schools (e.g., auto repair, welding) or even separate schools, now with recent calls for twenty-first-century skills and for every student to learn computer science and programming languages, K–12 schools have focused on careers by pushing *all* students to enter college before embarking on their careers. In effect, one direct outcome of the standards-based reform movement has been the total vocationalizing of public schooling.[25]

K–12 vocationalized schooling. One does not need a PhD to figure out that in the nearly forty years of the standards-based movement (I use the *A Nation at Risk* report from 1983 as a benchmark), reform-driven coalitions have forged strong links between the economy and public schooling. The primary purpose of the reform-driven standards, testing, and accountability movement in K–12 schools has been preparing each child for college and career.

So becoming college-ready means that higher education is really another vocational experience that provides a ticket to a decent-paying job. But a wrinkle in the expected step-by-step progression has occurred. Today, high-tech entrepreneurs, CEOs of technology companies, and advocacy coalition leaders lament the need to outsource coding to other countries and import software engineers from Asia and elsewhere. They point to the lack of US graduates skilled in programming, systems analysis, and computer support. And job growth in this sector will continue. The US Bureau of Labor Statistics estimated that computer and information technology jobs would grow by a half-million from 3.9 million in 2016 to 4.4 million by 2020.[26]

Keep in mind, however, that the US economy employed over 150 million workers (2018, prior to the coronavirus pandemic). Those estimated technical jobs in 2020 would have represented less than 3 percent of the overall workforce. According to projections, far larger growth in jobs will occur in health care and social assistance (almost six million), professional and business services (nearly four million), and construction (nearly two million), far surpassing computer and information technology (a half-million).[27]

An obvious question: Should all students learn coding to prepare for jobs that represent less than 3 percent of the workforce?

The strong smell of Silicon Valley self-interest accompanies these proposals to improve schooling. Behind Code.org and other advocacy groups are the thick wallets of donors and technology companies carrying iconic names. They push state and local education officials to enhance the standards-based movement by requiring computer science for high school graduation, classifying the subject as a fourth "science" in the secondary curriculum, substituting it for a foreign language requirement, and having five-year-olds learn to code. Over these proposals wafts the scent of companies seeking graduates who can enter the computer and information workforce, a minute fraction of the entire US workforce.[28]

Backers of coding are a Who's Who of Silicon Valley firms and donors who see the necessity of coding and computer science being part of the required curriculum standards and practices in US schools, as they are in over fifteen European nations. The United Kingdom, for example, tossed out its previous curriculum on information communications technology and introduced computer science and coding in 2012. In the US, champions of coding and adding computer science to the curriculum have already succeeded in lobbying state policy makers to insert coding and computer science into current curriculum standards and graduation requirements.[29]

As in the 1890s, a "new" vocationalism, this one with an emphasis on twenty-first-century skills for an information-driven society, has emerged as the primary purpose for tax-supported schooling. Business and corporate leaders have supported and lobbied for vocational education as an integral part of public schools. The strategy of choice for accomplishing these outcomes has been the standards, testing, and accountability movement.[30]

As noted above, when vocational education lost its shine in the late twentieth century, business leaders and educational policy makers reinvented it as career and technical education, or CTE. Support from the business community for schools to prepare students for the workplace has been unflagging. Business leaders recognized in the 1890s as they do now that tax-supported public schools have a definite role to perform in growing a strong local, state, and national economy. That belief and its tacit assumptions remain unchallenged in 2021.

Core assumptions of business-inspired school reformers. The crisply stated beliefs that I list here did not spring full-blown from corporate brows; they emerged decades ago and became shared among business leaders, policy elites, parents, and educators. They evolved over time and unevenly across the country, growing in diverse economic, social, demographic, and political contexts. They drew also from the persistent American faith in schooling as the solution to many national problems, including a weak economy. Occasionally, these premises would be stated explicitly. For the most part, however, these assumptions remained implicit in framing the problem of failing schools but became obvious in school-driven proposals to solve problems, then and now.

The first three assumptions deal with the relationship between the economy and schools, while the final two presume a fundamental similarity between businesses and schools, particularly that successful strategies borrowed from businesses can produce success in public schools:[31]

- Strong economic growth, high productivity, long-term prosperity, including a higher standard of living, and increased global competitiveness depend upon a highly skilled workforce.
- Public schools are responsible for equipping students with the necessary knowledge and skills to compete in an information-based workplace.
- Most public schools do a poor job of preparing high school graduates for college and the workplace, especially most urban schools.
- Schools are like businesses. The strategies that have made businesses successful can be applied to schools to produce structural changes that will improve academic achievement as measured by standardized tests, end the skills mismatch, and increase public confidence in schools.
- Higher test scores in school mean future employees will perform better in college and the workplace.

These taken-for-granted assumptions—occasionally contested in academic journals and by lone voices in op-ed columns—have driven school reform for nearly four decades

Strategies to improve schools. Acting on these core beliefs, US presidents, governors, and corporate leaders since the late nineteenth century promoted diverse ways to solve the problems afflicting public schools and thereby strengthen the nation's economy. Vocational education was the business-inspired strategy over a century ago. In its reincarnation as CTE, it remains a key part of the reformers' agenda.

Since the 1970s, another strategy for tying education more closely to the economy has emerged. Bipartisan agreement from national political leaders and policy elites arose that called for centralizing federal and state policy authority and applying corporate practices to public schools.

Through US Supreme Court decisions and legislation to correct inequalities arising from segregation, poverty, and racial, ethnic, and gender discrimination, federal authority for education coalesced sub-stantially since the 1950s. Although the passage of the Civil Rights Act (1964) and the Elementary and Secondary Education Act (1965) made federal authority a presence in state and local school decisions, the No Child Left Behind legislation (2001) cast the federal government as an active decision maker in local school affairs. Through funding and accountability regulations, US Department of Education officials now reached down into the nation's classrooms to determine whether a quali-fied teacher was present and whether every urban, rural, and suburban child improved their academic achievement.[32]

With increased federal funding since the mid-1960s, state control over educational policy also increased, albeit at an uneven pace, given the varied state political cultures in such places as New York, Vermont, Minnesota, Georgia, and California. Nonetheless, almost four decades after *A Nation at Risk* appeared, nearly all states raised curriculum stan-dards, administered annual tests, and held districts responsible for stu-dent test scores. States exerted far greater control over schooling than had existed prior to 1983.

By the second decade of the twenty-first century, few policy makers questioned increased centralization of state and federal authority over schools. Also, few questioned the current wisdom that business expertise and market success could (and should) be applied to schools.

Consider that by the end of the 1980s, corporate chiefs and writers boasted of firms that had gone from bankruptcy to high performance. Innovative companies crowed about their achievements. At the height of the automakers' slump, the semi-independent Saturn Corporation, for example, in an agreement crafted by General Motors and the United Auto Workers union, established high standards (e.g., zero defects in finished cars), measured workplace performance continually, delegated authority to make decisions to teams of workers (including those on the assembly line), and linked pay and job security to results.

To cite another example, Delaware governor Pierre S. du Pont IV at a 1989 Heritage Foundation–sponsored conference entitled "Can Business Save Education?" told corporate participants that fixing public schools in the 1990s would depend on putting into practice the "tried and true prin-ciples that have helped each of your businesses prosper over the years."

In these years, civic and corporate leaders urged school officials to adopt businesslike measures, such as establishing quality-control procedures, and market competition, such as letting parents choose schools—especially after the seeming victory of capitalism over communism when the Soviet Union collapsed in 1991.[33]

Educators easily borrowed innovations from the "corporate closet" that business leaders claimed had turned around Ford Motor Company, General Electric, and other major firms. Not only did many superintendents and school boards mimic business practices by adopting management by objectives, strategic planning, restructuring units, participatory management, holding midlevel executives responsible for achieving goals, and linking salaries to outcomes, as did modern technologically advanced companies, they used the vocabulary of *customers, return on investment,* and *productivity*. Educators wanted schools to look more like successful businesses as they accepted competition, choice, and teacher participation in decision-making. Traveling this path, they believed, would produce school results that would renew public trust in schools.[34]

Throughout the 1980s and 1990s, districts easily incorporated these business-inflected lessons into standards-based, testing, and accountability reforms:

- Set clear organizational goals and high standards for everyone.
- Restructure operations so that managers and employees who deliver the services decide what to do.
- Reward those who meet or exceed their goals. Shame or punish those who fail.
- Expand competition and choice in products and services.[35]

Throughout the 1990s, districts often packaged these reforms into the phrase "systemic reform."[36]

Broad political coalitions that included practitioners, union officials, policy makers, researchers, business leaders, and elected public officials offered a public face of agreement on "systemic reform" but often glided over conflicting strategies to improve schools. Free-market advocates among coalition partners, for example, wanted vouchers; others believed in broad parental choice with public schools—charters and intra- and interdistrict transfers. Efficiency-driven critics wanted ex-CEOs with managerial moxie to lead school systems and contract out tasks to the private sector. Corporate leaders and elected officials wanted more and faster system-wide reform (and computers as well) and less sluggish school-by-school change. Even with these frequent conflicts, the popular systemic reform model of standards-based reform, tests, accountability, and parental choice, initially pushed by business leaders, was largely embraced by states and districts by the early 2000s.[37]

Except for vouchers, standards-based reform has become de facto national policy written into the No Child Left Behind Act and its replacement, the Every Student Succeeds Act. That national and state policy continues today. Its life span as a reform movement now challenges the half-century reign of Progressive education. How long the standards-based movement will continue remains unknown.

In 2021, as I write in the midst of the COVID-19 pandemic, when most in-person schooling has been shuttered for nearly a year and when public schools have had to shift to remote instruction immediately, I have not noted any groundswell of opposition to the Common Core State Standards and mandated state tests. More important, I have detected no organized resistance to districts, schools, and students being held responsible for annual test scores.[38] The US Secretary of Education did waive states administering standardized tests in the fall of 2020. Beyond that, many states have requested waivers for giving tests in 2021. With the election of Joe Biden as president, the next US Secretary of Education will make those decisions.

What I have noticed is that the rationale for business involvement in the 1890s and 1980s remains nearly the same in the 2020s. From the Business Roundtable, a group of CEOs drawn from all sectors of the economy, this statement on education might well have gained nods from their forebears a century earlier:

> U.S. companies are the backbone of the country's economy, and the U.S. education system is what makes Americans the best workforce in the world. But in an economy that looks vastly different than it did 20 years ago, a traditional approach to education is struggling to equip students with the skills in the most demand among the nation's leading businesses.

Rigorous academic standards in K–12 English language arts and mathematics are critical to ensuring all students graduate from high school ready for college and the workforce. Business Roundtable supports the full adoption and implementation of high-quality education standards and aligned assessments to raise the performance of U.S. students. Business Roundtable also supports policies and programs that ensure all students read on grade level by the end of third grade.[39]

🙚

This is the "long" story of the standards-based reform movement.

Yes, I do prefer the long to the short story of this reform movement. Just as the historical context of the Progressive and civil rights movements revealed a chain of interconnected events and interest group actions occurring over an extended period of time, a more nuanced and deeper political and organizational perspective on school reforms arises.

The actions of business and civic leaders at two different times in the history of the US both show the permeability of tax-supported public schools to external stakeholders and, of even greater importance, illustrate how politically vulnerable public schools are to major economic, social, and cultural currents in the nation. That permeability to societal currents was surely in evidence when I became superintendent in Arlington, Virginia, in the early 1970s.

REFLECTIONS ON THE STANDARDS-BASED REFORM MOVEMENT IN ARLINGTON (1970S–1980S)

A midsized urban district across the Potomac River from Washington, DC, the Arlington Public Schools has been blessed with a long-standing solid funding base and a string of long-tenured superintendents. Arlington had also avoided federal court intervention by desegregating its few all-Black schools in the early 1970s, permitting the district to respond wholeheartedly to subsequent state-mandated standards and tests. Even by that time, Virginia business and civic elites examining standardized test scores—like their counterparts elsewhere—feared that the state was falling behind in producing sufficiently educated graduates to enter college and a swiftly changing job market increasingly tied to a knowledge-based economy.

In these years, Business Roundtables composed of corporate CEOs sought school reform across the US. Such groups made the following assumptions:

- Lack of appropriate training in high school causes unemployment.
- Improving high school performance on tests will produce better-trained graduates.
- State-mandated standards will improve high schools' academic performance.

Virginia business leaders adopted these views. In 1976, the Virginia state legislature required districts to set curriculum "standards of quality" and also "specific minimum Statewide educational objectives in reading, communications, and mathematics skills." The state board of education also mandated that for students to graduate from high school they had to pass "minimum competency tests."[40]

The five-member Arlington County School Board, which was appointed by the elected county board and to which the schools were dependent for funding, hired me as their superintendent.

The school board wanted me to design a program that would respond to the changing demographics in the county—that is, a largely white school population had shrunk while Hispanic immigrants and Blacks increased to where they made up about one-third of the students. A growing perception among white taxpayers and voters was that as the county enrollment shrank and more diverse students entered the schools, falling test scores meant a decline in academic quality. Now with increasing state demands for higher academic standards and a minimum competency test, the board reasonably expected their new superintendent to make that test part of a portfolio of changes to county schools. Those were my marching orders when I entered the superintendent's office in 1974.

Within a year, Arlington schools required high school students to pass a competency test in order to graduate. If they failed it, they could take it until they did pass and, with sufficient credits, receive their diploma. Information on the kinds of math and reading skills that would be included on the competency test circulated to all elementary and secondary teachers. By the end of the decade, over 95 percent of Arlington students passed both reading and math competency tests.[41]

The state board of education also mandated achievement tests (developed by Science Research Associates) in reading, math, science, and social studies to be administered annually in both elementary and secondary school grades.

Passing the tests mattered to districts since their scores were public, and such evidence was harnessed to judgments of the academic quality in the county. A few districts, including Arlington, went further and published school-by-school scores for parents and taxpayers to examine. State and district administrators also used test scores to determine whether schools would be accredited. Moreover, individual students would be promoted or held back in the lower grades on the basis of their scores. Accountability measures in Arlington and other districts, then, were built into the state curriculum and testing program.

Within that hectic first year—which I describe in chapter 6—I designed a managerial program where every one of the thirty-five elementary and secondary schools created an Annual School Plan mirroring the school board's goals, using test scores as one measure of school improvement.

In short, then, the standards, testing, and accountability movement had already moved into high gear in Virginia well before *A Nation at Risk* appeared nearly a decade later.

CHAPTER 6

From Teacher to Superintendent to Professor (1972–Present)

It was a hot august day in 1974. My palms were sweating. I could see out of the corner of my eye my wife, Barbara, and two daughters, Sondra and Janice, seated to my right among the 1,200 teachers and administrators spread out before me in the Thomas Jefferson Junior High School gymnasium. As I waited to be introduced by a school board member, I remembered that two months earlier, I had been a graduate student finishing the final pages of my dissertation. Twenty-six months earlier, I had been teaching US history to Roosevelt High School students in the District of Columbia. And now Arlington County public school teachers and administrators would hear for the first time their new, thirty-nine-year-old superintendent.

I knew clearly how I wanted to begin my talk, given the two years of intense wrangling between teachers and my predecessor, whom they viewed as indifferent to their classroom issues.

Finally, the board member turned to me; the polite applause rippled toward the stage as I stepped up to the podium. "The last job I had before Arlington," I began, "was teaching high school across the river." The teachers let out a roar, and the mild handclapping that greeted my introduction erupted into shouts, feet stamping, and vigorous clapping. I began my superintendency in Arlington with teacher applause ringing in my ears.[1]

There had been little applause when Barbara, Sondra, Janice, and I parked in front of 83B at Escondido Village, the housing provided for Stanford graduate students, in early September 1972. After three weeks of driving across the country from Washington, DC, we were tired, excited, and scared. We had come to Stanford so that I could get a doctorate and then get a superintendency somewhere. Each of us had many questions about living on a campus, making friends, living within a tight budget, doing new things, and a dozen other concerns that flitted in and out of our minds.

As it turned out, the two years that we lived at Stanford were ones that we recall decades later with great affection both as a family and individually. I remember it as being almost like an adolescent again, without the worry of acne. But I did hear a clock ticking. I had told David Tyack, my adviser and ultimately my dear friend, that I wanted to get the doctorate swiftly and begin superintending.

With an abiding interest in history, I not only pursued courses in the history of education with Tyack but also studied politics of education, economics, and organizational sociology. It was a movable feast, an intellectual smorgasbord that immersed me in a community of like-minded practitioners and scholars who differed among themselves about aspects of public schooling but possessed in common a passion for understanding. If motivation and readiness are prerequisites for learning, I had them in excess.

My experiences in public schools were rich but specific. Discovering connections with the past, seeing theories at work in what I had done, and, most important for me, coming to understand the worth of seeing the world through multiple lenses drove me to reexamine my classroom and administrative experiences. Lectures, long discussions with other students, close contact with a handful of professors, and work on a dissertation about three big-city superintendents wrestling with desegregation made the two years an intensely satisfying intellectual experience.

Historian David Tyack's patient but insightful prodding made research and writing a scholarly pleasure. Even though he was my advisor, only four years separated us in age. We both loved biking and became fast friends. From social scientist Jim March, I learned the importance of looking at the world in multiple ways, of learning to live with uncertainty, of the tenacious hold that rationalism has on both policy makers and practitioners, and of understanding that ambiguity and conflict are part of the natural terrain of organizational life. In my second year, a committee approved my proposal and I gathered data for my dissertation, finishing it in the spring of 1974. I earned a doctorate in the history of education. So whenever I read about or hear from superintendents and principals who found their graduate preparation either insufferable or inadequate, I recall how different my experience was.

In pursuing history and social science while investigating the superintendency, I found the two years at Stanford to be a first-rate preparation for the job that I sought. But it was not easy getting that job. Beginning in the fall of 1973, I began applying for superintendencies around the country.

The six months of job searching put my family and me on a roller-coaster ride of moods that is distasteful to recall. I applied for fifty-three vacancies, forty-five urban superintendencies, and eight principalships. By June 1974 I had been rejected by all of them, including a district to which I had not applied. The closest I came to being selected was in the Harrisburg and York school districts in Pennsylvania, where I went through elaborate interviews only to be named the runner-up. What became clear to me in this painful process was that my dream of serving as a superintendent was close to becoming a fantasy. Rejection letters and interviewers kept telling me that jumping into a superintendency from being a high school teacher (without ever having served as a principal), even with some administrative experience, was a grandiose leap of faith. To say that I was depressed in June was an understatement.

The only application left was in Arlington, Virginia. The school board chairman had written me to say that I was a finalist and invited me to come for an interview. Of course, I went, but my spirits were low and self-confidence battered.

Arlington was the largest district I had applied to. It had had twenty thousand students a few years ago but was dropping yearly in enrollment. Across the river from Washington, DC, Arlington's reputation as a politically conservative jurisdiction suggested there would be risks involved in choosing a superintendent whose prior service was across the bridge in the Black, low-income schools of a city that one Arlingtonian called "Sodom on the Potomac."[2]

Interviews with school administrators, parents, students, and the school board raised my hopes somewhat, especially with the appointed board. This board was different from any that I had met in the previous year of interviews. Four women, including the first Black to serve on the school board, and one man formed a politically liberal majority looking to hire their first superintendent.[3]

The board had just forced the resignation of the previous superintendent. They wanted someone who would address openly the teacher-administrator split, falling test scores, shrinking enrollment, and the growing presence of Black, Hispanic, and Southeast Asian students. All of the board members had children in the schools and were concerned about the lack of serious attention to these issues. They were enthusiastic. They had the endorsement of the reigning political majority in the county, and they wanted to move now.

The chemistry between this board and me during the dinner-long interview was unusual. The questions and answers were punctuated by genuine conversation and raucous laughter. Afterward, in describing it to Barbara and my daughters, I told them that it was closer to a family gathering than an interview.

Two weeks later, the chairman of the school board called to ask if I would accept the superintendency. Without hesitation I said yes, but with two conditions: that I could spend the first six weeks visiting schools and classrooms before taking on the formal position of superintendent, and that I could hire one assistant. She called back immediately to say that the conditions were acceptable to the school board. Arlington had a new superintendent.

Let me describe Arlington briefly before dealing with the conflicts that were central to my seven-year tenure. Once a middle-class, politically conservative white suburb with segregated schools, Arlington was the first Virginia county to desegregate its schools five years after the *Brown* decision. An influx of US government workers and political appointees had begun to give the county's political demography a more liberal cast. Moreover, other migrations altered the county's population.

By the early 1970s Arlington had become a city with an expanding multiethnic population. In those years Arlington had gotten smaller, older, and culturally diverse. The population dropped from almost one hundred eighty thousand in 1966 to about one hundred sixty thousand in 1980. There were fewer families with school-age children; the number of young singles and adults over fifty-five years of age spiked. Scores of different nationalities moved into the county, swelling the minority population that had already existed in two largely Black neighborhoods in the county.

These demographic changes altered schooling. Pupil enrollment dropped from a high of twenty-six thousand in 1968 to eighteen thousand in 1974; from nearly forty schools in 1968, the number fell to thirty-five in 1974. Also, from less than 15 percent minority students in 1969, the numbers doubled by 1974. The jump came most sharply among non-English-speaking minorities, particularly Hispanic and Vietnamese children.[4]

If population changes altered the face of county schools, so did the rising cost of schooling. Diminished revenues in the mid-1970s coincided with double-digit inflation, rising school costs, and employee demands for higher salaries, squeezing the school board and superintendent from different directions.

Since the appointed five-member school board was fiscally dependent on the elected five-member county board, state and federal revenue shortfalls plus inflation punctured school budgets badly in these years, precisely at the time that the effects of changing populations were being felt.

What prevented the pinch from hurting Arlington schools too badly was its prime location across the Potomac from the nation's capital, which was improved further by a new subway system and the county board's cautious fiscal policies, giving it the lowest tax rate in the metropolitan area in 1980. Because of the high assessed valuation of property, the county was wealthy. That wealth somewhat eased the painful transition from suburb to city, especially during economic recessions.

Nonetheless, the county board had to struggle with the politics of retrenchment. Irate property owners, most of whom no longer had children in school, wanted reduced school budgets and lower taxes as their property increased in value. Their demands competed with requests from other citizens who wanted higher school budgets to keep pace with inflation, subsidies for the elderly, improved police protection, and broader recreation and social services. Caught politically like everyone else in the recession of the mid and late 1970s, county officials cut budgets. Schools, particularly, bore a major share of the cutbacks. The county emerged from the recession with most services intact, the lowest tax rate in the area, and a school system that had become an annual target for reducing expenditures.

Political change also occurred. There had been a gradual but persistent shift from a Republican county board in the 1960s to one consisting of a coalition of Democrats and independents. By 1971 this liberal bloc had taken over the five-member elected county board and appointed like-minded school board members.

The school board that appointed me in 1974 was troubled over the consequences of a shrinking enrollment, declining test scores, a growing dissatisfaction among parents over school quality, rifts between teachers and administrators, and what board members saw as an experienced instructional staff that was either unaware of or resistant to the changes prompted by a diverse student population. But they had appointed a politically inexperienced superintendent, one who learned quickly about local politics on the job.

In deciding what to do and how to do it, I worked initially on establishing a reputation as a superintendent who would be accessible to all stakeholders in the district and who would listen to (but not necessarily agree with) anyone. The board allowed me six weeks—the deputy superintendent ran the district during that time—to visit hundreds of classroom teachers in dozens of schools. I gained an enormous amount of information about the quality of schooling, the troubles that could not be ignored, and the political dilemmas that I would face as superintendent.

I began holding "Open Doors" at a different school each week, where I would listen to complaints, take notes, and discover emerging issues. Parents, students, teachers, citizens, and administrators dropped in. Open Doors became a useful early warning system for problems and a clear signal to the entire school community that I was reachable.

The board's insistence on doing something about the shrinking numbers of students—at a time when the county board told the school board to reduce their budget—quickly translated into pursuing mergers of very small schools (less than 250 students). While schools had been closed in Arlington because of desegregation or inadequate facilities, none had been closed because of too few students. The schools with the least number of students, however, were in affluent parts of the county, where most of the school board and county board members lived. A political clash over which schools to close was inevitable, I discovered.

By 1975, a step-by-step decision-making process for school consolidation was in place. The board and I agreed that I would provide the data, suggest criteria for them to use in deciding which schools to close, and establish the process of sifting the data through simulations of possible school closures. They would examine the data and each criterion and go over options in public work sessions. I would then recommend which school to close prior to public hearings so that the board would have the benefit of my thinking and could listen to the community's response to my recommendation.

Publicly and privately, I advised the board that if a decision to close a school was to appear as rational policy, it must be anchored in data. But there were criteria they approved and values that each member had to weigh and consider. The decision the board reached would be, ultimately, a data-informed, value-based, political decision.

I recommended that the small Madison Elementary School in an affluent neighborhood be closed. Hearings brought out residents vociferously pointing out all of the strengths of the school. The board voted 4–1 to close Madison. That decision reverberated throughout the district, foreshadowing grueling years to come when other schools closed.

By 1980, the board had closed five elementary schools and two junior highs. Moreover, the board approved a secondary school reorganization that moved the ninth grade to the high school and converted the remaining junior high schools into intermediate schools with seventh and eighth grades.

The other central task that consumed much of my time was creating an organizational framework for improving instruction and student performance. While the state had curriculum standards in place, state officials left districts much flexibility in adhering to them. There was a state test that had to be administered annually across both elementary and secondary schools. Moreover, the state published the district scores, thereby creating public awareness and an informal accountability for gains and losses in student performance.

By 1976, the staff and I had put into place the scaffolding for district improvement as measured by state test scores. The pieces to that framework were as follows:

1. The school board established a set of district instructional goals (e.g., improving reading, math, writing, and thinking skills; deepening students' understanding of humanities and human relations).
2. The staff and I constructed an organizational mechanism called the Annual School Plan (ASP) that converted those board goals into school priorities and targets to be met. Every principal met with staff and parents to build the ASP, including the School Academic Profile, which listed student outcomes (e.g., test scores; survey results from students, teachers, and parents) that were linked to the district's goals.
3. Every district office administrator (including the superintendent) had to have an ASP showing links between their department, board goals, and performance.
4. I then met with each principal to discuss the degree of alignment of ASP objectives with school board goals and instructional materials, including textbooks and county and state tests. I expected school staffs to analyze state tests item by item to see how their students performed. Based on these outcomes, they would make corrections in grade-by-grade instruction and set new targets for next year's plan.
5. District administrators evaluated school principals on the degree to which they met the goals and objectives they had set in their ASPs; I evaluated district office administrators to see how they met or did not meet the goals they set in their annual plans.
6. The district published annually school-by-school scores on the state test at the second, fourth, sixth, eighth, and eleventh grades.

This managerial framework for instructional improvement and accountability tightened the generally loose links between district goals, curriculum, individual school goals, texts and materials, tests, and evaluations to allow the instructional staff to concentrate on raising students' academic achievement.

My personal involvement in reading each ASP, meeting with district office administrators, principals, and teachers to discuss changes in plans, teaching workshops on thinking skills, and offering written comments on ASPs established clearly, I believe, that this process ranked high on my agenda for district improvement.

I did discover, however, some disturbing trends toward the end of my tenure that caused me to temper my enthusiasm for the tight coupling of district goals to curriculum, texts, state tests, and student performance. For example, I saw a strong, irresistible tug toward a uniform curriculum with the adoption of similar textbooks, workbooks, and other materials. I had not anticipated that a press toward standardization would occur.

In visiting schools and conferring with principals, teachers, and parents, I began to hear echoes of the previous century's reformers who sought a single, best curriculum for all students. I also saw a press toward the use of those classroom practices cited in research findings as raising test scores. In my visits to schools every week I saw less variety in pedagogy. The rich, broad array of practices I had seen in my first year visiting Arlington teachers seemed to shrink. I sensed a tendency toward more whole-group instruction, active monitoring of student work, and lecturing, and less emphasis on small-group activities, student participation, and independent work.

I felt that this drift might stamp a set of practices as the single best way of teaching, something that I, because of my experience as a teacher and my historical awareness of pedagogy, rejected. This push for curricular and instructional uniformity is neither a strength nor a weakness; every school district strikes some balance between diversity and standardization in teaching. It could, however, go too far. I saw flashing yellow lights.

This bothered me. When I came to Arlington with teachers' applause ringing in my ears, I sought to establish the central importance of teaching in the district and in the community. Placing a high value on teaching and student performance was linked to my goal of improving county schools.

My weekly visits to classrooms for seven years made it obvious to the staff where my priorities lay. I would come unannounced, observe, and, if possible, speak with the teacher about what had occurred while I was in the classroom. If I couldn't, I would write a note.

And I did more than visit teachers. Within the first year, I located enough money in the budget to establish a Teachers Innovation Fund similar to the one I had begun in the District of Columbia. In addition, I offered workshops for principals on constructing goals and assessing their ASPs. When we retooled the evaluation system for administrators and teachers, a small group of principals asked me to teach skills on conferencing and observing classroom teachers.

My particular favorites, however, were workshops on developing thinking skills through questioning. I began these when the board adopted the goal of improving thinking skills. Each year I would offer a workshop, and anywhere from ten to fifteen teachers and principals would work together for four sessions. One summer, twenty teachers and I constructed multicultural units (e.g., historical and contemporary experiences of Blacks, Hispanics, and Asian Americans) with these skills embedded in lessons.

Finally, from time to time I would teach students—for example, as a substitute for an hour in an elementary school class or, on one occasion, for three days in a sophomore world history class. Not only did I find the direct contact with teachers, principals, and students invigorating, but I also knew that I conveyed to those inside and outside the school much more than the particular content of the lessons or workshops.

Did all of these goals, strategies, and tactics make a difference in school performance? I don't know. I discovered that determining my influence on the district, amid shouts of acclaim and screams for dismissal, continually danced just beyond my reach. I settled for proxies. The fact that the school board renewed my contract for four years after I had received glowing annual evaluations merely demonstrated that the board was satisfied with my work, not a trivial achievement.

There also were biennial parent surveys. They recorded increasing satisfaction with the schools between 1972 and 1980. Moreover, administrators who annually assessed my performance moved from acute hostility to moderate support. While board evaluations and surveys of stakeholders became increasingly positive after an initial chill, such messages are only surrogates for effectiveness, quite removed from schools except as linked to a positive district climate for academic performance. In even mentioning performance, the inevitable question arises: What about Arlington test scores?

TEST SCORES

In Arlington, scores on state and national tests (especially the Scholastic Aptitude Test) had become the political coin of the realm well before I arrived. For the next seven years, state test scores for elementary school students climbed consistently. The bar charts we presented to the board and at press conferences looked like a stairway to the stars. Those charts thrilled school board members.

Even in the face of my repeated admonitions that these welcome results were a very narrow measure of what occurred in Arlington classrooms and that scores were largely inadequate as direct assessments of individual teachers or school performance, Arlington parents, community members, and staff tracked results religiously. And for good reason, since gains in test scores were a strong political signal that fears of declining school quality were unfounded. The district was in fact delivering high-quality education, according to the metric that political figures, both liberal and conservative, used time and again.

Reporters and board members hungered for numbers. After the release of school-by-school test scores, the next day's headlines and articles displayed the results. School board members, like superintendents and other public officials, have so few direct measures of effectiveness that they often seek surrogates, paste pearls for natural ones, that with a wink of the eye may pass for the real item. One incident tattooed that insight into my mind.

A *Washington Post* article in 1979 showed Arlington to have edged out eight districts in the Washington metropolitan area in having the highest Scholastic Aptitude Test (SAT) scores (yes, I know it was by one point, but when test scores determine winners and losers as in horse races, Arlington won).

I knew that SAT results had nothing whatsoever to do with how our schools performed. It was a national standardized instrument to predict college performance of individual students; it was not constructed to assess district effectiveness. I also knew that the test had little to do with what Arlington teachers taught. I told that to the school board publicly and anyone else who asked about the SATs. Few listened.

Nonetheless, the *Post* article with the district-by-district box score produced personal praise, testimonials to my effectiveness as a superintendent, and, I believe, acceptance that the school board's policies and actions had, indeed, improved county schools, more than any single event during the seven years I served. From that experience I concluded that SAT scores are ridiculous measures of district or school performance but, nonetheless, politically potent indicators that satisfy a public craving for measures of improvement.

Yet I still saw my primary task as reshaping the community's perception of excellent schools as more than higher test scores. I pursued that task in my monthly articles for a local newspaper, where I explained state tests' inherent limits and negative consequences. Annual press conferences on test score were a ritual that made as much sense to me as trying to find water using a divining rod. But I held them nonetheless. My on-the-job learning of school politics in Arlington had paid off.

The school board became so used to my concern over excessive stress on standardized test scores that in public sessions, when I presented glowing annual results, they would repeat aloud and in chorus what I was about to say before I could say it, prompting great laughter from the audience.

Academic progress, as measured by state test scores, was less evident, however, at junior and senior high schools. Moreover, we also identified for the school board and community substantial gaps in academic achievement between minority and white students. We were one of the few districts in the metro area that disaggregated test scores by ethnic and racial groups, revealing large gaps in performance and drawing the attention of the board, administrators, teachers, and parents to curriculum changes and shifts in pedagogy to reduce the performance gaps.

In short, I made a major effort in the initial three years to become personally accessible and responsive to instructional issues while directly wrestling with the powder keg of closing schools. Results were ambiguous. Effectiveness measures were uncertain. This summary of the early years of my tenure in Arlington may suggest that events and decisions involving me, the school board, the staff, and community interest groups flowed smoothly. Far from it.

POLITICAL CONFLICTS

From the very first week after I was appointed, the conservative wing of the local Republican Party challenged my credentials. Because I had not taken one prescribed administrative course to be eligible for a Virginia superintendent's license, I was called "unqualified."

What course did I lack? Plant maintenance, or the care of school buildings, the Virginia Department of Education said. So I arranged to take a course at George Washington University from a professor I knew, who couldn't contain his laughter when I explained the situation. I wrote one paper on school mergers, which I later published as an article in a professional journal. The Virginia Department of Education notified me in 1975 that I was now fully credentialed as a superintendent. However, other conflicts arose.

The essence of public schooling is political. It is a fact. After all, tax-supported public schools were inventions of the federal government going back to the Northwest Ordinance of 1787. Likewise, during my years in Arlington, I rediscovered that fact. Competing goals, various stakeholders, and limited resources made political conflict inevitable. Friction ebbed and flowed between community activists and the board, between the board and superintendent, superintendent and administrators, teachers and principals. And do not forget parents and students.[5]

Consider teacher salaries. In 1975, when the state and nation were in an economic recession and deep cuts in state funding occurred, I recommended to the board that teachers receive only a 2 percent salary increase. Angry teachers likened the decision to a slap in the face. Resentment over this 2 percent increase smoldered in subsequent years, erupting in 1979 when again I recommended a small increase in teacher salaries because of increased inflation, the economy slipping into a recession, and the county board's slackened revenue flow. The union decried the low percentage I recommended. A majority of union members voted to ask for my resignation.

By that time, though, I had served five years and my contract had already been renewed, although not without a flurry of political attacks from those who continued to argue that I was unqualified and bringing the schools to rack and ruin. My relationship with the school board was solid. We saw ourselves as a team. Actually "marriage" was a common metaphor we used to describe how closely we worked together. Even though new board members came and veteran ones went, the norms established by the five that hired me persisted:

- When you hear a rumor or complaint, check with the superintendent first.
- The superintendent keeps board members informed of any breaking news that may have moderate to serious consequences for the district.
- Don't surprise board members.
- Everyone has a responsibility to air disagreements prior to a vote being taken, including the superintendent. But once the vote is taken and implementation is underway, no backstabbing second thoughts.

I worked hard at cultivating those norms and practicing openness on sticky issues through weekly conferences with the board chair to discuss upcoming meeting agendas, conferring with individual members, public bimonthly sessions of the board, and our annual retreat to set the next year's goals. Moreover, we evaluated one another.

The board assessed my performance based on my ASP. I shared with them my views of their strengths and limitations. The mutual trust that marked our formal and informal relationship for six of my seven years permitted me to implement a jointly constructed agenda of school improvement without looking over my shoulder every day.

The first year I served, however, produced a barrel full of political controversy that sorely tested that growing trust. I transferred a veteran high school principal to the central office. I made the decision based on what I learned from months of dealing directly with the principal, what I saw in the school, and what I heard from a number of teachers, students, parents, and board members.

In visiting the school often—it was next door to the district office—I had discovered that this principal was just waiting to retire in five years, yet the board faced a deteriorating academic program and a million-dollar renovation of the building that needed immediate and close attention.

A large portion of the veteran teaching staff, who recalled a "golden age" when the student population was largely white and middle class, confused academic excellence with just doing business as usual. These staff members exerted great influence on the principal. Here was a school coasting on a tattered reputation. I found in the principal little motivation, much less energy to overhaul a declining program in a school about to undergo construction of a new wing. If anything, the principal saw the school as being in excellent condition and wanted me to disappear.

Delegating a large part of managing the school to an assertive assistant principal, he also distanced himself from facing daily issues of school improvement. I wanted someone in that building who could work closely with students, teachers, and parents in imagining, constructing, and carrying through new instructional programs matched to the emerging needs of a different school population without sacrificing standards of academic excellence. It was a political tightrope walk, but it had to be done. This principal was simply not up to the task.

The school board unanimously approved my transfer. No one saw anything unusual in moving a principal from one post to another. Within forty-eight hours of my speaking with the principal, however, he had leaked the board decision to teachers and parents, and political fires were lit.

Within two months, Republicans who served on the county board organized a public protest. The principal hired a lawyer, who filed an age-discrimination suit. I had taken a tired administrator waiting to retire, hardly admired by most staff, students, or parents and created a cause célèbre.

Finally a settlement was reached between the school board's lawyer and the principal's lawyer that kept him at the high school for one year, after which he would move to the central office. We immediately launched a national search for a new principal.

The incident dogged our heels throughout the next few years. It provided political ammunition for Republicans to attack the superintendent and the school board on many issues. It provided a rallying point for conservatives frustrated by the liberal majority on both the county board and school board.

After he retired, the principal's loyalty to this conservative bloc was rewarded in 1979. The county board now had a conservative majority and appointed the ex-principal to the school board. A year later, a conservative majority on the school board named the former principal chairman of the board. For those who had railed against the school board for years, this was a delicious victory.

While the principal's transfer in 1975 momentarily claimed much board and superintendent attention, the fact is that the hullabaloo over a principal's transfer was a minor conflict compared with the dozens of other matters that the school board and I faced in the daily whirl of events. Closing schools, putting ASPs into practice, reorganizing secondary education, collective bargaining with five unions, and dealing with instances of teacher and principal misconduct consumed far more energy, emotion, and time than transferring a principal. Most important to me was the central lesson I learned over seven years. I learned that schooling was as much a political process as it was managerial and instructional.

THE PERSONAL SIDE OF SUPERINTENDING

The superintendency was both exhilarating and exhausting. As a line from a song put it, "Some days were diamonds; some days were stones." What values I prized about serving the public and educating others were enacted daily; what skills I had were tapped frequently, but even more important, the job jolted me into learning new skills, especially in working with a wide array of stakeholders inside and outside the school system. In short, being superintendent stretched me in ways I keenly felt were worthwhile, albeit demanding. I enjoyed the job immensely.[6]

But (invariably there is a "but") a number of job-related issues that arose over the years softened my rosy assessment, forcing me to face the inevitable trade-offs that accompany being a politically appointed top school official. Especially with my family.

What initially turned our lives topsy-turvy was the time I had to spend on the job. After two years as a graduate student with plenty of time available and before that as a teacher when I would be home most days by 4 p.m., superintending began early in the day and ended late at night.

The days for my family and me in Arlington usually began at 6:30 a.m., when I would get up, with Barbara joining me in the kitchen around 7 a.m. Sondra and Janice would come down for breakfast shortly after that. If I had an early morning meeting, I would leave and Barbara would get the girls off to elementary and intermediate schools. I would get into the office most of the time around 8:00 a.m., with the day often ending after 6 p.m. Two or three nights a week, I had evening meetings with community groups or board budget meetings, and then I would get home after 10 p.m.

On those long days, I would race home for dinner at 5:00 p.m. and leave two hours later for a board meeting, work session, or some other community event. During the week, I saw my family for a few minutes in the morning and at dinner. Fatigue tracked me relentlessly the first few years; I'd fall asleep watching the evening news and take long afternoon naps on weekends.

While we had not given too much thought to the issue of privacy, Barbara and I had made a few decisions about our family's time together. We agreed that Friday evening dinners to celebrate the Sabbath were high priority. I asked the school board to be excused from obligations on Friday evenings, and they honored my request for seven years.

A listed telephone number proved to be less of an issue than we had anticipated. I rarely received more than a half-dozen calls a week at home from parents, students, or citizens, except during snowstorms or when I made a controversial recommendation to the board. Surprisingly, we received few crank or obscene phone calls.

Buffering the family from the demanding job was tough enough. Deciding what to do about those social invitations, where much business was transacted informally, without reducing time spent with my family, troubled me.

The first week on the job, for example, a principal who headed the administrators' union invited me to join a Friday night poker game with a number of principals and district office administrators that met twice a month. My predecessor, he said, had been a regular player for three years. Moreover, it would offer me a splendid chance to meet some of the veteran staff away from the office in relaxed surroundings. Aware of the political advantage in playing poker twice monthly and the costs to my family in missing Sabbath dinners, I thanked the principal for the generous invitation but said no.

Another piece of the "no" decision was the simple fact that I would be making personnel changes, and a certain amount of social distance from people I supervised might be best. Over the seven years I was superintendent, I moved or replaced at least two-thirds of the principals.

Dinner invitations also proved troublesome for Barbara and me. Invariably at these affairs, conversations would center on school matters and juicy political gossip. These evenings became work for me and difficult for Barbara, who was then immersed in completing her undergraduate degree. The last thing either of us wanted to hear on a Saturday night out was more about the Arlington schools. Except for socializing with the few longtime friends in DC and new ones in the county with whom we could relax, we turned down many invitations after our second year in town.

We remained, however, part of the ceremonial life in Arlington. I ate chicken at Boy Scout dinners, sampled appetizers at chamber of commerce affairs (until I dropped out of the organization because of its persistent attacks on our school budgets), spoke at church suppers, and represented the school board at civic meetings.

I can see now, in ways that I could not have then seen, that entering the community as an outsider and remaining separate from existing social networks prevented the job from completely swallowing our lives. But, of course, its shadow, with all of its pluses and minuses, still fell over the family.

For example, our daughters (ages nine and twelve in 1974) were not only singled out, both positively and negatively, by teachers; they also had to deal with all of the complications of being emerging teenagers, losing old friends, gaining new ones, and coping with schoolwork and family issues. The desire to be accepted as newcomers to their schools put a constant strain on both girls; from early on they were seen as being different because of their father's position and their religion.

Active and smart, Sondra and Janice both enjoyed and hated the attention. While some teachers were especially sensitive to the awkward position the girls were in, others were callous. Principals of the schools they attended were very understanding and tried to help, but little could be done with the occasionally insensitive teacher in a classroom lesson.

When salary negotiations with the teacher union heated up, for example, two of their teachers made caustic remarks about their father's lack of concern for teachers' economic welfare. The pressures were such that our eldest daughter wanted to try another school. It proved to be the hardest decision that Barbara and I made while I was superintendent. For us, her welfare was more important than concerns over what others might think of a superintendent pulling his daughter out of the public schools. We transferred her to a private school in Washington, DC, where she began to thrive academically and socially. Of course, the local newspaper carried an article about it. Our other daughter went to a private school for one year but wanted very much to return to the Arlington schools and did so for her high school years.

Barbara was clear on what she wanted. She did not wish to be "the superintendent's wife." She wanted to complete her undergraduate degree and enter a profession. In seven years, she finished her degree at George Washington University, earned a master's in social work from Catholic University, and completed internships for a career in clinical social work. Between caring for a family, doing coursework, research papers, and tests, and coping with a tired husband, Barbara had little time or concern for meeting others' expectations of how a superintendent's wife should act.

Yet, try as we might, it was difficult to insulate ourselves from the fact that I was the district superintendent and a political figure in the county. My efforts, for example, to keep my family and my job separate when serious decisions had to be made often did not work. Firing a teacher, determining the size of a pay raise, recommending which schools to close, and dozens of other decisions had to be made. After listening to many individuals and groups, receiving advice from my staff, and hearing all the pros and cons from my closest advisers, I still had to make the decision.

At these times, I often discussed a pivotal decision with Barbara. Equally as often, however, there were family concerns that required our attention instead. Nonetheless, I would still come home with the arguments ricocheting in my mind about a recommendation I had to make to the board or a personnel choice; I would carry on an internal dialogue while I was eating dinner, raking leaves, playing with the girls, or on a weekend trip with the family. I was home, but not there. Over the years, with Barbara's help, I became more skilled at telling my family that something from the job was bothering me and that if I seemed distracted it had nothing to do with them. But I never fully acquired the knack of leaving serious issues on the doorstep when I came home.

Sometimes, escaping the job was impossible. Newspaper articles or television news on the schools entered our home whether we liked it or not. What did stun me, however, were the lengths that some people would go for political advantage, including destroying someone's reputation. Elected officials, accustomed to political infighting, might find such rumormongering trivial. But it jolted my family and me. One example will do.

Shortly before the school board reappointed me for another four years, a board member called to ask if I had ever been arrested in Washington, DC, on a drug charge. No, I hadn't, I told her. She said that there was a story that would appear in the next day's newspaper stating that I had been arrested and put in jail for possession of heroin. Within the next hour, I received a dozen calls from county officials, parents, friends of school board members, and the head of the teacher union asking me if the newspaper story was true and if they could help.

Finally, a newspaper reporter called to say that they were printing the story and did I have any comments to make. I told the reporter that there was no basis for the allegation and that before printing such a lie they would do well to get a record of the alleged arrest and other documentation. The newspaper did not print the story. What shocked me most was the fragility of a professional reputation, the willingness of people to believe the worst (this occurred a few years after Watergate), and the lengths some people would go to destroy a political enemy.

The seven years as superintendent taught me a great deal about district politics and mixing public and private lives for officials like myself. More prosaic than senators who party or congressmen who resign or presidents who lie daily, our experiences still map an unfamiliar terrain for a superintendent and family who tried to maintain privacy.

LEAVING THE SUPERINTENDENCY AND
RETURNING TO TEACHING

By early 1980, two years before my contract was up and the year when my slim three-two majority on the school board would disappear with the appointment of two more Republicans, I decided that it was time to leave.

While there was a chance that I could make a public battle over seeking reappointment for another term, I had no appetite for another political skirmish, one I would surely lose. Moreover, a school board should have someone who reflects their values. The liberal board I had served would now have a majority of political conservatives whose appointments were aimed at a set of policies different from the ones earlier boards and I had adopted. Finally, the conservative majority on the county board wanted a low-profile, fiscally cautious superintendent who could put a ceiling on school costs, rather than one who pressed annually for expanded programs and higher teacher salaries.

I had come to Arlington because a new school board wanted someone who mirrored their values; now that had changed. That was the game. No superintendent is a man or woman for all seasons. In any case, seven years was the most time I had spent in any one job in my lifetime. The shuttling I had previously done between teaching and administration was again an option. Also, I wanted time to write, think, and teach.

So, in making plans for leaving the post, I applied for a research grant from the National Institute of Education (NIE) to study how teachers had taught over the last century. When I received the grant in the summer of 1980, I announced that I would not seek renewal of my contract.

In drafting my resignation letter for early 1981, I tried to recapture the meaning of the seven years I had served. I reexamined the major issues in 1974 and what had occurred over the time I had served. Admittedly a highly personal estimate, my letter to the board concentrated on how a district, in the midst of getting smaller and culturally diverse, closing schools, fiscal retrenchment, and high-profile firings, could maintain academic excellence and increase parental satisfaction as measured by conventional indicators of success. I counted that as a major victory for both the school board and superintendent during hard times. Of course, longtime critics would see my tenure differently.

After announcing the research grant and my departure, I was asked to apply for a number of other superintendencies. I refused. Far more attractive to me were offers to teach at a university. The idea of having time to teach, write, and think was like serving ambrosia to a starved traveler. When Stanford University began its search for an education professor, the chair of the search committee called to ask if I would come for an interview. I did, and afterward the dean offered me a job. I asked for and got a five-year contract as an associate professor since I was planning to return to an urban superintendency.

Barbara went to Palo Alto and bought a house while I wrapped up the school year. Sondra had already left for college, and Janice decided to take her senior year at a new high school. She and I drove cross-country to California.

For five years, I taught four courses a year and researched questions that had bugged me about policies, schools, and classroom work. I went on an initial writing spree, completing two books; advised a handful of doctoral students; and organized superintendent roundtables that brought district leaders to campus monthly. I loved the work.

But it was hard at first. I held twice-weekly office hours and posted sign-up sheets with half-hour time slots. After the first month, I would often come home with a massive headache. By then Barbara had become a therapist at a family service agency, and she listened carefully as I told her how hard it was for me to focus on a conversation with students and colleagues for more than fifteen minutes. After some gentle nudging from her, I slowly realized that those headaches came from switching from being a superintendent to being a professor.

In superintending, you never have long conversations; everything is boom, boom, boom. Crises occur and decisions have to be made and bam, bam, all day. Now at Stanford, I was sitting across from a graduate student in a small office; I listened carefully to what the person was saying. Head nodding was not enough. You had to respond on point to what the student just said or asked. Barbara's insight into the shift in work environments, especially when it came to listening intently, helped me considerably. As I became more practiced in longer exchanges with students and colleagues, the headaches disappeared.

By the third year of being a professor, teaching, writing, and working with doctoral students, I had become familiar with the ebb and flow of a professor's annual teaching and researching schedule. I began planning to fulfill a dream that I had had for the past decade but never as a superintendent had the time to do: a cross-country bike trip.

In June 1984, I left Portland, Oregon, with a group of ten bikers—I was the oldest at forty-nine; the youngest was nineteen. Seventy-five to one hundred miles a day on mostly rural roads, camping each night, taking turns fixing dinner, we crossed the Rockies by the end of July. I wrote daily to Barbara and where there were pay phones, called.

I had told my fellow bikers when I joined them in Portland that I would leave the group in Kansas to have the experience of biking alone and staying with friends and family in St. Louis, Missouri; Richmond, Indiana; Cleveland, Ohio; and Pittsburgh, Pennsylvania. My friend Bill Plitt, who was part of the Cardozo Project years earlier and who had introduced me to riding a ten-speed bike, joined me in Pittsburgh, and we took three days to complete the last leg of the trip to Washington, DC.

I had been gone three months. I flew home two weeks before Stanford began its fall quarter. In overcoming the physical and psychological demands of daily biking and seeing the ever-changing, grand beauty of the nation, I had fulfilled my dream.

My university contract was nearing an end, so in 1985 I tried to return to a superintendency. I applied for those city posts that I felt would stretch me while offering me the chance to improve schooling. While I made the short list for five urban districts, no offer was made. I was very disappointed.

With no superintendency in sight and my contract expiring, the then dean asked me if I would like to stay and apply for a tenured post. I had two books under my belt and was working on a third; students had just voted me teacher of the year. I said I would. The faculty approved both tenure and a full professorship in 1986. I continued as a professor until 2001, when I retired.

I was blessed with superb students over the twenty years I taught and researched. Fifty of them received their doctorates under my guidance. Many more were in my classes on "good" schools, leadership, and organizational theory. The blessing that inheres in being a professor is that a few of my students moved from being advisees to becoming close friends after they moved into their careers.

Close friendships with faculty also unfolded. I had team-taught with Ed Bridges and Elliot Eisner, often having weekly coffee meet-ups with each. David Tyack and I biked weekly. We became very close friends. We also created a history of school reform course that we team-taught for eleven years and that became the basis for our *Tinkering Toward Utopia*.

Since retiring in 2001, I have researched and written about the policy-to-classroom path, always with a historical perspective. While I continued to teach a seminar every other year on "good" schools until 2013, seeking answers to questions about the history of policy, district politics, and how policies are converted into classroom lessons drove me to interview superintendents, principals, and teachers while observing lessons and school practices. I continued to research schools and write about what I found until 2019, before the pandemic closed schools. My retirement, then, was as close as I could come to a researcher's Nirvana.

Barbara also made a professional and satisfying life for herself. After coming to California in the early 1980s, Barbara became a licensed social worker at a family service agency. In 1995, she started what became a flourishing private practice. When I retired in 2001, I began doing more cooking for dinners—with much coaching from Barbara. Both of our daughters completed college and entered careers as full-fledged professionals. Sondra earned a doctorate and researched global migration of women, and eventually became a professor in adult and higher education. Janice moved from journalism to writing in different capacities for Silicon Valley firms as a marketing consultant. She started her own business as an independent contractor that continues in 2021.

Life was good for the Cubans until it was not.

Barbara and I traveled throughout the US and Europe before and after I retired. We visited our daughters wherever they worked in the US and abroad. As we got older, Barbara saw a future where our two-story home, in which we had lived for a quarter-century, would become difficult to take care of both inside and outside. She found a one-story home in the same neighborhood, and we moved there. She had a designer's eye and refurbished the house while maintaining her private therapy practice. Me? All I did was read, research, write, bike daily, and learn to cook, with much help from my wife.

In 1993, Barbara fell ill with lymphoma just before opening her private practice. She had surgery to remove a tumor in her stomach. After chemotherapy, her private practice expanded. Her cancer was in remission until 2004, when the cancer returned. After more surgery and chemotherapy, she returned to being a psychotherapist, but the tumors reappeared in 2008, two years after we moved into the house that she had found and redecorated. The surgery and chemo third time around left Barbara exhausted and severely ill. She died a few months later.

That was a crushing loss for all of us. My daughters and I mourned a mother, wife, and friend whom we loved dearly and were loved by in return and had now lost. We still grieve.

A year after Barbara died, Sondra was living in England, where she was a professor at Lancaster University researching migration of Eastern European women to the United Kingdom. She got pregnant and delivered a child that she and her then husband named Barbaraciela—they call her Ciela, but I prefer her full first name. It was a joyful gift to the Cuban family for which I am forever grateful. Barbaraciela is now eleven. They travel from Seattle to my home, and Janice and I take trips to their home. We are a small but a raucous family, one that Barbara would have loved dearly.

CHAPTER 7

Reform Movements Before and After COVID-19

Writing final chapters has been hard for me. And *Confessions of a School Reformer* is no exception. In earlier books on school reform, I laid out policy recommendations in the last chapter that were anchored in the book's analyses and hopes for the future.

In this closing chapter, however, I offer no recommendations. Not because I have lost hope in the future of public schools—I remain a tempered optimist about what schools can do for individuals and the practice of democracy in the larger society—but mostly because this book analyzes three twentieth-century reform movements and then scrolls through my life as a student and reform-minded teacher, administrator, and professor during these massive efforts to improve public schools. In combining analyses and personal experiences, I reveal inexperience, mistaken beliefs, and errors in judgment. So as a scarred school reformer, I have no special credentials that would make me sufficiently believable to deliver recommendations to readers, especially as I write this final chapter during a pandemic.

Instead, this chapter summarizes my answers to the questions I posed in the introduction. Then I unpack my confessions as a teacher, administrator, and researcher who has worked to reform schools for the past half-century. And, lastly, I consider the COVID-19 pandemic's impact on existing public schools and what I see occurring after vaccines safely restore in-person classrooms in the US.

As a historian of educational policy, I know well the dangers of writing in the moment when a pandemic has come to an end and unexpected events continue to unfold. Risks of being horribly wrong nudge at me as I write these paragraphs, thus making wobbly any predictions about which reforms have staying power and which will disappear like a morning's dew. If I had a strong record of forecasting, I would be confident in the guesses I render here. But that is not the case, for my record as a historian of school reform who tries to look around the corner is at best mixed and at worst blemished. With that admission, yes, another confession: I offer neither predictions nor recommendations accompanying my assessment of schooling in a post-COVID era.

ANSWERING THE QUESTIONS

Past generations of reformers in these three movements ignored, occasionally considered, but seldom grappled with publicly the linkages between individuals, families, schools, and society. These linkages and the questions they pose remain unanswered and too often ignored by contemporary crusaders:

- How much of a child's academic success or failure in school is due to family background?
- Can schools, reflecting the larger society's faith in perfecting individuals and institutions, alter the effects of family background in children and youth while seeking to reform society?

Sociologist James Coleman answered the first question through the seven-hundred-plus pages of the *Equality of Educational Opportunity* report in 1966. Surveying six hundred thousand students and sixty thousand teachers from four thousand schools, the US Congress's mandated study came up with findings that even today resonate but remain largely unimplemented:

- The most important variable in a child's success was neither the condition of the buildings students went to nor the level of funding; the most important factor was a child's family background joined to a diverse socioeconomic mix of students in classrooms.
- A huge achievement gap exists between Black and white students in the nation's schools.[1]

In the six decades since the Coleman Report was published, during the civil rights movement and subsequently the standards, testing, and accountability reforms, a constant flow of federal, state, and local policy interventions have flowed over the nation's schools. Yet deeply rooted societal problems remain unsolved, so the answer to the second question is, in a word, no.

At a conference marking the fiftieth anniversary of the Coleman Report, Johns Hopkins University professor Stephen Morgan said, "Too many proposals for innovative educational reforms fail to recognize how important family is. Policymakers have dropped the ball on that insight." And when it comes to the achievement gap that Coleman and his team of researchers made plain, at the same conference Stanford University professor Eric Hanushek said, "We know how large the achievement gaps were in 1965, and we know what they are today, so how much have they changed? . . . At this rate of improvement and if we continue at the pace we've been going on, it will take two and a half centuries to close the achievement gaps between blacks and whites in our public schools."[2]

While Progressive educators driven by efficiency concerns sought to improve America's public schools well before the Coleman Report appeared, civil rights reformers and champions of standards-based reforms were aware of these conclusions. The evidence is clear that these well-intentioned, fervent champions focused instead on who the students were and their imperfections while working hard to improve how age-graded schools worked.

THE REFORM MOVEMENTS

Early to mid-twentieth century Progressives, imbued with the "science" of education and brand new tools of achievement and intelligence testing, largely answered the first question by taking credit for students' academic successes in age-graded schools while blaming individual students and their families for failure. Common terms Progressive educators used in these decades to describe students deviating from the behavioral and academic regimen of the age-graded school were *pupils of low IQ, low division pupils, ne'er-do-wells, sub-z group, limited, slow learner, laggards, overage, occupational student, mental deviates, occupational student,* and *inferior.*[3]

These terms allocating blame for students' performance seldom softened most Progressives' rock-hard Deweyan belief in the power of the school to reshape both individuals and society. Pursuing their faith in democratic schooling as they defined it, Progressives developed and installed new subjects and textbooks called civics courses and "problems of democracy." Some Progressives, such as George Counts, from their pulpits on university campuses even called for schools to be the vanguard of socially reconstructing American society. Little happened.[4]

As the civil rights movement emerged in the South and moved northward, desegregating schools was on activists' agendas. One influence of the civil rights movement was that school reformers shifted from Progressives' perspective of blaming children and their families for inadequate performance to blaming poverty, crime-ridden neighborhoods, unemployment, shabby housing, and age-graded schools. It is not the students or their families, civil rights reformers said, it is the school structures located in segregated neighborhoods that produce low academic performance in minority children and youth. These reformers, then, reversed the customary causal direction of students determining school failure.

So these reformers shifted labels toward schools and poverty-ridden neighborhoods damaging students. They called students *the rejected, educationally handicapped, forgotten children, educationally deprived, culturally different*, and *pushouts*. But older habits of distributing blame remained embedded in labels like *socially maladjusted, terminal students, marginal children, immature learners, educationally difficult, unwilling learners*, and *dullards*.[5]

As for schools improving society, *Brown v. Board of Education* and subsequent federal court decisions desegregating schools throughout the 1960s and 1970s were markers of faith in schools remedying a flawed society. More to the point of schools solving social problems was President Lyndon B. Johnson's vision and program called the "Great Society." The federally funded "War on Poverty," the Civil Rights Act of 1964, and the Voting Rights Act of 1965 became milestones in the civil rights movement and small inroads in desegregating classrooms.

Belief in the federal government intervening to right wrongs and advance bottom-up political coalitions to move society toward a better day threaded through the civil rights movement. As Martin Luther King

Jr. said in 1968, "We shall overcome because the arc of the moral universe is long but it bends toward justice."[6]

But the civil rights movement ebbed in the 1970s, and as racially and socioeconomically segregated classrooms persisted, another school reform movement emerged. The economy-driven standards, testing, and accountability movement accelerating in the mid-1980s began reshaping the nation's schools over the next four decades.

Presidents, state governors, and local school boards raised graduation requirements and curriculum standards. They mandated tests to determine gains and losses, distributing both rewards and sanctions for results. Nonetheless, de facto segregated schools and their core structures, including the grammar of instruction, remained largely as is. This standards-based reform movement, aimed at strengthening the national economy, concentrated on improving students' academic performance and launching graduates into careers. It was in high gear before and after the COVID-19 pandemic of 2020–2021.

The norms and structures of the age-graded school require students to conform. They must meet grade-level standards of performance. They must fit into a hierarchy of academic performance—honor roll students, those just passing with a D—and they must meet behavioral norms—no running and shouting when changing classrooms.

Thus, labeling students and schools that either fit or deviate from school norms has persisted since *A Nation at Risk* appeared in 1983, continued through the crusade for national goals and higher standards in the 1990s, and remained in place during the No Child Left Behind (2001–2015) era. As the standards, testing, and accountability movement unfolded over recent decades, then, the age-graded school's attachment to labels remained, but individual blame softened into institutional euphemisms.

Names for students run the gamut. *At risk, Title I, English language learners,* and *students identified with specific disabilities* are just a few. Likewise, schools failing to post satisfactory test scores or meet curriculum standards are called *low performing* or *underperforming.* Some states and districts award letter grades to school performance on tests and other measures that make clear whether a school is exemplary, meeting standards, or failing. Euphemisms abound, with *urban* and *inner-city schools* as placeholders for poor neighborhoods. But the stubborn fact remains that resegregated schools have continued largely untouched by federal, state, and local policy makers. Yet labels endure.[7]

Names Progressive reformers used to categorize individual children have been defanged, but stigma persists for those who carry institutionalized labels, such as *Title I children* who are pulled out of a class for more reading instruction or *English language learners* who are assigned to special classes. Or students who are designated eligible for *free and reduced-priced lunches.*[8]

During the standards-based reform movement, the quest for schools to reshape both individuals and society persevered. While angst over "failing" schools has been widespread, fed by constant attacks on schools and the growth of publicly funded charter schools since the early 1990s, one would reasonably expect to also see the erosion of Americans' faith in their schools. That has not been the case.

Public confidence in what schools can do for both individuals and communities has grown in the past decade, even during the COVID-19 crisis. Such growing public confidence—an all-important political fact—reveals again a cast-iron faith in schools as escalators taking individuals to where they want to go and, of equal importance, as an avenue for renewing those American ideals found in the Declaration of Independence, the US Constitution, and the words inscribed on the pedestal of the Statue of Liberty.[9]

In the standards-based movement stretching from the early 1980s to today, school and district reformers worked hard with children and schools to connect every student to a growing economy while ending the "soft bigotry of low expectations." Many of these reformers and their predecessors during the civil rights movement (e.g., Title I of the Elementary and Secondary Education Act of 1965, the War on Poverty) earnestly pressed for social justice within both the school and the larger community.[10]

While soaring rhetoric and well-spent dollars are crucial, the quest for social justice outside and inside schools requires more than words and money. Ideas drive social movements. Again and again, beliefs in social justice mattered as reformers reached far beyond improving teachers' and individual students' performance or merely sandpapering rather than altering substantially school structures within which they lived. Social justice meant school improvement and community development.

SOCIAL JUSTICE

Markers of grassroots activism pushing social justice can be seen in the Google Books Ngram showing the sharp spike in use of the phrase in books, articles, and printed matter since the 1980s. Rhetoric is important in mobilizing support for a movement, but organized activism in schools and neighborhoods trumps words.[11]

In the past decade, for example, community groups have mushroomed across the country in response to social justice issues, including the Me Too movement to call attention to men harassing and assaulting women, and Black Lives Matter groups to protest police killings of Black men and women. Both whites and Blacks have organized and protested the lack of equal treatment in the criminal justice system.

Mirroring society, many public schools have embraced "social justice," even including the phrase in their names, such as School of Social Justice High School in Chicago; Charter High School for Law and Social Justice in the Bronx, New York; and Social Justice Humanitas Academy in Los Angeles Unified District.[12]

Beyond school names, curricular content shows up in schools that include social justice in their mission. Depending on students' ages, some schools deal directly with the subject through courses and units of study on structural racism and economic and social inequalities in American life. Other schools will include lessons built into kindergarten and primary classes in elementary schools and as part of English, social studies, math, and science courses.[13]

Then there are middle and high school-based programs such as restorative justice. Aimed at helping administrators, teachers, and students reduce racist disciplinary practices such as suspension and expulsion, these programs focus on having students "talk things out" and using nonpunitive actions. Have efforts to install social justice programs squarely into schools' curricula, instruction, and disciplinary practices altered student outcomes? This question is one that current school reformers often ask. Perhaps, but past and current research on these programs remain unpromising.[14]

Recall the two conclusions that the Coleman Report (1966) reached over a half-century ago—that is, the key variables that determine student outcomes are family background and with whom children attend school.

Both variables remain largely unchanged by the current school reform movement in 2021. And during the decades since the Coleman Report, I was a teacher, district administrator, superintendent, and researcher. If anything, I could do very little to alter the variables that Coleman identified.

THE COLEMAN REPORT

In the late 1960s and early 1970s, the Coleman Report entered and exited policy discussions time and again. But I had worked in Cleveland, a segregated school district, and then taught in Washington, DC, another segregated system. Moreover, I had worked briefly at the US Commission on Civil Rights, whose report *Racial Isolation in Public Schools* reanalyzed data in the Coleman Report. And as a graduate student at Stanford University, I had taken courses with policy experts who assigned their classes readings from the report. So I knew well the data-supported conclusions of the Coleman Report.[15]

As a teacher, district office administrator, and later superintendent, however, I could do little to put any of the report's conclusions into practice. Not for a lack of will or knowledge but simply because I worked *within* school systems for reforms, which meant, at best, incremental changes in school structures and the daily business of teaching and learning.

By choosing to work inside rather than outside school districts, as I had for decades, fundamental changes in who attends school, such as desegregation and altering the age-graded school structures, were largely beyond my grasp—even as a superintendent beholden to a school board. Such fundamental changes usually come from outside schools as part of social and political movements. I chose—a political decision—to work inside the system.

Is this a confession? Yes, it is. One of many that I have reflected on over the six decades I have worked in and around public schools. Let me be clear about the word.

Confession has a small *c* as I use it. So I do not use "confession" in the religious sense of admitting sinfulness. Nor do I use the word to absolve myself of poor judgments I have made or to make spicy disclosures. After much reflection, I use the word simply to be honest with myself in being a school reformer my entire adult life.

I have not lied or been dishonest in seeking school reforms. It is only that when I championed changes in schools, I heightened the advantages and minimized the disadvantages. I was a salesman for particular school reforms. Salespersons pride themselves on promoting their product, not candor about its defects. Even more so, these confessions reveal how my ideas about what reforms are best and work under what conditions have changed over time.

CONFESSIONS

I begin by returning to my first job teaching history at Cleveland's Glenville High School between 1956 and 1963. What I discovered about reforming both teaching and the classroom curriculum convinced me then that engaged teachers creating lessons with multiethnic and racial content tailored to student interests could get Black students to participate and learn in segregated classrooms. That belief in sharp, committed teachers wielding relevant content and skills getting students to not only engage but also learn I carried to the District of Columbia's Cardozo High School to train new and committed teachers to teach in similar ways.

Turns out I was only partially correct. I came to see after being a teacher in Cleveland for seven years and then a teacher and administrator for another nine years in DC that my view of reform was blinkered, even myopic. I had not even imagined that classroom and school reform was a political process.

In moving from the granular classrooms of Glenville and Cardozo High School and then to the district office of the DC schools, my view of reform expanded to encompass the politics of getting something to happen beyond classrooms at a school or in a district. Mobilizing resources and people to focus on a particular idea or program took bureaucratic moxie and forging relationships with like-minded people inside and outside schools. I began to see different units or sites for reform—classroom and school—nested within one another. Both had to be altered in order for reforms to have the most effect on both teachers and students.

And that view further enlarged when I administered a districtwide staff development program from my office in DC. My experiences within the bureaucracy and budgetary ties to the DC government and both municipal and school finances linked to the US Congress forced me to see how relationships, resources, and reform were intimately bound together. I came to a broader view that the district was nested within the federal bureaucracy and that they together constituted a larger political system in need of change for schools and classrooms to get better. The intersecting of various systems became clear to me in ways that I had not known as a teacher at Glenville High School.

And yet there was even a larger picture that I slowly became aware of as I reflected on the intersection between classroom, school, district systems, and the larger society. As a researcher at Stanford, I went into many California districts and came to grasp better how the politics of state and federally driven school reforms did and did not translate into district and school programs. I came to realize that a district system was itself nested within larger socioeconomic, political, and caste-like structures (e.g., market-driven society focused on individual action, economic inequalities, racist structures), all of which hemmed in what superintendents, principals, teachers, and students could do in making classroom, school, and district changes. I realized that a social and political coalition (e.g., the civil rights movement) struggled to change those societal structures and in some instances made incremental improvements.

Writing in 2021, all of this seems self-evident. But it wasn't to me in 1956 when I began teaching. What I have described is the growing awareness of school reform as a political process and the complexity of schools as I moved from teacher and administrator to researcher—the journey of a toddler, so to speak, to an adult. I was innocent of the difficulties in grasping the interconnectedness of politics, relationships, resources, and systems. I had to pull together my experiences in schools and think about them time and again. That's my first confession.

The second confession comes from my years as Arlington County superintendent.

I entered that post saturated with experiences in Washington, DC, classrooms and the central office and filled with ideas learned at Stanford about organizations and how they worked. Experiences with racial divides and political infighting at the administrative headquarters in the

DC system echoed in my mind. And in Arlington, I presented myself to the community and teachers as someone who prized the art and science of classroom teaching. All of these things ran smack up against serious political problems over a largely white district shrinking in enrollment while becoming increasingly minority and fearing a loss in academic quality. The fact is that even after my experiences in the DC bureaucracy and taking courses at Stanford in politics of education, I was inexperienced, even naive, about the political role I played as superintendent.

Chapter 6 described how the Arlington County school board and I in our first few years, amid constant political conflicts over closing schools, reframed problems in ways that would restore community faith in its schools. A key part of those efforts was tightening up organizational links between what happened in classrooms, schools, and the district to students' academic outcomes. My staff and I developed a management mechanism that applied to all principals and district administrators called the Annual School Plan. And here is where I offer my next confession.

The Annual School Plans were successful in concentrating the entire staff's attention on students' performance, so that within three years I began to see organizational, curricular, and instructional changes that I believed could lead to a mindless conformity, ultimately producing a system geared to cranking out high test scores and operating with less imagination and creativity. And that worried me, because I was very proud of the high level of teacher competence and creativity across Arlington classrooms. While I did not dial back the push for higher test scores to meet local and state standards, my concerns over increasing uniformity grew. I regret that I could not articulate the peril of mindless standardization.

My third confession involves my initial embrace as a young man of the Deweyan notion that public schools are in the vanguard of societal reform. My ideas about schools both altering and being altered by society slowly formed as I thought and wrote about my experiences as a high school teacher for sixteen years in de facto segregated Black schools, as a school-based and district office administrator in the DC schools, and as superintendent in Arlington.

In thinking about those personal experiences during these decades, I discovered that political, social, and economic events outside of schools mattered greatly. I got married; Barbara and I raised two daughters; and we did so during the civil rights movement, the Vietnam War, economic recessions, and growing inequalities between the very rich, middle class, working class, and poor Americans. Our daughters became adults and entered careers that have given them some of the rewards they sought. And there is a granddaughter who will see, I hope, a changed society from the one her grandparents and mother inherited.

As a professor for decades, I have had the precious time to reflect on these personal and professional experiences, do additional research, and write. So I confess that the five-year-old first grader readers met in chapter 2, the twenty-year-old teacher in chapter 4, and the thirty-nine-year-old superintendent in chapter 6 has at the age of eighty-seven pulled back from his Progressive roots as a reform-driven educator. I confess that I have tempered the unvarnished optimism I had initially about the power of schools to mold individuals and societal institutions. I have come to understand the political and organizational forces at work inside and outside schools whenever reformers see their rhetoric of change morph into a mud-filled slog.

My experience- and research-produced knowledge over the decades has blended into a mix of what schools can and cannot do in a decentralized national system of schooling driven by an abiding faith in schools as an all-purpose solvent for individual, institutional, and societal problems. I have come to see that schooling is embedded in a society where economic, social, and political winds shape and reshape the dunes we call public schools. I have learned over decades that schools rather than altering a capitalist democratic society mirror it. Events occurring outside schools shape children and youth as much if not more than the fifteen thousand hours they spend in classrooms and schools during their careers in age-graded schools. Yet what appears like a lot of time is only 20 percent of the total time children and youth spend outside of school. Eighty percent of their time is spent in the home, neighborhood, and religious institutions with families, friends, and others. In brief, then, children spend far more time outside of school than inside. An obvious but too often neglected fact in a nation beholden to the power of schools to bend lives.

None of this is meant to say that schools do not matter. They do. The 20 percent of time spent in schools is a significant fraction, but only a fraction. In chapter 2, I recount events that occurred in my life that had a momentous impact on my family and me. Within the first decade of my life, the Great Depression, World War II, moving from a mostly Black neighborhood to an Irish and Italian neighborhood where anti-Semitism was common, and then getting polio shaped who I was and what I did, I believe, far more than school did.

As an educator, recognizing that schooling is important but not all-important is a conclusion that took me many years to arrive at. That events outside of schools, from hurricanes to pandemics to being wealthy or unemployed and homeless, weigh far more heavily in shaping lives than the considerable influence that schooling exerts is a conclusion I have uneasily reached.

So schools in a capitalist democratic society surely matter. Yet public faith that schools can reshape or alter society, as Deweyan Progressives believed and contemporary reformers claim, well, that is unfounded in both historical evidence and my experiences in and around schools. Regardless of what I think and write, however, popular trust in schooling solving national problems continues to resonate among those who want improvements. That trust became evident during the pandemic of 2020–2021.

THE COVID-19 PANDEMIC AND SCHOOL REFORM

In the US, the coronavirus that causes the disease of COVID-19 began its first surge in the early months of 2020, causing most states and cities to order residents to stay home. While the president and Congress twice appropriated billions of dollars to soften the harsh economic damage of businesses closing and massive layoffs of employees during the first year of the pandemic, it was discouraging to see presidential press conferences and tweets that sent mixed messages as governors and mayors scrambled for personal protection equipment (e.g., masks, gloves, shields) for health-care workers, quick and effective tests to determine if Americans had the virus, and ways of tracking the spread of the infection.[16]

Even more telling was President Donald Trump and White House aides wearing no masks as the pandemic unfolded. Nor did it help when the president and White House aides undercut the federal Centers for Disease Control and Prevention's and Food and Drug Administration's guidelines in press conferences and tweets even before and after the president contracted COVID-19 and lived to tell about it.[17]

The initial lack of coordinated national leadership contributed to nearly 350,000 Americans dying from the disease by the end of 2020.

What the president did do, however, was jump-start the national search for vaccines, and by the end of 2020 at least two were created and being distributed in the US and other countries. By early 2021, as I complete this book, millions of Americans have received doses of the vaccines.

The lack of a national policy grounded in available scientific knowledge became even more evident when it came to school closures and the swift, wholesale move to remote instruction across the nation's districts for the rest of school year 2020 and much of 2021. (I use *remote, online,* and *distance* to describe the noun *instruction* rather than the noun *learning* simply because there is only scattered evidence that *online learning*—or similar descriptors—does, indeed, benefit students.) In the US's decentralized educational system, thirteen thousand-plus school boards and superintendents stumbled through sporadic reopening and closings of schools for in-person instruction. New York City, for example, relied on online instruction, reopened schools in the fall for limited in-person instruction, and then closed down the system before Thanksgiving 2020 as infections surged then and after the winter holidays in 2021.[18]

Anxious about economic recovery, President Trump called for all schools to open in the fall. Again, as he had done with mask wearing, Trump weaponized the opening of schools, complimenting Republican-led states that left businesses and schools open and demonizing states and cities led by Democrats that closed schools and businesses.[19]

If any observer of past school reform ever questioned the strong linkages between the economy and public schooling, the COVID-19 crisis revealed starkly how the two were bound together. Parents, worried about endangering their children by exposing them to the virus in crowded buildings (and possibly infecting not only teachers but themselves and grandparents as well), had to decide family by family whether to send their children to school or quit their job and supervise their sons' and daughters' remote instruction at home.[20] Into this maelstrom of confusion, uncertainty, and mounting deaths, there were calls for rethinking US schools and yes, yet again, noisy demands for wholesale reform.[21]

Those calls for school reform got me thinking about other natural catastrophes such as the flu pandemic in 1918–1919 and Hurricane Katrina in 2005, which wreaked devastation on New Orleans.

New Orleans closed all public schools following the hurricane. Teachers were fired. What schooling children did receive was haphazard, with large swaths of mostly poor Black children and youth not attending parish schools. The state intervened and within a few years established a market-driven model of schooling. As researcher Douglas Harris reported, the district changed dramatically from parish-run public schools to independent charter schools enrolling nearly all students. Such an outcome for the US—the spread of charters—after the coronavirus ebbs is highly unlikely.[22]

My knowledge of school reform movements in the past century, particularly after disasters, tilted me more toward what happened to schools following the 1918–1919 influenza pandemic. Influenza killed over fifty million across the globe and around 675,000 Americans (ten times more than died in World War I). That pandemic closed US businesses and schools. Mask-wearing was encouraged and crowd gatherings were banned, as they were in the current coronavirus crisis. Schools eventually reopened (Tacoma, Washington, closed its schools October 11, 1918, and allowed students to return on November 14).[23]

Prior to and during the flu pandemic, educational Progressives installed a series of governance, organizational, curricular, and instructional reforms in various urban, suburban, and rural districts across the country. These reforms (e.g., governing efficiently through bureaucratic hierarchies; new curricula focused on children and youth working on projects; widespread intelligence testing to sort students into different courses of study; schools as medical, social service, and community centers) had become incorporated into thousands of districts' policies and practices. After the influenza crisis, these reforms largely continued. No shift in direction or substantive changes occurred as a result of the pandemic.

So when public schools reopened their doors to children in 2021, unlike post-Katrina New Orleans, there were few substantive changes in those standards-based reforms that had been in place nearly forty years. I summarize the reforms that seem to be emerging after 2021 and, finally, a few that may have staying power for the rest of the 2020s.

Continuing Trends

Reforms initiated since the mid-1980s to closely link tax-supported public schools to the workplace will persist. Those reforms—such as raising graduation requirements, encouraging all high school students to attend college, state tests, and accountability structures, along with increased parental choice of schools, particularly with charters—I expect to chug along pretty much as they had prior to COVID-19.

I do expect some short-term effects in the use of instructional technologies and on school calendars. But for schools to continue with remote instruction as a full-time or even half-time option for students, I do not expect to occur.

Online Teaching

Beginning in early 2020, K–12 schools closed across the country. Districts responded to the emergency with a blanket mandate of remote teaching. What became obvious within a few weeks was digital inequality. Those children from affluent and middle-class families with easy access to the internet and multiple devices eclipsed working-class and poor families with fewer or no computers at home and spotty access to the web.

Likewise, online instruction disadvantaged preschool and primary grade children and students with disabilities. Lower attendance rates of these students—that is, showing up for Zoom classroom meetings—worsened as the pandemic stretched out over two school years. Researchers have often pointed out the erosion of achievement that usually occurs every summer for these groups of children, but the duration of the pandemic worsened such a loss and was tagged as the "COVID Slide."[24]

The rush to provide schooling online so that students could continue learning uninterrupted offered incentives to technologically driven reformers to promote even more online instruction once schools reopened. And there are economic incentives for adopting "distance education," as it once was called, since such instruction tends to cost less schooling the young (e.g., fewer teachers, larger classes). But even with the federal stimulus packages passed in 2020–2021 containing funds for

K–12 schools to expand remote instruction, these incentives may not lead to clear growth in distance instruction.

Incremental Changes

Instead of expanding remote instruction after the pandemic, age-graded schools and in-person classrooms will return as before but with a few pandemic-induced wrinkles.

In writing these paragraphs in early 2021, I have read research reports, followed articles in newspapers and magazines, and listened to television news and parents (including my immediate family, friends, and former students), and what has become obvious to me is increased appreciation among single mothers, families with two working parents, and extended families for the custodial function of schools.

All American children ages five to sixteen have to go to school (ages vary by state). Compulsory enrollment legally requires schools to take care of students. Minors in the eyes of the law, children have to learn content and skills, interact with peers and adults, and receive community services, including meals, while within brick-and-mortar buildings. After schools were closed in early 2020 and children and youth were at home for months, only then did the full force of the loss of in-person classrooms in age-graded schools hit families squarely between the eyes. Once schools reopened and a sense of normalcy in daily routines for work and school returned, I did not sense any popular support for initiatives to substantially alter current policies or the age-graded school and its grammar of schooling.

Will there be, however, accelerated support for online instruction in K–12 schools? I expect that many underfunded public schools—most states have cut back on funding public schools in the past three decades—will increase remote instruction as a cost-saving move. The economic tremors following the pandemic may reduce school funding even further, as happened after the Great Recession of 2008.[25]

The Obama administration did pour additional funds into schools then for rehiring teachers who had been let go and other services. In the last weeks of the Trump administration, Congress did allocate further funds, some of which went to the nation's schools for repair and replacement of heating and air-conditioning equipment to minimize subsequent airborne infections, additional funding for Title I schools, and in-school childcare.[26]

So I do expect when in-person schooling has resumed fully an uptick in online instruction during and after the school day. Overall, however, such increases will remain peripheral to the core work of teachers teaching content and skills to children and youth daily in classrooms.

In the immediate future, I expect that there will be changes in the annual school calendar and shortened summers for incrementally greater use of remote instruction. Districts will skip over altering age-graded school structures, dropping Common Core curricular standards, or making major reductions in testing or substantive changes to prepandemic forms of teaching.

Here is why I believe that any reforms during and after the 2020–2021 crisis will be incremental, even superficial, much like throwing a flat stone on a pond to see ripples flow. Not only has COVID-19 frozen in place prior reforms, but it also saw schools swiftly spread devices and software before the pandemic to ensure that all students would embrace online instruction. Districts provided families with laptops and tablets like popcorn. What reforms that occur, if any, will be familiar to current educators, parents, and policy makers. Technology enthusiasts must keep in mind, however, previous moments when policy makers turned to a total reliance on technologies.

Twice in the past century, technology has been the primary medium of instruction for each and every teacher and student. One was planned and the other unplanned.

In the mid-1960s, the federal government established television as the primary means of instruction in American Samoa. Daily lessons would appear on a monitor in the front of the classroom, airing what content and skills were to be learned by elementary and secondary school students in each grade. A classroom teacher would then follow up the televised lesson. By the mid-1970s, however, Samoan schools had reverted back to in-person classroom instruction, with televised lessons being used as supplements to the curriculum.[27]

A generation earlier, an unplanned example of reliance on technology of the day occurred in Chicago during the polio epidemic of 1937, when nearly 325,000 students were sent home for three weeks. The radio in the classroom became the primary teaching device. Once school resumed, goodbye radio; it lost its central place in the teaching of Chicago students. Fast-forward to 2020.[28]

Over thirteen thousand districts responsible for over fifty million students shuttered schools in March 2020, slowly reopening to limited in-person classes over the summer and early fall. According to the US Census Bureau, 93 percent of people living in households with school-age children reported midsummer 2020 some form of distance instruction going on in their homes. Yesterday it was the radio; today it is the laptop.[29]

After wholesale in-person instruction resumed in 2021 following mass distribution of vaccines, daily distance learning at home became, for the most part, an unpleasant memory. Screens went dark. Nearly all lessons became face to face for the simple reason that voters and taxpayers (including parents, of course) expected schools to return to their core social, moral, and civic functions. But a residue of this emergency turn to online instruction remained.

If anything, doubters that the economy was connected to public schooling saw clearly how schools are intimately tied to the workplace insofar as permitting moms and dads to work at home, the shop, or the office. Presidential tweets demanding that schools resume in September were clearly linked to reopening the economy by freeing moms and dads to return to the workplace and also to shop, since consumer purchasing is a huge chunk of the US economy. Pushback from parents and educators concerned about the health risks to their children and themselves turned reopening of schools into a hopscotch mix of plans across thirteen thousand-plus school districts.[30]

Reopened schools in 2021 brought sighs of relief to parents and students while revealing anew inequalities that had gone untouched during the pandemic. States had cut back on school funding because of drops in tax revenues, which led to laid-off teachers and enlarged class size.[31]

Since then, online instruction has become the default option for schools when they close for snow days, torrential rains, and contagious diseases. Students wanting to gain extra units for graduation or make up for failed subjects are channeled to online courses during the school year and summer. It is the same for those individual students who have prolonged illnesses or are unable to attend school because of suspension or expulsion. For those students, laptop screens have become the medium for instruction.

But other questions about online instruction were ignored during the pandemic and remain unanswered today. Student attendance slid downward over time as social interaction shrank, screen-based pedagogy narrowed, and boredom grew. Additionally, teachers and parents asked reasonable questions about online assessment of students' academic performance. How should students be graded for their online responses to instruction, homework, and teacher-made tests taken in kitchens and living rooms? And how to factor into student grades existing gaps in urban and suburban teacher inexperience with remote instruction, quality of instruction, and student access to devices and the internet?

Many districts initially responded by abandoning letter grades (A–F) in exchange for pass/fail judgments. For high school students looking toward college and maintaining a high grade-point-average, letter grades were crucial for getting admitted and being awarded scholarships. Many districts later in the school year reverted back to the familiar grading system.[32]

And what about state standards, tests, and accountability—the nearly four-decade long reform movement—in the post-COVID era?

Then US Secretary of Education Betsy DeVos granted state waiver requests for the 2020–2021 administering of standardized tests. While there has been certainly much talk and some action in reducing standardized tests (e.g., fewer colleges using the SAT for admission), the rush to return to normal will include annual state testing. The machinery for taking such tests is already in place, since taking computer-based tests began well before the pandemic struck.

District and school accountability for test scores, however, has been sharply reduced. Ending No Child Left Behind in 2015 removed the coercive accountability that had grown dramatically since 2002. The Every Student Succeeds Act (2015) returns decisions of what to do with low performing schools and districts to the states. And across the states— again I speculate—the appetite to punish low academic performance, as measured by standardized tests, has shrunk greatly. That shrinkage began well before COVID-19 struck.

Still, the above point about online standardized testing does not directly deal with the contentious and unresolved issue of assessing student performance during and after remote instruction. Participation in lessons and homework can be graded. Mastery of content and skills, however, is difficult to assess online without knowing what students at home or in other locations knew before of the content and skills and what they gained from remote lessons—and especially so with glaring inequalities in US schools continuing to be part of the "normal" that children and youth face as they re-enter schools.

So my guess is that remote instruction in sharply reduced fashion will remain in public schools as the default option for teachers to use when students cannot attend school. Apart from that, I have yet to detect any groundswell of reform talk, much less policy action, since schools have reopened about altering the familiar school organization, Common Core curriculum, or existing accountability measures. Nor do I sense any political coalition of reformers offering concrete policies that can reduce the stark differences in funding and staffing schools in urban and sub-urban districts that have become, in a word, resegregated.

THE END . . .

So I come to the end of a century of school reform, when three social and political movements to alter school goals and classroom practices were politically and organizationally successful to a degree. Progressives, civil rights reformers, and standards-based promoters all left their thumb-prints on public schools, yet, in the final analysis, these fervent reform-ers changed only surface features of the basic organizational structures and processes of schooling that had been put into place in the nine-teenth century.

The COVID-19 catastrophe—as all disasters do—offered many would-be reformers the chance to make deep changes when schools turned on a dime in mandating remote instruction. But no such politi-cal coalition emerged advocating deep changes in schooling to remove long-standing inequalities or even rework the current standards-based reforms that have dominated public schools for nearly four decades.

Instead, there was a great deal of talk about fundamental changes but as of 2021 little action, much less implementation of reforms aimed at existing policies and classroom practices. During and after the COVID-19 pandemic, the age-graded school and the grammar of schooling remain secure. Most Americans continue to have faith in public schools and accept the system, including many urban and rural districts where inequalities in teaching and learning have been left untouched.

Any reformer eager to tackle the age-graded school and its grammar of schooling must keep in mind that there are nearly one hundred thousand schools located in thirteen thousand-plus school districts in fifty states. States govern districts. They allow local school boards within the state to make policy for students, teachers, and administrators within their boundaries. There is neither a federal superintendent of schools nor a national ministry of education. There is, instead, a fragmented, decentralized system that governs US public schools.

Certainly, as I have noted previously, the age-graded school and its grammar of schooling have incrementally changed over time. Where once there were bolted-down desks, now movable furniture dominates classrooms. Where once large-group instruction occurred in elementary school classrooms, now the prevailing pattern is a mix of small-group, partner activities, individual work, and whole-group instruction. Where there were once fifty-plus students in many classrooms, there are now twenty-five-plus. Where once high school schedules contained daily forty-minute periods, many schools now have blocks of time when teachers meet with students for sixty to ninety minutes a few days a week.

By the mid-twentieth century, minimal high school graduation requirements were the norm. But over the past four decades, states and districts have ratcheted up those requirements. Districts, schools, and teachers are directly held responsible for student outcomes contrary to the laissez-faire attitude of state and local school boards toward accountability a half-century ago. While still the authority figure, the teacher today is better trained in content and skills, much less formal in attire, far more knowledgeable of children's behavior, and increasingly avid in working individually with students than her great-grandmother who taught in the 1930s.

Such adopted changes preserve stability. Social scientists label such organizational adaptations "dynamic conservatism." Like many other organizations, public schools bob and weave in order to retain their "real" school structures. They "fight to remain the same." Hardly any of these incremental changes that the three reform movements have engineered would please contemporary critics of the age-graded school who want grander, deeper, and wholesale changes closer to a transformation than to nip-and-tuck surgery.[33]

Yet remaining in place are the larger societal inequalities in wealth distribution, employment insecurity, the lack of adequate housing for large swaths of American families, and the persistent ebb and flow of racism. The deep-seated political reluctance, or will, to challenge residential segregation and the inexorable resegregation of schools in the last half of the twentieth century continue to undermine the American Creed and tarnish the democracy that others and I prize.

In the decades to come, school reformers need to have bifocal vision. Looking closely at the goals, structures, and processes of schooling as shaping teacher and student behaviors is crucial, and just as essential for reformers is to work with others who see the larger societal forces that shape what schools are supposed to do and how they affect both adults and children in classrooms. Such bifocal vision remains uncommon in 2021 but oh so necessary for the next generation of school activists.

Notes

INTRODUCTION

1. Andrew Carnegie, *Triumphant Democracy* (New York: Scribner's Sons, 1886), 79.
2. W. E. B. Du Bois, "The Talented Tenth," in *The Negro Problem*, ed. Booker T. Washington (New York, 1903; Project Gutenberg, 2005), https://www.gutenberg.org/files/15041/15041-h/15041-h.htm#The_Talented_Tenth.
3. Lyndon Johnson, "Remarks in Providence at the 200th Anniversary Convocation of Brown University, September 28, 1964," *Public Papers of the Presidents of the United States: Lyndon Johnson* (Washington, DC: US Government Printing Office, 1965), 1140.
4. Aaron Sorkin, screenwriter for season 1, episode 18, has presidential speechwriter Sam Seaborn make this statement to an aide. See *Fandom*, "West Wing Wiki," https://westwing.fandom.com/wiki/Sam_Seaborn.
5. Gustavo Carreon et al., "The Importance of Presence: Immigrant Parents' School Engagement Experiences," *American Educational Research Journal* 42, no. 3 (2005): 465–93. Quotation is on p. 476.
6. Henry Perkinson, *The Imperfect Panacea: American Faith in Education, 1865–1990* (New York: McGraw-Hill, 1991); Carl Bankston and Stephen Caldas, *Public Education—America's Civil Religion: A Social History* (New York: Teachers College Press, 2009).
7. I surely wish I could take credit for the phrase "steady work," but I cannot. Richard Elmore and Milbrey McLaughlin used it as a central theme in their work *Steady Work: Policy, Practice, and the Reform of American Education* (Santa Monica, CA: RAND Corporation, 1988).
8. Warren Susman, "The Persistence of Reform," in *Culture As History* (New York: Pantheon Press, 1984), 86–98; David Rothman, *Conscience and Convenience: The Asylum and Its Alternatives in Progressive America* (New Brunswick, NJ: Transaction Publishers, 2012); Carl Kaestle, "Social Reform and the Urban School," *History of Education Quarterly* 12, no. 2 (1972): 211–28. While the dates of these twentieth-century movements indicate separate decades, all three were linked in their goals and strategies to previous generations of nineteenth-century reforms insofar as they shared a belief in the perfectibility of individuals and institutions. I foreshadow these linkages in the introduction and elaborate on the overlap and interconnectedness in the final chapter.
9. US Commission on Civil Rights, *Racial Isolation in the Public Schools* (Washington, DC: US Printing Office, 1967), vol. 1.

10. Gary Orfield and Erica Frankenberg, *Brown at 60: Great Progress, a Long Retreat and an Uncertain Future* (Los Angeles: The Civil Rights Project, May 15, 2014), 13–15, https://www.civilrightsproject.ucla.edu/research/k-12-education/integration-and -diversity/brown-at-60-great-progress-a-long-retreat-and-an-uncertain-future /Brown-at-60-051814.pdf.
    For how government policies created segregated housing in the US, also see Richard Rothstein, *The Color of Law* (New York: Liveright, 2017).

11. Elise Gould, *State of Working America: Wages 2018* (Washington, DC: Economic Policy Institute, February 20, 2019), https://www.epi.org/publication /state-of-american-wages-2018/. For unemployment, see Olugbenga Ajilore, *On the Persistence of the Black-White Unemployment Gap* (Washington, DC: Center for American Progress), https://www.americanprogress.org/issues/economy /reports/2020/02/24/480743/persistence-black-white-unemployment-gap/.

12. Thomas Dee et al., "Effects of NCLB on School Resources and Practices," *Educational Evaluation and Policy Analysis* 35, no. 2 (2013): 252–79; Vivian Wong et al., "Did States Use Implementation Discretion to Reduce the Stringency of NCLB? Evidence from a Database of State Regulations," *Educational Researcher* 47, no. 1 (2017): 9–33.

13. US Department of Education, "Duncan Says 82 Percent of America's Schools Could 'Fail' Under NCLB This Year," press release, March 9, 2011, https://www .ed.gov/news/press-releases/duncan-says-82-percent-americas-schools-could-fail-under-nclb-year; Matt Barnum, "No Child Left Behind Is Dead," *Chalkbeat*, August 4, 2017, https://www.chalkbeat.org/2017/8/4/21102738/no-child-left-behind-is-dead-but-have-states-learned-from-it.

14. Carl Bankston and Stephen Caldas, *Public Education—America's Civil Religion: A Social History* (New York: Teachers College Press, 2013); Henry Perkinson, *The Imperfect Panacea: American Faith in Education* (New York: McGraw-Hill, 1995).

15. Wikipedia, s.v. "Carnegie Library," https://en.wikipedia.org/wiki/Carnegie_library.

16. Bill Hussar et al., "Racial/Ethnic Enrollment in Public Schools," in *The Condition of Education 2020* (Washington, DC: National Center for Educational Statistics, 2020), https://nces.ed.gov/programs/coe/pdf/coe_cge.pdf; Steve Suitts, *A New Majority: Low Income Students Now a Majority in the Nation's Public Schools* (Atlanta: Southern Education Foundation, January 2015).

17. See James S. Coleman et al., *Equality of Educational Opportunity* (Washington, DC: Government Printing Office, 1966). For two-thirds in poverty, see Cynthia Hudley, "Education and Urban Schools," *The SES Indicator Newsletter*, May 2013, https:// www.apa.org/pi/ses/resources/indicator/2013/05/urban-schools; Cara Jackson and Kecia L. Addison, *Understanding the Relationships Between Poverty, School Factors and Student Achievement* (Rockville, MD: Montgomery County Public Schools, 2018), https://files.eric.ed.gov/fulltext/ED598342.pdf; Misty Lacour and Laura D. Tissington, "The Effects of Poverty on Academic Achievement," *Educational Research and Reviews* 6, no. 7 (2011): 522–27, https://sustainablefreedomlab.org /wp-content/uploads/2015/11/Effects-of-Poverty-on-Academic-Achievement.pdf; Sean Reardon, "School Segregation and Racial Academic Achievement Gaps," *The Russell Sage Foundation Journal of Social Sciences* 2, no. 5 (2016): 35–57.

18. David Kirp, *Improbable Scholars: The Rebirth of a Great American School System*

and a Strategy for America's Schools (New York: Oxford University Press, 2015); Jay Mathews, *Work Hard. Be Nice* (New York: Algonquin Books, 2009).

19. Drew Desilver, "School Days: How the U.S. Compares with Other Countries," Pew Research Center, Washington, DC, Fact Tank, September 2, 2014, https://www .pewresearch.org/fact-tank/2014/09/02/school-days-how-the-u-s-compares-with -other-countries/; Mona Chalabi, "American Kids Will Spend an Average of 943 Hours in Elementary School This Year," *FiveThirtyEight*, September 4, 2014, https:// fivethirtyeight.com/features/american-kids-will-spend-an-average-of-943-hours -in-elementary-school-this-year/.

20. Roger Wilkins, *A Man's Life: An Autobiography* (Woodbridge, CT: Ox Bow Press, 1991); Alex Kotlowitz, *There Are No Children Here* (New York: Doubleday, 1992); Coleman et al., *Equality of Educational Opportunity*; High Scope, Perry Preschool Project, https://highscope.org/perry-preschool-project/.

CHAPTER 1

1. The framework of a "short" and "long" story to social movements comes from Jacquelyn Hall, "The Long Civil Rights Movement and the Political Uses of the Past," *Journal of American History*, 2005, 91, no. 4 (2005): 1233–63.

2. William Reese, "The Origins of Progressive Education," *History of Education Quarterly* 41, no. 1 (2001): 1–24.

3. Ibid.

4. Samuel Hays, *Response to Industrialism, 1885–1914* (Chicago: University of Chicago Press, 1957); Robert Weibe, *The Search for Order, 1877–1920* (New York: Hilland Wang, 1966); Richard Hofstadter, *The Age of Reform* (New York: Vintage, 1960); Jill Lepore, *These Truths* (New York: W.W. Norton, 2019).

5. On crowded conditions in New York City, see Jeffrey Scheuer, *Legacy of Light: University Settlement's First Hundred Years* (New York: University Settlement Society of New York, 1985), https://socialwelfare.library.vcu.edu/settlement-houses/ university-settlement-of-new-york-city/.

6. Lepore, *These Truths*, 365–66. Quotation is from George Mowry, *The California Progressives* (Berkeley and Los Angeles: University of California Press), 88–89; cited in Hofstadter, *The Age of Reform* (New York: Vintage, 1955, 145).

7. The historiography of Progressivism is best captured by the following historians of education: Robert Westbrook, *John Dewey and American Democracy* (Ithaca, NY: Cornell University Press, 1991), 182–84; David Gamson, *The Importance of Being Urban: Designing the Progressive School District, 1890–1940* (Chicago: University of Chicago Press, 2019), 269–70.

8. See Jimmie Franklin, "Blacks and the Progressive Movement: Emergence of a New Synthesis," *OAH Magazine of History* 13, no. 3 (1999): 20–23.

9. Wikipedia, s.v. "Goo-goos," https://en.wikipedia.org/wiki/Goo-goos.

10. Doris Kearns Goodwin, *The Bully Pulpit* (New York: Simon and Schuster, 2013); Wikipedia, s.v. "Goo-goos," https://en.wikipedia.org/wiki/Goo-goos. For the Pure Food and Drug Act, 1906, see Wikipedia, s.v. "Pure Food and Drug Act," https://en.wikipedia.org/wiki/Pure_Food_and_Drug_Act. For details on which states have the initiative and referendum process, see "State I&R," *Initiative &*

Referendum Institute at the University of Southern California, https://web.archive
.org/web/20160211180917/http://www.iandrinstitute.org/statewide_i%26r.htm.

11. Pamela Tolbert and Lynne Zucker, "Institutional Sources of Change in the Formal
Structure of Organizations: The Diffusion of Civil Service Reform, 1880–1935,"
Administrative Science Quarterly 28 (1983): 22–39.

12. Education historian David Gamson makes that point clearly in *The Importance of
Being Urban*.

13. Margaret Berry, *The Settlement Movement, 1886–1986*, (Richmond, VA: Social Welfare History Project, n.d.), https://socialwelfare.library.vcu.edu/settlement-houses/
settlement-movement-1886-1986/. First published by United Neighborhood Centers of America (Milwaukee, WI).

14. Philip Jackson, "Black Charity in Progressive Era Chicago," *Social Service Review*
52, no. 3 (1978): 400–417.

15. Wikipedia, s.v. "White Rose Mission," https://en.wikipedia.org/wiki/White
_Rose_Mission; Charles Hounmenou, "Black Settlement Houses and Opposi-
tional Consciousness," *Journal of Black Studies* 43, no. 6 (2012): 646–66, https://
doi.org/10.1177/0021934712441203.

16. Lewis Harlan, *Booker T. Washington* (New York: Oxford University Press, 1983);
William McFeely, *Frederick Douglass* (New York: W.W. Norton, 1991).

17. Kenneth O'Reilly, "The Jim Crow Policies of Woodrow Wilson," *Journal of Blacks
in Higher Education*, no. 17 (1997): 117–21; Mark Benbow, "Birth of a Quotation:
Woodrow Wilson and 'Like Writing History with Lightning,'" *Journal of the Gilded
Age and Progressive Era* 9, no. 4 (2010): 509–533.

18. Trace Steffes, *School, Society, and State: A New Education to Govern Modern Amer-
ica, 1890–1940* (Chicago: University of Chicago Press, 2012), 26–28; Joseph Cronin,
The Control of Urban Schools (New York: The Free Press, 1973), 92–93; David Tyack,
The One Best System (Cambridge, MA: Harvard University Press, 1974), 126–27.

19. Steffes, *School, Society, and State*, 26–28.

20. Pingree, quoted in Tyack, *The One Best System*, 95; Greg King, "The California
State Civil Service System," *Public Historian* 1, no. 1 (1978): 76–80; Anirudh Ruhil,
"Urban Armageddon or Politics As Usual? The Case of Municipal Civil Service
Reform," *American Journal of Political Science* 47, no. 1 (2003): 159–70.

21. Cronin, *Control of Urban Schools*; Tyack, *One Best System*.

22. Steffes, *School, Society, and State*, 83–118.

23. Joseph Rice, *American Education* (New York: Arno Press and the New York Times,
1969), 88–89, 229.

24. Adele Shaw's observations quoted in Tyack, *The One Best System*, 230–31.

25. Jack Campbell, *Colonel Francis W. Parker: The Children's Crusader* (New York:
Teachers College Press, 1967); Robert Westbrook, *John Dewey and American
Democracy* (Ithaca, NY: Cornell University Press, 1991); Lawrence Cremin, *The
Transformation of the School: Progressivism in America Education, 1876–1957* (New
York: Vintage, 1961); David Labaree, *Someone Has to Fail* (Cambridge, MA: Har-
vard University Press, 2010).

26. David Tyack and Elisabeth Hansot, *Managers of Virtue* (New York: Basic Books,
1982), 105–144; David F. Labaree, "How Dewey Lost: The Victory of David Sned-
den and Social Efficiency in American Education," in *Pragmatism and Moderni-
ties*, ed. Daniel Trohler, Thomas Schlag, and Fritz Osterwalder (Rotterdam: Sense

Publishers, 2010), 163–88; David Labaree, "Limits on the Impact of Educational Reform: The Case of Progressivism and U.S. Schools, 1900–1950," (paper presented at the conference "The Century of the School: Continuity and Innovation During the First Half of the 20th Century," Ascona, Switzerland, September 2007).

27. Ronald Cohen, *Children of the Mill: Schooling and Society in Gary, Indiana, 1906–1960* (New York: Routledge, 2002); John Dewey and Evelyn Dewey, *Schools of To-morrow* (New York: E. P. Dutton, 1915).

28. Dewey and Dewey, *Schools of To-morrow.*

29. Paul Chapman, *Schools as Sorters, 1890–1930* (New York: New York University Press, 1988); Raymond Callahan, *Education and the Cult of Efficiency* (Chicago: University of Chicago Press, 1962); Harold Rugg, "Curriculum-Making and the Science of Education Since 1910," *Curriculum Theory Network* 4, no. 4 (1975): 295–308.

30. Ellen Condliffe Lagemann, "The Plural Worlds of Educational Research," *History of Education Quarterly* 29, no. 2 (1989): 185.

31. David Gamson offers an astute and insightful analysis of the historiography of educational Progressivism (*The Importance of Being Urban*, 269–70).

32. Nina Vandewalker, *The Kindergarten Movement in American Education* (New York: Macmillan, 1908); Barbara Beatty, *Preschool Education in America* (New Haven, CT: Yale University Press, 1995).

33. Kenneth Simon and Vance Grant, *Digest of Education Statistics*, Bulletin No. 18, OE-10024-64 (Washington, DC: Office of Education, US Department of Health, Education, and Welfare, 1964), 45.

34. Ibid., 56.

35. Edward Krug, *The Shaping of the American High School*, Vol. 2, *1920–1941* (Madison: University of Wisconsin Press, 1972); Diane Ravitch, *Left Back: A Century of Failed School Reforms* (New York: Simon and Schuster, 2000); Herbert Kliebard, *Struggle for American Curriculum, 1893–1958* (New York: Routledge & Kegan Paul, 1986); William Wraga, "From Slogan to Anathema: Historical Representations of Life Adjustment Education," *American Journal of Education* 116, no. 2 (2010): 185–209.

36. For a contemporary, positive, and breathless description of each of these innovations, see Agnes De Lima, *Our Enemy the Child* (New York: New Republic, 1926), 82–97. De Lima was a journalist who had been swept away by pedagogical Progressives of the day in her visits to and descriptions of these programs.

37. Arthur Zilversmit, *Changing Schools: Progressive Education Theory and Practice, 1930–1960* (Chicago: University of Chicago Press, 1993); Kate Rousmaniere, *City Teachers* (New York: Teachers College Press, 1997); Nancy Hoffman, *Woman's "True" Profession: Voices from the History of Teaching* (Cambridge, MA: Harvard Education Press, 2003); Craig Kridel, *Progressive Education in Black High Schools* (Charleston, SC: Museum of Education, University of Charleston, 2015); Larry Cuban, *How Teachers Taught* (New York: Teachers College Press, 1993); Vanessa Siddle Walker, "African American Teaching in the South: 1940–1960," *American Educational Research Journal* 38, no. 4 (2001): 751–79.

38. Cuban, *How Teachers Taught*, 55.

39. De Lima, *Our Enemy the Child*, 21.

40. Ibid., 26–27, 29–30.

41. Cuban, *How Teachers Taught*, 273.

42. Francis Couvares, *The Remaking of Pittsburgh: Class and Culture in an Industrializing City* (Albany: State University of New York Press, 1984), 81.

43. Lincoln Steffens, "Pittsburgh: A City Ashamed," *McClure's Magazine*, May 1903, http://www.historicjournalism.com/liincoln-steffens.html.

44. Loomis Mayfield, "Voting Fraud in Early Twentieth Century Pittsburgh," *Journal of Interdisciplinary History* 24, no. 1 (1993): 56–84.

45. Steffens, "Pittsburgh."

46. Ibid.

47. Ibid.

48. Mayfield, "Voting Fraud," 67.

49. Quotation is from Robert Woods, "A City Coming to Itself," *Charities and the Commons: The Pittsburgh Survey*, vol. XXI, *February 6, 1909* (New York: The Charity Organization Society of the City of New York, 1909), 786; also see Couvares, *Remaking of Pittsburgh*, 128–29.

50. Samuel Hayes, "The Politics of Reform in Municipal Government in the Progressive Era," *The Pacific Northwest Quarterly* 55, no. 4 (1964): 157–69.

51. "Historical Sketch of the Pittsburgh Public Schools," Guide to the Records of Pittsburgh Public Schools, 1870–1980, Historic Pittsburgh, https://historicpittsburgh.org; *Pittsburgh Post-Gazette*, June 20, 1933 (cited in Cronin, *Control of Urban Schools*, 98).

52. For Marcus Aaron's biography, see "The Aaron Family," Rauh Jewish Archives, Senator John Heinz History Center, Pittsburgh, PA, https://www.jewishfamilieshistory.org/entry/aaron-family/; The Board of Public Education, School District of Pittsburgh, *Twenty-Ninth Annual Report*, 1940, p. 273, Pittsburgh Public School Records, MSP 117, Detre Library & Archives, Heinz History Center, https://www.heinzhistorycenter.org/detre-library-archives/collection-highlights/pittsburgh-public-schools.

53. Richard Altenbaugh, "Teachers and the Workplace," *Urban Education* 21, no. 4 (1987): 365–89. Quotation is on p. 378.

54. Richard Kristufek, "The Immigrant and the Pittsburgh Public Schools, 1870–1940" (PhD diss., University of Pittsburgh, 1975), 79.

55. Ibid., 80; *Twenty-Ninth Annual Report*, 28.

56. The Board of Public Education, School District of Pittsburgh, "Report of the Superintendent of Buildings," *Twenty-Sixth Annual Report*, 1937, p. 27, Pittsburgh Public School Records, MSP 117, Detre Library & Archives, Heinz History Center.

57. George Strayer, *The Report of a Survey of the Public Schools of Pittsburgh, Pennsylvania* (New York: Teachers College, Columbia University, 1940), 318–19; *Twenty-Sixth Annual Report*, 14–26.

58. Strayer, *Report of a Survey of the Public Schools of Pittsburgh*, 318–20.

CHAPTER 2

1. Liana Loewus, "The Nation's Teaching Force Is Still Mostly White and Female," *Education Week*, August 15, 2017, https://www.edweek.org/ew/articles/2017/08/15/the-nations-teaching-force-is-still-mostly.html.

2. Hillary Clinton, "Remembering My School Days," *AFTVoices*, September 8, 2015, https://aftvoices.org/remembering-my-school-days-2d060cb60d87.

3. Kate Haas, "I Was Haunted by Painful School Memories—Until My Son's Fifth Grade Promotion," *ParentMap*, June 4, 2019, https://www.parentmap.com/article/ i-was-haunted-painful-school-memories-until-my-sons-fifth-grade-promotion.

4. Primo Levi, *The Drowned and Saved* (New York: Simon and Schuster, 2017), 13.

5. National Center of Education Statistics, "School and Staffing Survey 2007–2008," https://nces.ed.gov/surveys/sass/tables/sass0708_035_s1s.asp.

6. I have used family photos, taped interviews with my mother, handwritten documents, marriage certificates, visa applications, and US Census returns for 1920 and 1930 to compile this chronology of my parents after they immigrated to the United States in 1911 and 1912. All of these are in the author's possession.

7. George Strayer, *The Report of a Survey of the Public Schools of Pittsburgh, Pennsylvania* (New York: Bureau of Publications Teachers College, Columbia University, 1940), 426.

8. The Board of Public Education, School District of Pittsburgh, "Pittsburgh Public Schools," *28th Annual Report*, 1939, p. 15, Pittsburgh Public School Records, MSP 117, Detre Library & Archives, Heinz History Center, https://www.heinzhistorycenter .org/detre-library-archives/collection-highlights/pittsburgh-public-schools.

9. George Strayer, *The Report of a Survey of the Public Schools of Pittsburgh, Pennsylvania* (New York: Bureau of Publications Teachers College, Columbia University, 1940), 426; *28th Annual Report*, 15.

10. Historian David Gamson notes in *The Importance of Being Urban: Designing the Progressive School District, 1890–1940* (Chicago: University of Chicago Press, 2019) that of the four Progressive districts he examined in these decades, only Portland adopted platoon schools.

11. Reviewer Dwight Garner quotes writer Christopher Hitchens (himself quoting a friend) talking about failing memories as "CRAFT syndrome." CRAFT is an acronym for "Can't Remember a F— Thing." *New York Times Book Review*, November 8, 2020, 13.

12. Taylor-Allderdice English teacher Dorothy Albert, a veteran of eighteen years of teaching, had been a member of the Communist Party. Superintendent Earl Dimmick cited the state school code forbidding teachers to be members of organizations that sought the overthrow of the US government. Dimmick fired her. Albert appealed the decision to the state superintendent of instruction and lower state courts on the grounds that she was prevented from offering evidence that contradicted what Superintendent Dimmick had said about the party. She lost her appeals at every level. The Pennsylvania Supreme Court finally ruled in 1952 that her dismissal was legal under the state school code. Albert Appeal, 92 A.2d 663 (Pa. 1952), https://casetext.com/case/albert-appeal.

13. I recovered the names of the teachers cited here from *The Allderdice*, the 1951 Yearbook, http://www.donslist.net/PGHLookups/TAHS1951L.shtml.

14. For similar observations that a life education exceeds formal schooling in shaping the trajectory of one's lifetime, see Roger Wilkins, *A Man's Life* (New York: Simon and Schuster, 1991) and Tara Westover, *Educated: A Memoir* (New York: Random House, 2018).

CHAPTER 3

1. Cynthia Brown, *Ready from Within: Septima Clark and the Civil Rights Movement* (Navarro, CA: Wild Trees Press, 1986), 104–105.
2. Ibid., 106–107.
3. Ibid., 110.
4. Septima Clark, interview by Peter Wood, February 3, 1981, tape recording, Highlander Archives, Charleston, South Carolina. Cited in David Levine, "The Birth of the Citizenship Schools: Entwining the Struggles for Literacy and Freedom," *History of Education Quarterly* 44, no. 3 (2004): 405.
5. Brown, *Ready from Within*, 110.
6. For a brief description of the school, see *The Martin Luther King, Jr. Encyclopedia*, s.v. "The Highlander Folk School," https://kinginstitute.stanford.edu/encyclopedia/highlander-folk-school.
7. Quoted in Levine, "Birth of the Citizenship Schools," 408–409.
8. See Levine ("Birth of the Citizenship Schools," 402) for quotation taken from Jerome D. Franson, "Citizenship Education in the South Carolina Sea Islands, 1954–1966" (PhD diss., Peabody College for Teachers, 1977), 82.
9. Brown, *Ready from Within*, 17.
10. Wikipedia, s.v. "Rosa Parks," https://en.wikipedia.org/wiki/Rosa_Parks.
11. Wikipedia, s.v. "Septima Poinsette Clark," https://en.wikipedia.org/wiki/Septima_Poinsette_Clark.
12. Wikipedia, s.v. "Freedom Schools," https://en.wikipedia.org/wiki/Freedom_Schools.
13. Jacquelyn Hall, "The Long Civil Rights Movement and the Political Uses of the Past," *Journal of American History* 91, no. 4 (2005): 1233–63.
14. Gunnar Myrdal, *An American Dilemma* (New York: Harper and Brothers, 1944), vol. 1.
15. Ibid. Like historians Manning Marable and C. Vann Woodward, I distinguish between the First and Second Reconstructions. The dates of the First Reconstruction are far clearer than the dates for the Second Reconstruction, which begin immediately following World War II or after the *Brown v. Board of Education* decision in 1954. I suspect that dates will vary as well for the Third Reconstruction. The movement for racial justice appeared in the early 2010s with such events as Occupy Wall Street and the Women's March and organizations such as Black Lives Matter. Even during the 2020 pandemic, marches for social justice erupted after George Floyd was killed by police officers. Max Ufberg, "The Decade We Marched for Our Lives," *Medium*, December 11, 2019, https://gen.medium.com/the-decade-we-marched-for-our-lives-2c8198018e86; also see Manning Marable, *Race, Reform, and Rebellion: The Second Reconstruction in Black America, 1945–2006* (Jackson, MS: University Press of Mississippi, 2007); C. Vann Woodward, *The Strange Career of Jim Crow* (New York: Oxford University Press, 1966).
16. Eric Foner, "Rights and the Constitution in Black Life During the Civil War and Reconstruction," in "The Constitution and American Life: A Special Issue," *The Journal of American History* 74, no. 3 (1987): 863–83. Quotations on p. 871.
17. W. E. B. Du Bois, *Black Reconstruction in America, 1868–1880* (Cleveland, Ohio: The World Publishing Co., 1935), 600–604.

18. Quoted in Christopher Span, *From Cotton Field to Schoolhouse: African American Education in Mississippi, 1862–1975* (Chapel Hill, NC: University of North Carolina Press, 2009), 3.

19. W. E. B. Du Bois, "Reconstruction and Its Benefits," *American Historical Review* 15, no. 4 (1910): 781–99. Quotation is on p. 797.

20. James Anderson, *The Education of Blacks in the South, 1860–1935* (Chapel Hill, NC: University of North Carolina Press, 1988), 20–21.

21. Eric Foner, *Reconstruction: America's Unfinished Revolution, 1863–1877* (New York: Harper, 2014).

22. Wikipedia, s.v. "Knights of the White Camelia," https://en.wikipedia.org/wiki/Knights _of_the_White_Camelia.

23. For this section I leaned on C. Vann Woodward's *Reunion and Reaction* (Boston: Little, Brown and Company, 1951) and subsequent criticism of Woodward's interpretation represented fairly, I believe, in Woodward's *Thinking Back: The Perils of Writing History* (Baton Rouge, LA: Louisiana State University Press, 1986), 48–57.

24. Isabel Wilkerson, *Caste* (New York: Random House, 2020), 154–55.

25. James Patterson, *Brown v. Board of Education: A Civil Rights Milestone and Its Troubled Legacy* (New York: Oxford University Press, 2001). Charles S. Johnson's *Shadow of the Plantation* (New Brunswick, NJ: Transaction Publisher, 1996) gives detailed descriptions and photos of rural southern Black schools.

26. Woodward, *The Strange Career of Jim Crow*, 107.

27. Wikipedia, s.v. "Civil Rights Movement," https://en.wikipedia.org/wiki/Civil _rights_movement.

28. Peniel Joseph, *Stokley: A Life* (New York: Basic Civitas, 2014), 102–108; Wikipedia, s.v. "James Meredith," https://en.wikipedia.org/wiki/James_Meredith.

29. David Garrow, *Bearing the Cross* (New York: William Morrow, 1986), 473–81.

30. Ibid., 482.

31. Joseph, *Stokley: A Life*, 105.

32. Holly Yan, "'Black Lives Matter' Cases: When Controversial Killings Lead to Change," CNN, May 4, 2017, https://www.cnn.com/2017/05/04/us/black-lives-matter -updates-may-2017/index.html; Adam Serwer, "For the First Time, America May Have an Anti-Racist Majority," *The Atlantic*, October 2020, https://www.theatlantic .com/magazine/archive/2020/10/the-next-reconstruction/615475/.

33. Ellen Barry, "They Made History in the 1960s, and See It on the March Again," *New York Times*, June 19, 2020, A1.

34. Larry Cuban, "A Strategy for Racial Peace: Negro Leadership in Cleveland, 1900– 1919," *Phylon* 28, no. 3 (1967): 299–311.

35. Kenneth Kusmer, *A Ghetto Takes Shape: Black Cleveland, 1870–1930* (Champaign: University of Illinois Press, 1978), 283, 183.

36. Edward Miggins, "'No Crystal Stair': The Cleveland Public Schools and the Struggle for Equality, 1900–1930," *Journal of Urban History* 40, no. 4 (2014): 683–84.

37. Kusmer, *A Ghetto Takes Shape*, 237–38.

38. Ibid.

39. Kusmer, *A Ghetto Takes Shape*, 157–73; David Van Tassel, ed., *The Encyclopedia of Cleveland History* (Bloomington: Indiana University Press, 1996), 595–99.

40. Kusmer, *A Ghetto Takes Shape*, 170–71; Miggins, "'No Crystal Stair.'"

41. The United Freedom Movement split apart in 1966 over whether to support Black candidates for mayor. See *Encyclopedia of Cleveland History*, s.v. "United Freedom Movement," https://case.edu/ech/articles/u/united-freedom-movement-ufm.

42. Leonard Moore, "The School Desegregation Crisis of Cleveland, Ohio, 1963–1964," *Journal of Urban History* 28, no. 2 (2002): 135–57. Quoted statistics on p. 140.

43. Descriptive phrases for "riots" often depend on the perspective of the viewer or reader and frequently occur after the event. See Karen Sternheimer, "Civil Unrest, Riots, and Rebellions: What's the Difference?," *Everyday Sociology*, May 3, 2012, https://www.everydaysociologyblog.com/2012/05/civil-unrest-riots-and-rebellions-whats-the-difference.html; *Wikipedia*, s.v. "Hough riots," https://en.wikipedia.org/wiki/Hough_riots.

44. Wikipedia, s.v. "Carl Stokes," https://en.wikipedia.org/wiki/Carl_Stokes.

45. Lauren Pearlman, *Democracy's Capital: Black Political Power in Washington, D.C., 1960s–1970s* (Chapel Hill: University of North Carolina Press, 2019).

46. Wikipedia, s.v. "Demographics of Washington, D.C.," https://en.wikipedia.org/wiki/Demographics_of_Washington,_D.C.; Constance Green, *The Secret City: A History of Race Relations in the Nation's Capital* (Princeton, NJ: Princeton University Press, 1967), 151.

47. Green, *The Secret City*; Haynes Johnson, *Dusk at the Mountain* (New York: Doubleday, 1963).

48. Green, *The Secret City*, 129.

49. James Borchert, *Alley Life* (Champaign-Urbana: University of Illinois Press, 1980); Haynes Johnson, *Dusk at the Mountain*, 28–29.

50. Green, *The Secret City*, 128, 190–94.

51. Haynes Johnson, *Dusk at the Mountain*, 32–33.

52. Joan Quigley, "How DC Ended Segregation a Year Before Brown v. Board of Education," *Washington Post*, January 15, 2016, https://www.washingtonpost.com/opinions/the-forgotten-fight-to-end-segregation-in-dc/2016/01/15/1b7cae2a-bafc-11e5-829c-26ffb874a18d_story.html.

53. Pearlman, *Democracy's Capital*, 196–97.

54. Ibid., 14; Wikipedia, s.v. "Vehicle Registration Plates of Washington, D.C.," https://en.wikipedia.org/wiki/Vehicle_registration_plates_of_Washington,_D.C.

55. Wikipedia, s.v. "Marion Barry," https://en.wikipedia.org/wiki/Marion_Barry.

56. Pearlman, *Democracy's Capital*, 34.

57. Pearlman, *Democracy's Capital*.

58. George Musgrove and Chris Asch, "D.C. Statehood Is Good for Democracy," *New York Times*, October 2, 2020, A23; "Republicans Know D.C. Needs Voting Rights, but Their Own Power Takes Precedence," Opinion of the Editorial Board, *Washington Post*, November 15, 2020, https://www.washingtonpost.com/opinions/republicans-know-dc-deserves-to-be-a-state-but-their-own-power-takes-precedence/2020/11/15/ca38ad86-248f-11eb-a688-5298ad5d580a_story.html.

59. Perry Stein, "D.C. Public Schools Reports Enrollment Rise of 2 Percent," *Washington Post*, November 7, 2018, https://www.washingtonpost.com/local/education/dc-public-schools-reports-enrollment-rise-of-2-percent/2018/11/07/43084252-e2bc-11e8-b759-3d88a5ce9e19_story.html; Perry Stein and Fenit Nirappil, "Latest Star Ratings for D.C. Schools Show Citywide Improvement Even as Gaps Persist," *Washington Post*, November 26, 2019, https://www.washingtonpost.com/local/

education/latest-star-ratings-for-dc-schools-show-citywide-improvement-even
-as-gaps-persist/2019/11/26/acf97162-1052-11ea-bf62-eadd5d11f559_story
.html.

CHAPTER 4

1. John Dewey, *My Pedagogic Creed* (New York: E. L. Kellogg & Co., 1897), 16.

2. When I began writing this section, one phrase kept returning in my memory, "The Morrison Plan." So for these paragraphs I looked up who Henry Morrison was, his career (teacher, district and state superintendent, professor), and the 1926 text that I used in the methods courses. See Wikipedia, s.v. "Henry C. Morrison," https://en.wikipedia.org/wiki/Henry_C._Morrison; Henry C. Morrison, *The Practice of Teaching in the Secondary School* (Chicago: University of Chicago Press, 1926).

3. Leonard Moore, "The School Desegregation Crisis of Cleveland, Ohio, 1963–1964," *Journal of Urban History* 28, no. 2 (2002): 135–47. Within the school, I quickly learned from experienced colleagues that the district personnel department customarily assigned young, white, inexperienced teachers like me to mostly minority schools to see if they would survive.

4. Kenneth Kusmer, *A Ghetto Takes Shape: Black Cleveland, 1870–1930* (Champaign: University of Illinois Press, 1978), 157–73; David Van Tassel, ed., *The Encyclopedia of Cleveland History* (Bloomington: Indiana University Press, 1996), 595–99.

5. Kusmer, *A Ghetto Takes Shape*, 170–71.

6. A reader knowledgeable about Progressive thought in the early twentieth century could easily point out that the connection I made was within Progressive educators' thinking decades earlier.

7. For the reference to David Muzzey's US history textbook, see Larry Cuban, "Jim Crow History," *Negro History Bulletin* 25, no. 4 (1962): 84–86. The ditto machine (or "spirit duplicator") came into schools in the 1940s. It did not need electricity to run. The machine was basically a crank-turned drum to which I attached a stencil that I had typed up. I inserted paper in the tray and turned the handle until I had enough copies for my lesson. The finished copies were purplish with the distinct fragrance of alcohol (which was in the drum). The purple type ran occasionally, and after producing many copies my hands were often bluish. With the introduction into schools of the electronic copy machine in the 1970s, ditto machines became another footnote to classroom teaching.

8. Sam Wineburg, "Historical Thinking and Other Unnatural Acts," *Phi Delta Kappan* 80, no. 7 (1999): 488–99; Roy Rosenzeig, "What Is Historical Thinking Matters," *Historical Thinking Matters*, http://historicalthinkingmatters.org/about/. In 1962, I was asked to present at a national conference of social studies teachers on the ethnic and racial content lessons I had created. A member of the audience, Ted Fenton, came up to me afterward and asked me if I would write a volume for his Scott Foresman series on problems in American history. I said I would, and in 1964, *The Negro in America* appeared in the series (it came out in a second edition in 1971 retitled *The Black Man in America*). It was the first book that I published.

9. I got a master's in history in 1958 at Western Reserve and then enrolled in its PhD program. I completed all of the coursework for the degree by 1963 and began

writing a dissertation on Black leadership in Cleveland since 1900. I did not complete the dissertation.

10. James Patterson, *Grand Expectations: The United States, 1945–1974* (New York: Oxford University Press, 1996), ch. 18 and 19; Clayborne Carson, "Martin Luther King, Jr.: Charismatic Leadership in a Mass Struggle," *The Journal of American History* 74, no. 2 (1987): 448–54; David Levering Lewis, "Martin Luther King, Jr. and the Promise of Nonviolent Populism," in *Black Leaders of the Twentieth Century*, ed. John Hope Franklin and August Meier (Urbana: University of Illinois Press, 1982), 277–304.

11. Ellwood Carlson, *The Lucky Few: Between the Greatest Generation and the Baby Boom* (New York: Springer Publishers, 2008); David Labaree, "Pluck versus Luck," *Aeon*, https://aeon.co/essays/pluck-and-hard-work-or-luck-of-birth-two-stories-one-man.

12. A more detailed description of Cardozo High School and the teacher-training project can be found in Larry Cuban, *Teaching History Then and Now* (Cambridge, MA: Harvard Education Press, 2016), 43–70.

13. *Separate and Unequal: The State of the District of Columbia Public Schools Fifty Years After* Brown *and* Bolling (Washington, DC: Parents United for the DC Public Schools Advisory Committee Report, March 2005), 8–9.

14. "Central High School (Cardozo Senior High School)," *D.C. Historic Sites*, https://historicsites.dcpreservation.org/items/show/77. A person walking up the steps to the school's entrance in 1963 would have seen that the engraved name of Cardozo High School above the front doors just barely covered the faded but still noticeable title of the former school: Central High School.

15. Eve Edstrom, "Slum Children a New Challenge to Peace Corps Group," *Washington Post*, September 8, 1963, E2; Maxine Daly, Urban Teacher Corps, 1963–1968, (Washington, DC: Public Schools of District of Columbia, Office of Staff Development, May 1968), 4.

16. That organizational approach to schooling lasted until the track system was abolished by a US court decision in 1967. See Alexander Bickel, "Skelly Wright's Sweeping Decision," *New Republic*, July 7, 1967, https://newrepublic.com/article/90822/skelly-wrights-sweeping-decision.

17. In 1966, the US Congress authorized the National Teacher Corps based on the teacher-training model created at Cardozo High School. I served on the advisory board for the National Teacher Corps. In 1971, after four years of recruiting and training teachers in the Urban Teacher Corps, a new Washington, DC, superintendent abolished the program. In 1981, President Ronald Reagan ended federal funding for the National Teacher Corps.

18. Maxine Daly, "The Teacher as Innovator: A Report on Urban Teacher Corps," *Journal of Negro Education* 44, no. 3 (1975): 385–90.

19. Marvin Caplan and his work starting Neighbors Inc. is summarized at "Marvin Caplan Plaque Dedication Ceremony," *DC North Star*, June 18, 2018, http://dcnorthstar.com/marvin-caplan-plaque-ceremony-highlights/.

20. For Stokely Carmichael, see Wikipedia, s.v., https://en.wikipedia.org/wiki/Stokely_Carmichael.

21. For Poor People's Campaign in 1968, see Wikipedia, s.v., "Poor People's Campaign," https://en.wikipedia.org/wiki/Poor_People%27s_Campaign.

22. Wikipedia, s.v. "1968 Washington, D.C. Riots," https://en.wikipedia.org/wiki/1968 _Washington,_D.C.,_riots; Denise Wills, "'People Were Out of Control': Remembering the 1968 Riots," *Washingtonian*, April 1, 2008, https://www.washingtonian .com/2008/04/01/people-were-out-of-control-remembering-the-1968-riots/.

23. Ibid.

24. Norman Nickens, "The Ineffectiveness of Education Reform" (PhD diss., University of Massachusetts at Amherst, 1972), https://scholarworks.umass.edu/cgi/viewcontent .cgi?article=3617&context=dissertations_1. Teachers College professor Harry Passow directed the study. The first finding was damning:

> Despite some examples of good quality education, of dedicated and creative professionals at all levels, of a pattern of improving financial support and of efforts to initiate new programs, education in the District is in deep and probably worsening trouble. Unlike most large city systems which have a core of "slum" schools surrounded by a more affluent ring, the District has a predominance of so-called "inner-city" schools. These schools include large concentrations of economically disadvantaged children, a largely re-segregated pupil population, a predominantly Negro staff, a number of over-aged and inadequate school buildings and inappropriate materials and programs.

A. Harry Passow, *Creating a Model Urban School System: A Study of the Washington, D.C. Public Schools* (New York: Teachers College, Columbia University, June 1967), 2.

25. Larry Cuban, *Reform in Washington: The Model School Division, 1963–1972* (Washington, DC: US Department of Health, Education, and Welfare, Office of Education, December 1972).

26. During the years I was at Cardozo High School working on the project (1963–1967), teaching at Roosevelt High School twice, working at the CCR, and finally administering a districtwide program (1967–1972), I kept a personal journal chronicling my activities and thoughts. The journal helped me considerably in recalling specific people and instances.

27. Steven Diner, *The Governance of Education in the District of Columbia: An Historical Analysis of Current Issues*, Studies in D.C. History and Public Policy Paper No. 2 (Washington, DC: University of the District of Columbia, Department of Urban Studies), https://files.eric.ed.gov/fulltext/ED218375.pdf; Mary Levy, *History of Public School Governance in the District of Columbia: A Brief Summary* (Washington, DC: Washington Lawyers' Committee for Civil Rights), http://www.21csf .org/csf-home/DocUploads/DataShop/DS_307.pdf.

28. Personal journal, vol. 7, May 23, 1969, to January 31, 1971. Entry for July 7, 1969. Describing these experiences within a large educational bureaucracy and coming face-to-face with the politics of governing schools is not the same as understanding their import on my thinking. Not until I was at Stanford University working on my dissertation about urban superintendents in 1973–1974 did I come to realize that my experiences in DC for nearly a decade had shaped my intellectual framework for understanding urban schools both organizationally and politically.

29. Carstensen and family later moved to Madison, Wisconsin, where she served for eighteen years on the Madison Board of Education.

30. Jonathan Kozol, *Savage Inequalities* (New York: Harper Perennial, 1991).

CHAPTER 5

1. Cited in Herbert Kliebard, *Schooled to Work: Vocationalism and the American Curriculum, 1876–1946* (New York: Teachers College, 1999), 29 (italics original).
2. Ad appearing in the *New York Times Magazine*, April 28, 1991, 21.
3. Lawrence Glickman, "How White Backlash Controls American Progress," *The Atlantic*, May 21, 2020, https://www.theatlantic.com/ideas/archive/2020/05/white-backlash-nothing-new/611914/.
4. Data on economy in the 1970s taken from David Vogel, *Fluctuating Fortunes: Political Power of Business in America* (New York: Basic Books, 1989), 113–114, 136, 230, 256.
5. Ibid., 256.
6. Paul Hirsch and Michaela De Soucey, "Organizational Restructuring and Its Consequences," *Annual Review of Sociology*, no. 32 (2006): 171–89; Henry Aaron, *Politics and the Professors* (Washington, DC:The Brookings Institution, 1978).
7. Quotations come from Carol Ray and Roslyn Mickelson, "Business Leaders and the Politics of School Reform," *Politics of Education Association Yearbook* (1989), 123.
8. Sreven Holmes, "School Reform: Business Moves in," *New York Times*, February 1, 1990, Section D, 1.
9. One of the better summaries of how schools had become the central problem to the future of the nation in the 1980s can be found in Chester E. Finn Jr., *We Must Take Charge: Our Schools and Our Future* (New York: The Free Press, 1991); also see Diane Ravitch, "The Test of Time," *Education Next* 3, no. 2, https://www.educationnext.org/thetestoftime/.
10. George W. Bush, "Speech to NAACP's 91st Annual Convention," July 10, 2000, https://www.washingtonpost.com/wp-srv/onpolitics/elections/bushtext071000.htm.
11. US Commission on Excellence in Education, *A Nation at Risk* (Washington, DC: US Government Printing Office, 1983), 18.
12. Jal Mehta, "Escaping the Shadow," *American Educator* 39, no. 2 (2015): 20–26, 44; Milton Goldberg and Susan Traiman, "Why Business Backs Education Standards," in *Brookings Papers on Education Policy*, ed. Diane Ravitch (Washington, DC: Brookings Institution Press, 2001), 75–129.
13. John Mintz, "George W. Bush: The Record in Texas," *Washington Post*, April 21, 2000, https://www.washingtonpost.com/archive/politics/2000/04/21/george-w-bush-the-record-in-texas/3fcc6109-7332-45a6-9658-de52abc4c4ed/.
14. Cited in Maris Vinovkis, "Horace Mann on the Economic Productivity of Education," *New England Quarterly* 43, no. 4 (1970): 550–71. Quotation is on p. 561.
15. Claudia Goldin and Lawrence Katz, *The Race Between Education and Technology* (Cambridge, MA: Belknap Press, 2010).
16. David Tyack and William Tobin, "The Grammar of Schooling: Why Has It Been So Hard to Change?," *American Educational Research Journal* 31, no. 3 (1994): 453–79.
17. Raymond Callahan, *Education and the Cult of Efficiency* (Chicago: University of Chicago Press, 1962), 97. Since the late 1960s, generations of reformers have given the metaphor of schools as factories a decidedly negative connotation. See Larry Cuban, "Why Has the 'School as Factory' Metaphor Persisted?," May 28, 2019, https://larrycuban.wordpress.com/2019/05/28/why-has-the-school-as-factory-metaphor-persisted/.

18. Herbert Kliebard, *Schooled to Work* (New York: Teachers College Press, 1999), 115–116.

19. Harvey Kantor, "Vocationalism in American Education: The Economic and Political Context, 1880–1930," in *Work, Youth, and Schooling*, ed. Harvey Kantor and David Tyack (Stanford, CA: Stanford University Press, 1982), 14–44.

20. Larry Cuban, "Enduring Resiliency: Enacting and Implementing Federal Vocational Education Legislation," in *Work, Youth, and Schooling*, ed. Harvey Kantor and David Tyack (Stanford, CA: Stanford University Press, 1982), 45–78.

21. Kliebard, *Schooled to Work*, 150–51.

22. Shaun Dougherty, *Career and Technical Education in High School: Does It Improve Student Outcomes?* (Washington, DC: Thomas Fordham Institute, April 2016); Howard Gordon and Deanna Schultz, *The History and Growth of Career and Technical Education in America* (Long Grove, IL: Waveland Press, 2020).

23. School-To-Work Opportunities Act, Pub. Law No. 103-239, 108 Stat. 568 (1994) (20 U.S.C.6 101-6235), https://www2.ed.gov/pubs/Biennial/95-96/eval/410 -97.pdf; "Fact Sheet: What Is the Perkins CTE, and How Does It Serve Immigrants?," *National Immigration Forum*, https://immigrationforum.org/article/fact -sheet-perkins-cte-serve-immigrants/.

24. *2018 State of Computer Science Education* (Code.org Advocacy Coalition and Computer Science Teachers Association, 2018), https://code.org/files/2018_state _of_cs.pdf.

25. Daniel Kreisman and Kevin Stange, "Depth Over Breadth," *Education Next* 19, no. 4 (2019), https://www.educationnext.org/depth-over-breadth-value-vocational -education-u-s-high-schools/.

26. US Bureau of Labor Statistics, Computer and Information Technology Occupations, in *Occupational Outlook Handbook* (Washington, DC: US Bureau of Labor and Statistics), https://www.bls.gov/ooh/computer-and-information-technology /home.htm.

27. Employment in the United States 2010–2020, *Statistica*, https://www.statista.com /statistics/269959/employment-in-the-united-states/; Bureau of Labor Statistics, US Department of Labor, "Employment Projections 2010–2020," news release, February 1, 2012, https://www.bls.gov/news.release/archives/ecopro_02012012.pdf.

28. Natasha Singer, "How Silicon Valley Pushed Coding into American Classrooms," *New York Times*, June 27, 2017, https://www.nytimes.com/2017/06/27/technology /education-partovi-computer-science-coding-apple-microsoft.html.

29. "Infographic: Coding at School—How Do EU Countries Compare?," *Euractiv*, October 16, 2015, https://www.euractiv.com/section/digital/infographic/infographic -coding-at-school-how-do-eu-countries-compare/; Stuart Dredge, "Coding at School: A Parent's Guide to England's New Computing Curriculum," *The Guardian*, September 4, 2014, https://www.theguardian.com/technology/2014/sep/04/coding -school-computing-children-programming; Allie Bidwell, "Making It Count: Computer Science Spreads as a Graduation Requirement," *U.S. News*, November 25, 2014, https://www.usnews.com/news/stem-solutions/articles/2014/11/25 /making-it-count-computer-science-spreads-as-graduation-requirement.

30. Bernie Trilling and Charles Fadel, *21st Century Skills* (San Francisco: Jossey-Bass, 2009).

31. I have drawn these assumptions from a voluminous collection of newspaper and

journal articles, trade books, research studies, and national commission reports over the past quarter-century. Citations below suggest the range of sources. For example, economists and widely respected analysts produced best sellers in these years that judged schools as failures in teaching students to think and solve problems. See Ray Marshall and Marc Tucker, *Thinking for a Living: Education and the Wealth of Nations* (New York: Basic Books, 1992); Robert Reich, *The Work of Nations* (New York: Vintage, 1992); and Lester Thurow, *Head to Head: The Coming Economic Battle Among Japan, Europe, and America* (New York: Warner Books, 1992). Many of the assumptions I offer are stated explicitly by national business organizations, individual corporate leaders, and ad hoc groups of public officials and corporate leaders. See Thomas Toch, *In the Name of Excellence* (Philadelphia: American Philological Association, 1991); in chapter 2, Toch briefly summarizes various business and governmental reports following *A Nation at Risk* that state the connections between educating youth and a stronger economy. Also see David Kearns and Denis Doyle, *Winning the Brain Race: A Bold Plan to Make Our Schools Competitive* (San Francisco: Institute for Contemporary Studies, 1988). Articles from the *Wall Street Journal* on public schools and *The National Review* offer views from the conservative side of the political spectrum. On the progressive side, articles from *The Nation* and *The American Prospect* offer views that often challenge what appears in these politically conservative journals.

32. Carl Kaestle and Michael Smith, "The Federal Role in Elementary and Secondary Education, 1940–1980," *Harvard Educational Review* 52, no. 4 (November 1982): 384–408.

33. For the history of the Saturn Corporation, see Wikipedia, s.v. "Saturn Corporation," https://en.wikipedia.org/wiki/Saturn_Corporation; Jeanne Allen, ed., *Can Business Save Education?*, The Heritage Lectures (Washington, DC: The Heritage Foundation, 1989), 1.

34. Carol Ray and Roslyn Mickelson, "Business Leaders and the Politics of School Reform," *Journal of Education Policy* 4, no. 5 (1990): 119–35; Dorothy Shipps, "Echoes of Corporate Influence: Managing Away Urban School Troubles," in L. Cuban and D. Shipps, *Reconstructing the Common Good in Education: Coping with Intractable American Dilemmas* (Palo Alto, CA: Stanford University Press, 2000), 82–106; David Kearns and Denis Doyle, *Winning the Brain Race: A Bold Plan to Make Our Schools Competitive* (San Francisco: Institute for Contemporary Studies, 1988); Nancy Perry, "Saving the Schools: How Business Can Help," *Fortune Magazine*, November 7, 1988, 42–46, 50–56. The quotation comes from two researchers who studied business participation in school reform in the early 1980s; see Marsha Levine and Roberta Tractman, eds., *American Business and The Public School* (New York: Teachers College Press, 1988), xxiii.

35. I have taken much of these prescriptions from case studies of business involvement in district school systems. See, for example, the in-depth case study of a corporate elite heavily involved in one city's school politics and reform by Dorothy Shipps, *School Reform, Corporate Style, 1880–2000* (Lawrence, KN: University of Kansas Press, 2006); also see Roslyn A. Mickelson, "Corporations and Classrooms: A Critical Examination of the Business Agenda for Urban School Reform," in *Challenges of Urban Education: Sociological Perspectives for the Next*, ed. Karen McClafferty,

Carlos Torres, and Theodore Mitchell (Albany: State University of New York Press, 2000), 127–73.

36. Influential educational policy makers had evolved a similar strategy during the 1980s and early 1990s that derived from the strategies used by California State Superintendent Bill Honig between 1983 and 1990. By the early 1990s, this strategy had come to be called "systemic reform" and nicely converged with the market-driven prescriptions for school reform. For the 1980s, see Paul Berman's chapter on California in Marsha Levine and Roberta Trachtman, *Corporate Involvement in Education* (New York: Teachers College Press, 1988). See Marshall Smith and Jennifer O'Day, "Systemic School Reform," in Susan Fuhrman and Betty Malen, eds., *The Politics of Curriculum and Testing: The 1990 Yearbook of the Politics of Education*, (Philadelphia: Falmer Press, 1991); also see Maris Vinovskis, *History and Educational Policy Making* (New Haven, CT: Yale University Press, 1999), 171–202. Currently, forty-nine states have implemented standards of what their students should know and do and established tests to assess their performance. The number of states that administer student tests that are aligned with published standards in at least one subject climbed from thirty-five in 1998 to forty-one in 2000. According to *Education Week* ("Quality Counts 1999: Rewarding Results, Punishing Failure," *Education Week*, January 11, 1999), twenty-seven states rate schools primarily on the basis of test scores; fourteen states have authorized their departments of education to close and take over low performing schools. In nineteen states, students who fail the statewide graduation test do not receive diplomas. For descriptions of actions taken at state and national levels, see Jodi Wilgoren, "For 2000, the G.O.P. Sees Education in a New Light," *New York Times*, August 2, 2000, A15; David Sanger, "Bush Pushes Ambitious Education Plan," *New York Times*, January 24, 2001, A1, A14.

37. See, for example, the US Chamber of Commerce's policy position on education at http://www.uschamber.com/government/issues/education/education.htm.

38. Michael Stratford, "DeVos to Enforce School Testing Mandates amid Pandemic," *Politico*, September 3, 2020, https://www.politico.com/news/2020/09/03 /devos-enforce-school-testing-mandates-408626.

39. The Business Roundtable, "Modernizing K–12 Education," https://www .businessroundtable.org/policy-perspectives/building-americas-tomorrow-ready -workforce/pre-k-12-education.

40. Mary Commander, "Minimum Competency Testing: Education or Discrimination?," *University of Richmond Law Review* 4, no. 14 (1980): 769–90. Quotation is on p. 771.

41. Larry Cuban, "Corporate Involvement in Public Schools: A Practitioner-Academic's Perspective," *Teachers College Record* 85, no. 2 (1983): 183–203.

CHAPTER 6

1. This chapter is a revision of and addition to a chapter I wrote in *The Managerial Imperative and the Practice of Leadership in Schools* (Albany, NY: SUNY Press, 1988), 149–75.

2. In the early weeks of my coming to Arlington, I overheard the phrase in conversations with a number of politically conservative residents who were unhappy with my selection as superintendent.

3. Because Arlington desegregated its schools, the state legislature ended elected boards in the 1960s. Since then, the elected county board had appointed five school board members. In the mid-1980s, the legislature returned Arlington to its elected school board. See Wikipedia, s.v. "Arlington Public Schools," https://en.wikipedia .org/wiki/Arlington_Public_Schools.

4. In 2019, Arlington schools enrolled over twenty-eight thousand students. Nearly half were white and the rest were minorities. See Wikipedia, s.v. "Arlington Public Schools."

5. *Public Schools and the Original Federal Land Grant Program* (Washington, DC: Center on Education Policy, 2011).

6. A John Denver song, the lyrics of which can be found at https://www.azlyrics.com /lyrics/johndenver/somedaysarediamonds.html.

CHAPTER 7

1. James Coleman, *Equality of Educational Opportunity (Summary Report)* (Washington, DC: US Department of Health, Education, and Welfare, Office of Education, 1966).

2. Elizabeth Dickinson, "Coleman Report Set the Standard for the Study of Public Education," *Johns Hopkins Magazine*, Winter 2016, https://hub.jhu.edu/magazine/2016 /winter/coleman-report-public-education/.

3. Sarah Deschenes, Larry Cuban, and David Tyack, "Mismatch: Historical Perspectives on Schools and Students Who Don't Fit Them," *Teachers College Record* 103, no. 4 (2001): 525–47. Terms are on p. 532.

4. Columbia University Teachers College's Harold Rugg was the premier curriculum builder in the 1920s and 1930s. See Murry Nelson, "Rugg on Rugg: His Theories and His Curriculum," *Curriculum Inquiry* 8, no. 2 (1978): 119–32. For Progressives touting schools reshaping American society, see George Gutek, "George S. Counts and the Origins of Social Reconstructionism," in *Social Reconstruction*, ed. Karen Riley (Greenwich, CT: Information Age Publishing, 2006), 1–26. Also see David Tyack, *The One Best System* (Cambridge, MA: Harvard University Press, 1974) and Lawrence Cremin, *The Transformation of the School* (New York: Alfred Knopf, 1961).

5. Deschenes, Cuban, and Tyack, "Mismatch," 533.

6. Martin Luther King Jr., "Remaining Awake Through a Great Revolution," speech given at National Cathedral in Washington, DC, March 31, 1968. Available at https://www.si.edu/spotlight/mlk?page=4&iframe=true.

7. Margaret Placier, "The Cycle of Student Labels in Education: The Cases of Culturally Deprived/Disadvantaged, and At Risk," *Educational Administration Quarterly* 32, no. 2 (1996): 236–70; Wikipedia, s.v. "Inner City," https://en.wikipedia.org/wiki /Inner_city; Emma Garcia, "Schools Are Still Segregated, and Black Children Are Paying the Price," Economic Policy Institute, February 12, 2020, https://www.epi.org /publication/schools-are-still-segregated-and-black-children-are-paying-a-price/.

8. Amy Brown and Janna Bilski, "Fighting the Stigma of Free Lunch," Ford Foundation, September 29, 2017, https://www.fordfoundation.org/ideas/equals-change-blog/

posts/fighting-the-stigma-of-free-lunch-why-universal-free-school-lunch-is-good
-for-students-schools-and-families/.

9. Megan Brenan, "Amid Pandemic, Confidence in Key U.S. Institutions Surges," *Gallup News*, August 12, 2020, https://news.gallup.com/poll/317135/amid-pandemic -confidence-key-institutions-surges.aspx. For the words of the 1883 poem by Emma Lazarus inscribed at the base of the Statue of Liberty in New York City's harbor, see Wikipedia, s.v. "The New Colossus," https://en.wikipedia.org/wiki/ The_New_Colossus:

> "Keep, ancient lands, your storied pomp!" cries she
> With silent lips. "Give me your tired, your poor,
> Your huddled masses yearning to breathe free,
> The wretched refuse of your teeming shore.
> Send these, the homeless, tempest-tost to me,
> I lift my lamp beside the golden door!"

10. At the annual conference of the NAACP on July 10, 2000, George W. Bush, campaigning for president, used the "soft bigotry" phrase. See George W. Bush's speech to the NAACP's 91st annual convention, July 10, 2000, https://www.washingtonpost .com/wp-srv/onpolitics/elections/bushtext071000.htm.

11. Wikipedia, s.v. "Ngram," https://en.wikipedia.org/wiki/Google_Ngram_Viewer The Ngram for "social justice" can be found at https://books.google.com/ngrams /graph?content=social+justice+&year_start=1800&year_end=2019&corpus=26& smoothing=3&direct_url=t1%3B%2Csocial%20justice%3B%2Cc0.

12. See description of Chicago's School of Social Justice High School at "School of Social Justice High School," *US News & World Report*, https://www.usnews.com/ education/best-high-schools/illinois/districts/chicago-public-schools/school-of -social-justice-high-school-6637.
For the Charter High School for Law and Social Justice, see "Charter High School for Law and Social Justice," InsideSchools, https://insideschools.org/school/84X429. The website for Social Justice Humanitas Academy is http://www.sjhumanitas.org/.

13. I completed a case study of the Social Justice Humanitas Academy in 2018 in which I observed classes and interviewed teachers, students, and administrators. See Larry Cuban, *Chasing Success and Confronting Failure in American Public Schools* (Cambridge, MA: Harvard Education Press, 2020).

14. Jill Barshay, "The Promise of 'Restorative Justice' Starts To Falter Under Rigorous Research," *The Hechinger Report*, May 6, 2019, https://hechingerreport.org /the-promise-of-restorative-justice-starts-to-falter-under-rigorous-research/.

15. US Commission on Civil Rights, *Racial Isolation in Public Schools* (Washington, DC: Government Printing Office, 1967).

16. Wikipedia, s.v. "Covid-19 Pandemic in the United States," https://en.wikipedia.org /wiki/COVID-19_pandemic_in_the_United_States.

17. Michael Shear et al., "Trump's Focus as the Pandemic Raged: What Would It Mean for Him?" *New York Times*, updated April 22, 2021, https://www.nytimes .com/2020/12/31/us/politics/trump-coronavirus.html; Lawrence Wright, "The Plague Year," *The New Yorker*, December 28, 2020, https://www.newyorker.com /magazine/2021/01/04/the-plague-year.

18. Eliza Shapiro, "New York City to Close Public Schools Again as Virus Cases Rise,"

New York Times, November 18, 2020, https://www.nytimes.com/2020/11/18/nyregion/nyc-schools-covid.html.

19. Nat Malkus, "We Got the School Reopening Story Wrong," *The Hill*, October 20, 2020, https://thehill.com/opinion/education/521816-we-got-the-school-reopening-story-wrong.

20. Jon Valant, "School Reopening Plans Linked to Politics Rather Than Public Health," Brookings Institution, July 29, 2020, https://www.brookings.edu/blog/brown-center-chalkboard/2020/07/29/school-reopening-plans-linked-to-politics-rather-than-public-health/.

21. Alfie Kohn, "The Pandemic Pivot: Turning Temporary Changes into Lasting Reform," National Education Policy Center, September 3, 2020, https://nepc.colorado.edu/blog/pandemic-pivot; Yong Zhao, "Covid-19 as a Catalyst for Educational Change," *Prospects* 49 (2020): 29–33.

22. Douglas N. Harris and Matthew F. Larsen, *What Effect Did the New Orleans School Reforms Have on Student Achievement, High School Graduation, and College Outcomes?* Policy Brief (New Orleans: Education Research Alliance for New Orleans, July 15, 2018).

23. Douglas Jordan, "The Deadliest Flu: The Complete Story of the Discovery and Reconstruction of the 1918 Pandemic Virus," Centers for Disease Control and Prevention, n.d., https://www.cdc.gov/flu/pandemic-resources/reconstruction-1918-virus.html; Craig Sailor, "Tacoma's Last Pandemic Closed Schools, Turned a Church into a Hospital and Killed Hundreds," *The News Tribune*, March 12, 2020.

24. Of course, digital inequality is just a symptom of the economic gaps that have grown between the rich, middle-class, and poor. For "COVID Slide," see Amanda Getchell, "The 'COVID Slide': Study Shows Math, Reading Skills Now Deteriorating in Upper Elementary Students," *MassLive*, October 27, 2020, https://www.masslive.com/coronavirus/2020/10/the-covid-slide-study-shows-math-reading-skills-now-deteriorating-in-upper-elementary-students.html; Laura Meckler and Hannah Natanson, "'Lost Generation': Surge of Research Reveals Students Sliding Backward, Most Vulnerable Worst Affected," *Washington Post*, December 6, 2020, https://www.washingtonpost.com/education/students-falling-behind/2020/12/06/88d7157a-3665-11eb-8d38-6aea1adb3839_story.html.

25. Michael Leachman et al., *A Punishing Decade for School Funding* (Washington, DC: Center on Budget and Policy Priorities, November 29, 2017).

26. Wikipedia, s.v. "The American Recovery and Reinvestment Act of 2009," https://en.wikipedia.org/wiki/American_Recovery_and_Reinvestment_Act_of_2009; Rachel Siegel, Jeff Stein, and Mike DeBonis, "Here's What's in the $900 Billion Stimulus Package," *Washington Post*, December 20, 2020, https://www.washingtonpost.com/business/2020/12/20/stimulus-package-details/; Phyllis Jordan, "What Congressional Covid Funding Means for K–12 Schools," FutureEd, December 21, 2020, https://www.future-ed.org/what-congressional-covid-funding-means-for-k-12-schools/.

27. Wilbur Schamm, *Bold Experiment: The Story of Educational Television in American Samoa* (Stanford, CA: Stanford University Press, 1981).

28. Michael Hines, "In Chicago, Schools Closed During a 1937 Polio Epidemic and Kids Learned from Home—over the Radio," *Washington Post*, April 3, 2020, https://www.washingtonpost.com/education/2020/04/03/chicago-schools-closed-during-1937-polio-epidemic-kids-learned-home-over-radio/.

29. Kelvin McElrath, "Schooling During the COVID-19 Pandemic," US Census Bureau, August 26, 2020, https://www.census.gov/library/stories/2020/08/schooling-during-the-covid-19-pandemic.html.

30. Zack Friedman, "Trump: Schools Must Open This Fall," *Forbes*, July 7, 2020, https://www.forbes.com/sites/zackfriedman/2020/07/07/trump-schools-must-open-this-fall/?sh=3fd055126761; Robin Lake and Bree Dusseault, "We Reviewed the School Reopening Plans for 106 Districts Across the Country. Here's How They Square with Reality," *The 74*, October 16, 2020, https://www.the74million.org/article/analysis-we-reviewed-the-school-reopening-plans-for-106-districts-around-the-country-heres-how-they-square-with-reality/.

31. Daarel Burnette and Madeline Will, "Thousands of Educators Laid Off Already Due to COVID-19, and More Expected," *Education Week*, July 14, 2020, https://www.edweek.org/leadership/thousands-of-educators-laid-off-already-due-to-covid-19-and-more-expected/2020/07.

32. Ali Tadayon, "California School Districts Revert to A–F Grades This Fall—with More Flexibility for Some Students," *EdSource*, November 3, 2020, https://edsource.org/2020/california-school-districts-revert-back-to-a-f-grades-this-year-with-flexibility/641962; Valerie Strauss, "More Students Than Ever Got F's in First Term of 2020–21 School Year—But Are A–F Grades Fair in a Pandemic?," *Washington Post*, December 6, 2020, https://www.washingtonpost.com/education/2020/12/06/more-students-than-ever-got-fs-first-term-2020-21-school-year-are-a-f-grades-fair-pandemic/.

33. Donald Schön, *Beyond the Stable State* (New York: Norton, 1973), 32.

Acknowledgments

THE GENESIS OF THIS BOOK IS STRAIGHTFORWARD. I had finished *Chasing Success and Confronting Failure in American Public Schools* and was thinking of my next project (yes, I need to have projects to look forward to). The theme of *Chasing Success* was how ideas of success and failure in public schools have a long history in American life and showed up repeatedly during three major reform movements that blanketed the twentieth and twenty-first centuries. I wrote the book, but I could not get these surges of reform that roiled the nation, and to my surprise, my entire life, out of my head.

A century ago, the Progressive movement swept across the nation's schools and faded away only to be followed by the widespread quest for equality central to the civil rights movement. That then gave way to the business-inspired movement to tie school improvement to the nation's changing economy. The latter efforts resulted in the standards, testing, and accountability reforms that have marked the closing decades of the twentieth century and have continued into the early years of the twenty-first century.

But I was stuck intellectually. I didn't know what to do next. Slowly, I became unstuck as I began thinking of my life as a child and as a teacher, superintendent, and professor. I am in my late eighties and realized—not in any epiphany or REM-induced dream—that I had actually experienced all three of these twentieth-century reform movements: I had attended elementary and secondary schools in the latter years of the Progressive movement. I had been a history teacher during the civil rights era. And, finally, I served as a district superintendent during the early years of standards, testing, and accountability reforms, and then as a professor doing research on this last reform movement that remains intact in 2021. Could I tie my personal experiences to these larger movements?

Were my life experiences affected by these national reforms? The answers to these questions have become this book.

So the first confession is to simply acknowledge that *in my life and my career since the 1930s I have been helped* by family, friends, colleagues, and, of equal importance, luck in being in the right place at the right time. Sure, I would like to say that brains and talent mattered, and to some extent they did, but truth compels me to mention luck.

A central truth of my life and career is that while key people in my life nudged me in different directions over the years, chance played a large role in what I experienced and achieved. I cannot thank anyone for sheer luck. But I can thank many for the journey I have traveled in living a full life with family and friends I have loved, and been loved by in return, for nearly nine decades, and forging a career in teaching and writing that I have treasured.

Barbara, my wife of fifty years, whom I loved deeply, died twelve years ago, but her memory abides. Not a day goes by that I do not think of her. I miss very much her insight, alternative thinking, and wisdom. I miss her laughter and signal pride in helping others cope with life. And, of course, her love of our family. Daughters Sondra and Janice have grown into fine human beings, individuals who care about others and work to make this world better than it is now and have forged successful careers for themselves in education and business.

Without Barbara, Sondra, and Janice, there would not be the Larry I am now, as a husband, father, teacher/scholar, and friend. I should add "zayde," or grandfather, to that list since 2010. The family now includes Barbaraciela, a gift that Sondra has given to our entire family and my circle of dear friends.

And there is an extended family whose photos I look at when I do my thrice-weekly stretches in the living room. Barbara's nieces and nephews in Cleveland and Denver—Eddie, Caryn, and Jay—and my Dallas nephews Mark, Brian, and Jeff. All of them and their families have become part of my life, for which I am most grateful.

While family is of the highest importance to me, I want to acknowledge the dear friends of many decades whom I have known since I was a teenager—particularly Dave Mazer, Sam Balk, and Yus Merenstein (for whom this book is dedicated). We have stayed in close touch through frequent visits, phone calls, and email for over seventy years although we are separated by thousands of miles. I am most fortunate to have had these friends in my life.

I also have been lucky to have had former teacher colleagues, such as Bill Plitt and Jane David, not only stay in touch over the years but also become close friends. I have been rich in the students I have had as a high school and university teacher. In a few instances, those teacher-student relationships have morphed into cherished friendships, with Gary Lichtenstein, Joel Westheimer, Heather Kirkpatrick, Betty Achinstein, and David Brazer.

And that teacher-student relationship went in the opposite direction as well. When I was a middle-aged graduate student with family in tow, the Cubans spent two years at Stanford University. David Tyack was my adviser in my determined quest to secure a PhD so I could become a superintendent. He was a superb teacher from whom I learned a great deal. After I returned to Stanford as a professor following my superintendent years in Arlington, David and I biked weekly for the next three decades before he took ill and died. I lost a dear friend. Whatever gifts I have as a historian, writer, and friend—I received them from David.

And, as chance would have it, I have met along my journey people whose values, interests, and personality have meshed with mine and who have become beloved friends, such as Selma Wassermann, Harvey Pressman, and Sarah Blackstone. I have been both the recipient and giver of love to my family and friends.

While I acknowledge all of the above individuals for their love and friendship and in their own ways making possible this book, I would be remiss in not citing Harvard Education Press editor Jayne Fargnoli, whose support from the very first draft I submitted made this book a reality. After all of these bows to others, I nonetheless need to make clear that I did the writing, and no one in my family or close friends is responsible for any errors of fact or omissions. For that, dear reader, look only to me.

Larry Cuban
April 2021

About the Author

LARRY CUBAN is Professor Emeritus of Education at Stanford University. His background in the field of education prior to becoming a professor included fourteen years of teaching high school social studies in big-city schools, directing a teacher education program that prepared returning Peace Corps volunteers to teach in inner-city schools, and serving seven years as a district superintendent.

His major research interests focus on the history of curriculum and instruction, educational leadership, school reform, and the uses of technology in classrooms. In addition to his HEP books, he is also the author of *As Good As It Gets: What School Reform Brought to Austin* (Harvard University Press, 2010) and *Hugging the Middle: How Teachers Teach in an Era of Testing and Accountability* (Teachers College Press, 2009).

Index